Public Modalities

Rhetoric, Culture, and Social Critique

Public Modalities

Rhetoric, Culture, Media, and the Shape of Public Life

Edited by Daniel C. Brouwer and Robert Asen

THE UNIVERSITY OF ALABAMA PRESS
Tuscaloosa

Tuscaloosa, Alabama 35487-0380

Manufactured in the United States of America

Typeface: Goudy and Goudy Sans

∞

The paper on which this book is printed meets the minimum requirements of American National Standard for Information Sciences-Permanence of Paper for Printed Library Materials, ANSI Z39.48-1984.

Library of Congress Cataloging-in-Publication Data

Public modalities : rhetoric, culture, media, and the shape of public life / edited by Daniel C. Brouwer and Robert Asen.

p. cm. — (Rhetoric, culture, and social critique)

Includes bibliographical references and index.

ISBN 978-0-8173-1693-8 (cloth : alk. paper) — ISBN 978-0-8173-5585-2 (pbk. : alk. paper) — ISBN 978-0-8173-8361-9 (electronic) 1. Politics and culture—United States. 2. Rhetoric—Political aspects—United States. 3. Mass media—Social aspects—United States. 4. Mass media—Political aspects—United States. I. Brouwer, Daniel C., 1970– II. Asen, Robert, 1968–

JA75.7.P83 2010

306.20973—dc22

2009036546

Contents

Acknowledgments

Advocates of a project that affirms the unconventional, we find ourselves drawn toward conventional, earnest, and (we hope) effective modalities of giving thanks. Before attaining the form of this edited collection, our collaboration with each other and with our contributors developed through a series of formal and informal events across a significant span of time. These varied events permitted numerous encounters that were frequently enriching, illuminating, and deserving of tribute.

This project first took public form as a roundtable discussion at the November 2005 annual convention of the National (U.S.) Communication Association, where several of the contributors to this volume incubated their ideas about modalities. We had several opportunities to present versions and portions of the introductory chapter at colloquia sponsored by the Department of English in October 2006 and the Department of Communication Arts in February 2007 at the University of Wisconsin; the Department of Communication, Business, and Information Technologies at Roskilde Universitetscenter (Denmark) in March 2007; l'Institut de la Communication et des Médias at l'Université Stendhal Grenoble 3 in March 2007; the Department of Media, Cognition, and Communication at the University of Copenhagen in April 2007 and May 2008; and the Department of Communication Studies at the University of Texas in October 2008. We also presented portions of the introduction at the 2007 Alta Conference on Argumentation.

At these presentations and in innumerable informal conversations, many friends and colleagues offered trenchant criticism, engaged the project in various ways, and read portions of the manuscript. These wise commentators include David Cheshier, Jean Goodwin, Cynthia Willis-Chun, G. Thomas Goodnight, David Zarefsky, Debra Hawhee, Richard Graff, Nick Couldry, Vanessa Beasley, Lisa Storm Villadsen, Christian Kock, Christine Isager, Elisabeth Hoff-Clausen, Merete Onsberg, Cara Finnegan, Danielle Wiese, Barbara Biesecker, William Trapani, Lisa Foster, Alan Rubel, and Gordon Mitchell. We benefited immensely from their careful engagements.

Graduate students at Arizona State University and the University of Wisconsin, notably, Christina Colp-Hansbury, Marie-Louise Paulesc, Pam Conners, Rasha Diab, and Scot Barnett, edited portions of the project, interrogated it in their own work, or facilitated conversations with others, helping us to see the possibilities of our endeavor. At a late stage in the project, Vanessa Beasley and David Zarefsky offered sage and timely editorial advice. Randomly and tactically, mundanely and spectacularly, Charles E. Morris III, Prasad Boradkar, Angela Aguayo, Susan Zaeske, and Susan Robinson nourished our good spirits and perseverance toward this project by serving as workmates, playmates, gadflies, and pranksters. At the University of Alabama Press, the acquisitions editor and the series editor keenly alternated between support and patience. The two anonymous reviewers of the manuscript were incisive and expert.

To our contributors, we express again our heartfelt thanks for agreeing to be a part of this project. You are the sort of scholars whom we imagined to be best suited to bring this project to life, and our imagination has been rewarded by your efforts and talents. It bears remarking that, as in our first editing collaboration, work on this project was shared equally and has fortified our friendship with each other. Simply stated: I love you. (And *I* love *you.*)

We offer our labor in loving memory of Alexander Hivoltze-Jimenez, who died unexpectedly in May 2008. He was a beloved friend and a burgeoning scholar who excelled in imagining new possibilities, and the timing of his death on the verge of one of our formal presentations of our work bittersweetly marked his persistent and radiant impact on our personal and scholarly lives. Meow, Dear Alex Kitty.

Introduction

Public Modalities, or the Metaphors We Theorize By

Daniel C. Brouwer and Robert Asen

The public organizes through metaphor. Both its practitioners and theorists employ a rich range of metaphors when enacting and analyzing public activity. *Spheres, lines, networks, screens*—these terms render distinctly intelligible the qualities, realms, collectivities, or processes signified by multiple meanings of public. We have no recourse but metaphor, for public, so to speak, resists transparent representation. It resides neither in specific individuals nor in groups. It does not maintain a regular address. We cannot discover public in our physical environment. And yet public exerts a powerful force in our everyday lives, with significant symbolic and material consequences. The idea of a public may foster camaraderie among its members, and it may spur hatred of non-members. A public may discipline members to comport their behavior with widely shared norms, and it may encourage new and creative behaviors. A public may offer hope and solace, and it may elicit discomfort and alarm. Under conditions of strife, some individuals will kill for a public—whether themselves or others.

We need not invoke heroism and tragedy to discern the power of public. Consider the following quotidian case: In a *New York Times Magazine* article probing the implications of emergent social networking technologies, author Clive Thompson investigated the growing phenomenon of independent musicians who frequent Web sites like MySpace to establish direct, intimate connections with their fans. Unlike the Rolling Stones of the entertainment industry, these musicians post intricate details of their lives on blogs and spend hours every day answering fan emails. Thompson wondered if this trend would discourage talented young musicians from pursuing their passion. What about those shy souls whose muse felt uncomfortable with living in an online confessional? Yet, this very question, Thompson conceded, betrayed a generational bias. Teenagers understand public and private differently than their elders: "There are plenty of teenagers today who regard themselves as 'private' individuals, yet who post openly about their everyday activities on Facebook. . . . For that generation, the line between public and private is so blurry as to become almost nonexistent."[1] In short, public and private carry consequences. Thompson, who maintains a blog in addition to his regular contributions to print publications, appreciated these consequences for himself and others. His observation about teenagers suggests that public and private shape their worlds in ways vastly different from their parents and teachers.

Not only do public and private matter, but they matter in ways shaped by our language use. Thompson referred to *lines* of public and private, expressing anxiety over their increasingly *blurry* status. Lines connote boundaries or borders, often serving to delineate one realm (or, in common theoretical language, sphere) from another. In Thompson's writing, line marked two domains distinguished temporally by the practices of different generations. But what if he had written about a filter instead of a line? What if he exhibited anxiety about a tear in the filter? In standard usage, a filter allows some objects to pass through its membrane while preventing others. A filter between public and private may have functioned less to demarcate spheres and more to percolate experience differently. As these observations suggest, different word choices evidence wordplay and yet engender more than wordplay. *Line* and *filter* do not represent different names for the same things.

Our metaphors help construct the worlds in which we live. Theorists have long held that metaphor does not serve as a stylistic technique apart from the substance of discourse but instead functions prominently in our understanding of ideas and events. Writing in the early twentieth century, I. A. Richards challenged the notion of metaphor as "something special and exceptional in the use of language, a deviation from its normal mode of working, instead of the omnipresent principle of all its free action."[2] In our contemporary intellectual milieu, most scholars of language recognize its irreducibly metaphoric character and the constitutive power of metaphor.[3] This scholarly common sense has been motivated importantly by George Lakoff and Mark Johnson's germinal 1980 book, *Metaphors We Live By*. Through their notion of metaphorical entailment, Lakoff and Johnson explain how key metaphors invoke fundamental perspectives and normative frameworks. Our metaphors render events and contexts intelligible and commit us to particular values and beliefs, highlighting some conceptual connections while obscuring others.[4]

This collection of new essays, *Public Modalities*, interjects itself into ongoing scholarly conversations about metaphors and publics. More specifically, we intervene by drawing attention to the rhetoricity of prominent metaphors of publics and offering a new metaphor for the study of publics. That metaphor is, of course, *modality*. Modality references ways of being and studying public. In our rendering, modality entails a focus on multiplicity, movement and activity, and the mutual implication of theory and practice. Further, modality encourages scholars to pay attention to our language use, to recognize our own entailments. As critical scholars know well, no inquiry proceeds from an objective, value-free starting point. Our conceptual metaphors promise insights about our motives, values, and commitments. Like any metaphor, *modality* will live a life of its own—and we hope it does not die young. To grow robustly, modality will need many mentors and guardians. However, in our view, modality does not harbor imperial aspirations. We do not wish for modality to trump other metaphors, for we insist upon the enduring value of other metaphors' commitments, like those of sphere and networks, in which we have heavily invested. Nor, in a sense, is it possible for modality to replace other metaphors, for, as we demonstrate below, metaphors of public often share key entailments. Indeed, modality intersects with sphere and publicity, for example, to amplify analyses of public life.

In the remainder of this introduction, we first interrogate the dynamic lives and works of prominent metaphors—*sphere*, *networks/webs*, *publicity*, *screen*, and *culture*—advanced by scholars to study public, rendering explicit these metaphors' commitments and entailments and noting their convergences and divergences.[5] We then elaborate our *modality* metaphor. As a newer member in the constellation of public metaphors, modality foregrounds the *productive arts of crafting publicity*, a rendering that we route through the rhetorical tradition of *technē*. Our final section outlines the specific ways in which each of the contributions to this volume animates the metaphor of modality.

Sphere

Sphere stands as the most influential metaphor orienting studies of public, so much so that the term *public sphere* identifies a discrete line of inquiry, one that serves as a touchstone for other metaphors. On its own terms, a sphere metaphor presents advantages and disadvantages for studying publics. Sphere advantages scholarship by invoking a place for discourse. In his more recent writings on the subject, Jürgen Habermas explains that the public sphere refers to "the *social space* generated in communicative action."[6] As this definition suggests, sphere mediates metaphoricity on two levels: itself a metaphor, sphere also conjures up a metaphorical space of discourse. Although specific locales may host discourse, such as the steps of a town hall or the pages of a weekly magazine, these locales do not reductively literalize the public sphere. Conceptualizing a place for discourse spurs scholarship by contextualizing discourse practices. As a place, the notion of a public sphere has facilitated important scholarship revealing how ostensibly egalitarian forums encourage and discourage participation from variously situated individuals and privilege some discussion participants over others.

A sphere metaphor also lends itself to examining the politics of line drawing between public and private. Of course, lines can draw other shapes besides spheres, but spheres find themselves circumscribed by lines. Scholars have adopted this perspective to sketch how groups have fought to place putatively private matters on public agendas. In this spirit, Rita Felski and Nancy Fraser have investigated the efforts of feminist activists to raise public awareness of issues like sexual harassment.[7] In the work of scholars like Valeria Fabj, Matthew Sobnosky, and Catherine Palczewski, sphere metaphors have composed intriguing views of the interactions of diverse discourse practices.[8] Spheres comprise revealing pictures of the ways that agents and norms operating in different forums may partially overlap (as in a Venn diagram) or the ways that practices of different forums may share a common basis (as in concentric circles) or the ways that agents, norms, and practices circulate, conjoin, rearrange, and separate (as in the waxy globs of a lava lamp).[9] Starting from a relatively simple shape, through overlap, expansion, and centrifugation, spheres can model complex discursive practices and interactions.

Even as it has enabled important scholarship, a sphere metaphor threatens to contain discursive practices. Preferring a culture metaphor, Robert Hariman and John Lucaites critique spheres as "abstract, formally elegant, inherently rational, self-completing and self-regulating entities imagined to be freestanding in abstract space and seen from a macroscopic perspective."[10] In our view, this criticism goes too far, committing the very reductive conceptualizing it censures in spheres. Metaphors multiply potential meanings, enabling theorists and practitioners to take up metaphors in varied and not always consistent ways. We hold that Hariman and Lucaites's concerns would serve better as a caution against a particular metaphorical application, rather than a dismissal of spheres as inherently limiting. The spatial language of a sphere metaphor may wrongly suggest that publics possess impenetrable boundaries and essential cores.[11] Spatial language also may present a synchronic picture of publicity.

Spatial representations have difficulty conveying public engagement as a process that develops over time. Relations among publics and lines of public and private may change slowly or quickly, but both types of change inform and result from public engagement.

Two prominent theorists of the public sphere, G. Thomas Goodnight and Jürgen Habermas, have simultaneously used and struggled with the sphere metaphor in their germinal works. In his influential article "The Personal, Technical, and Public Spheres of Argument," Goodnight explains that sphere "denotes branches of activity—the grounds upon which arguments are built and the authorities to which arguers appeal."[12] Goodnight sometimes has been charged with propagating a reductive discourse typology,[13] and the peculiarity of this definition—its metaphor within a metaphor—may help explain both the inspiring and invective-eliciting qualities of his formulation. That is, although Goodnight promises to define a sphere, the most shapely aspect of his definition—a branch—is decidedly non-spherical. A branch suggests that argument shoots out in different directions, characterized variedly by straight lines, smooth curves, and irregular angles. Moreover, a branch connotes a common source for discursive activity, like the trunk of a tree or the main channel of a river. Goodnight's reference to activity indicates movement, as discourse flows or travels from one branch to another. Still, as the rhetorical tradition teaches us through concepts like *topoi*, specific instances of public discourse do not emerge *sui generis*, and sphere calls attention to shared features among diverse discourse practices. In this way, Goodnight both accepts and resists implications of a sphere metaphor.

Habermas's struggles with a sphere metaphor start with a problem of translation. Thomas Burger writes in his translator's note to *Structural Transformation of the Public Sphere* that the polysemic quality of Habermas's term *Öffentlichkeit*—with its plural meanings of the public, publicity, and the public sphere—is sacrificed in its uniform rendering as "public sphere."[14] Even as corollary terms recede, the notion of a public *sphere* allows Habermas to locate the critical power of a public, which capitalizes on its social location. Situated among the institutions of the state, market, and family, the bourgeois public sphere asserted independence from all three, enabling the bourgeoisie to leverage its critical distance in critiquing state actions. However, in this context, sphere also enforced a clear boundary between public and private. As he discusses the development of the bourgeois public sphere into the twentieth century, Habermas worries that an interpenetration of public and private issues has eclipsed the formation of public opinion altogether. Thirty years later, Habermas accepts this permeability, continuing to use a sphere metaphor while advocating explicit thematization of "boundary questions."[15]

Networks and Webs

Some scholars (including us) retain *public sphere* as a critical term but advance metaphors of *networks* and *webs* to substantiate the idea of a multiple public sphere. A move to multiplicity has been motivated by the recognition that modeling the public sphere as a singular arena devalues or excludes the contributions of less powerful members of society. Relative rather than absolute terms characterize this movement to multiplicity, for even the bourgeois public sphere, while conflating bourgeois and *homme,* enacted a public sphere through a range of broadsheets, coffeehouses, and salons. Yet the bourgeoisie excluded laborers and women, who formed public spheres of their own, and asserted its voice as the sole representative of public opinion. A networked or webbed public sphere challenges claims to singularity and centrality, rejecting the position that only one group may express public opinion or provide a privileged public perspective.

Discourse in the networks or webs of the public sphere takes place in innumerable, diverse forums varying in formality, access, power, privilege, breadth, visibility, interest, and style. In this spirit, Gerard Hauser writes that "the contemporary public sphere has become a web of discursive arenas, spread across society and even in some cases across national boundaries." Hauser holds that multiplicity does not serve solely as a critical concept. Its influence extends to the perceptions of participants themselves: "Our direct daily encounters with others who share our discursive spaces may be local, but our awareness of association with others who are part of this dialogue extends to locales and participants who are strangers and yet whose participation we heed and consider."[16] Well, not always. Hauser is right to note that participants in specific discursive exchanges often perceive that other members of society might hold a discussion about the same topic elsewhere, but heeding and considering their participation conveys an expression of faith rather than a statement of fact, as Hauser admits. Even in a multiple public sphere, participants in particular exchanges sometimes actively work to dismiss or exclude the involvement of others. As Catherine Squires observes, "not every group or individual enjoys the same access to public spaces, media resources, or other tools to participate in discursive activities. . . . Prevailing social norms may instill fear in citizens of marginalized publics that their ideas would at best be met with indifference, and at worst violence."[17] Importantly, network and web metaphors cannot eliminate exclusions, yet they may better explain the complexity of people's lives and the efforts of marginalized individuals and groups to advocate for their needs and interests. In these ways, network and web metaphors may offer potentially efficacious prescriptions for vibrant and inclusive discursive engagement.

Nodes and lines characterize a web or network. When we think about the arrangement of many networks, like a social network, we may focus our attention on intersections and sites without a center, as we have suggested above. This is not a necessary quality, since some computer networks, for instance, may operate through a hub-and-spoke system, but the spirit of multiplicity invokes decentralized networks. Along these lines, the blogosphere presents an excellent instantiation. Specific blogs host discussions about a range of social, cultural, economic, and political issues, while also linking to other discursive sites, whether blogs, newspaper Web pages, organizational Web pages, and others. Of course, blogs vary in their readership and influence. Some blogs, like the progressive public affairs blog Daily Kos, may receive hundreds of thousands of visits in a single day, whereas other blogs will attract the attention of only a small group of people.[18] These differences exemplify how nodes in a network will exhibit various connections, linking to a few forums or hundreds or thousands. Both a monthly book club that meets in members' living rooms and mass protests that occur on the National Mall in Washington, D.C., serve as sites in a networked public sphere.

Network and web metaphors invite greater consideration of relationality and temporality. In terms of relationality, connections across a network matter as much as—if not more than—specific sites themselves. One of the primary benefits of a network (in, say, a computer network) is that it enables otherwise disconnected sites to interact. Sites may share information, collaborate on various projects, and debate issues in previously unimagined ways. This is one way of reading Michael Warner's emphasis on circulation in his conception of public. Warner holds that "no single text can create a public." Rather, he calls attention to an "interactive relation" through the "potentially infinite axes of citation and characterization" that facilitates public discourse.[19] Unfortunately, Warner insists on a conceptual limit to circulation in his dismissal of dialogic models of public. A forced choice between spoken and written, auditory and visual communication appears oddly anachronistic in a conceptual movement (multiplicity) spurred by a desire to appreciate the complexities and inequities of public discourse. Circulation happens in many ways—we prefer to recognize all of them.

Temporality indicates that communication may circulate across a network at different rates. Some sites may link quickly, whereas others may interact slowly or require several intermediaries to connect. Particular issues, too, may engender faster or slower communication. In the immediate aftermath of the September 11, 2001, terrorist attacks, Henry Giroux observes, the Bush administration supplanted the deliberative, critical, and self-reflexive standards of "public time" with a version of "emergency time" that routed the affect of community toward sacrifice and loyalty with extraordinary efficiency. Many publics resolved quickly to support the president in locating the perpetrators and their accomplices of the attacks.[20] By contrast, activists' efforts to achieve full civil rights for gay and lesbian couples have proceeded more slowly, encountering greater reception from some publics and greater resistance from others. Networks and webs better appreciate these developments than spheres.

Publicity

Given some of the complications of the sphere metaphor noted above, some scholars have authored a simple but meaningful shift to *publicity* as an organizing metaphor.[21] Foregrounding action or activity and concrete examples, this metaphor also suggests the priority of phenomena and data over the integrity or validity of received concepts and theories. In the field of communication studies, publicity has been especially appealing to rhetorical scholars, especially those invested in enduring rhetorical principles of contingency and praxis.[22] Alongside his endorsement of a network metaphor, Gerard Hauser has linked activity with sphere, naming activity as one of the five rhetorical norms of the public sphere.[23] In this spirit, Erik Doxtader has aphorized "*counterpublic* is a verb" in order to draw explicit attention to activity; rendered thusly, the study of counterpublicity becomes the endeavor to observe "whether and how local speech acts invent the basis for dialogue and agreement."[24] Notably, both of these examples forward an investment in dialogue as a particularly valuable process of publicity. Emphasizing the recognition of publicity as activity, other scholars have described their line of inquiry as "publics theory."[25] This subtle shift recognizes that publicity-as-activity constitutes specific publics. These publics are not identical to the public sphere—a conceptual social space. They are empirical—things created through action. And yet, as we note above, the mutual implication of theory and practice reminds us that already existing theories of publics can motivate specific practices and that specific practices can generate theories of publics.

This story of subtle shifts and conceptual complementarity exhibits a decidedly comic attitude. Adopting a more tragic perspective, some scholars' commitment to publicity names the failure of sphere and other spatializing metaphors.[26] In contrast to Hauser's and Doxtader's model of publicity populated by human agents engaged in dialogue, Mimi Sheller and John Urry's publicity names the movements and flows of peoples, technologies, and systems that characterize the contemporary conditions of globalized life. Such conditions lead Sheller and Urry to launch a vigorous critique of sphere, objecting at least to its static and regional character. (For our response to the charge of its static character, see above in "Sphere"; for our response to its regional character, see below in "Culture"). The version of publicity-as-activity that they elaborate is mobility, which better captures, in their view, "how people (and objects) *move*, or desire to move, between the supposedly private and the public domains."[27] Global flows of people, objects, and information and the technological diversification of these flows expose the belief in distinct public and private domains as a debilitating fiction that forces us to tell the same story of public decline over and again. Conceptual revolution arises as the inevitable new order: "The distinction between public and private domains should be dispensed with since nothing much of contemporary social life remains on one side or the other of the divide. Thus the problems of (and hopes for) democratic citizenship must be theorized in relation to these dynamic, multiple mobilities of people, objects, information and images, especially as these move in powerfully fused or hybridized forms."[28]

We are, not surprisingly, reluctant to join others in the dismissal of the scholarly salience of public and private (and other) domains.[29] As we have argued elsewhere, these are socially meaningful categories that take material form and shape the conditions and experiences of many people's lives.[30] Further, we are concerned that investment in publicity-as-activity might be coupled with renderings of social fields in which people, objects, and information are imagined to have full, free reign, untroubled by centripetal forces. Even amidst conditions of perpetual action and movement and reconfigurations of social space through global and technological flows, we are well served by recognizing that precedents, habits, norms, sedimented articulations, and myriad institutions shape the constitution of publics. Consideration of the ambivalence of mobility illuminates this point. Mobility can be enriching, inspiring, and illuminating. Charting E. M. Forster's account of mobility in the novel *Howard's End*, Richard Sennett describes the novelist's rendering of mobility as a humane ethic: "Human displacements ought to jolt people into caring about one another, and where they are."[31] And yet mobility can be alienating. Global flows of capital can hold people captive and displace local modes of association. In the aftermath of passage of the North American Free Trade Agreement, for example, Raka Shome argues that migrant bodies at the U.S.-Mexico border experienced complicated (im)mobilities: "on the one hand, the border became more mobile and open for capital; on the other, it became more contained to control the effects of mobile capital—the movement of peoples northward." Shome's corrective to an overly ludic account of mobility is to recognize that "space matters." Space matters "as a component of power that penetrates all other social frameworks," though relations of power cannot be reduced to space.[32] In this vein, even if one rejects sphere as a hopeless, fatally static metaphor, as Sheller and Urry do, one should similarly reject enervated analyses that over-invest in activity.

Consideration of the dialectic of agency and structure further illuminates this point about activity: people engage others, but they do so within a field of constraint. On this score, performing publicity resonates with Judith Butler's observation that gender performances constitute "improvisation within a scene of constraint." Butler notes that one's gender sometimes may appear as "something that I author." And yet gender is not freely constituted: "the terms that make up one's own gender are, from the start, outside oneself, beyond oneself in a sociality that has no single author."[33] Similarly, agency is never free. Social actors sometimes may loosen constraints on publicity—reforming institutions, removing exclusions, reshaping norms. Other times, these constraints may sustain privilege, maintain marginalization, delimit modes of action. Public engagement is shaped by the specific conditions of its emergence even as it seeks to refashion these conditions.

Screen

In recent years, *screen* has emerged as a metaphor for assessing the implications of a media-scaped social environment for conceptualizing and studying publics. Increasingly, media scholars and publics scholars are interrogating the relationships between mainstream and alternative media, for example, and among media, publics, and states. Along these lines, many have expressed interest in new communication technologies and their roles in constituting publics and counterpublics, resulting in a wide range of conclusions about the abilities of media to constitute legitimate opposition on local and national levels and even to constitute something like a global public. On its own terms, *screen* stages important interventions into such investigations. Most obviously, it draws our attention to media not as neutral conduits but as structuring or constituting agents. This, in turn, goads more rigorous engagement between media theories of publics and discourse theories (rhetorical, deliberative, or other) of publics. More specifically, screen directs scholarly attention to both the fact and the significance of display, visuality, mediation. Especially when imagined in televisual, filmic, or digital forms, screen attends to nexuses of sound and sight and words and images, or the *multimodality* that Gunther Kress (alone and with colleagues) argues as the semiotic condition of existence.[34]

In the specific instance of its introduction by Kevin M. DeLuca and Jennifer Peeples, screen galvanized a line of criticism that directly confronts public *sphere* theory with the charges of iconophobia and iconoclasm.[35] Such charges are undoubtedly warranted. Among the prominent lines of critique against Habermas's germinal version of the public sphere, Jim McGuigan distills, is that the public sphere "misunderstand[s] the active powers of popular cultural consumption and reception as well as the opportunities that the modern and especially electronic media actually do and potentially afford informed public debate on serious issues."[36] It is not that Habermas and his progenitors in the Frankfurt School have ignored media. Instead, the Frankfurt School has crafted a consistently pessimistic take on media. Max Horkheimer and Theodor Adorno's thesis on the *Kulturindustrie* is one of the most famous indictments of mass media and media consumption.[37] Habermas's own attenuated version of that thesis, never entirely abandoned even in his more recent work, has been astutely characterized as a "distrust of [media] representation."[38] In short, DeLuca and Peeples and others conclude that the Frankfurt School tradition, from which emerges Habermas and his germinal account of the public sphere, does not adequately fund critical interrogation of contemporary mediations of publics.

DeLuca and Peeples offer screen as a "necessary supplement" to the allegedly stale metaphor of sphere, a supplement funded in large part by cultural studies and theories of postmodernity.[39] Their opposition to sphere stems from their concern about the power of dominant metaphors to restrict or misdirect social theory, a concern that motivates our own project. In their view, sphere is a faulty metaphor in part because it carries with it static notions of political identity, place, and action.[40] Drawing on Jacques Derrida, Jean Baudrillard, John Hartley, and others, DeLuca and Peeples argue that screen better captures new modes of knowledge, sociability, and democratic participation enabled by new communication technologies. Alongside the public sphere's investments in words, dialogue, and focus as exemplary media and qualities of communication, for example, the public screen values visuality, dissemination, and distraction as constitutive of social life.[41] Importantly, screen performs more than a simple and reductionist replacement of sphere. As supplements, the public screen and the public sphere "exist in a dialectic of remediation."[42]

DeLuca and Peeples's placement of screen and sphere in a dialectical relationship invokes Douglas Kellner's important observations about the differing investments of British cultural studies and the Frankfurt School. Reminding us that the two traditions shared significant commitments, such as concern about the co-optation of the working class into capitalist regimes, focus on mass culture as a significant means for co-opting the working class, recognition of culture as a fruitful site for resistance to capitalist ideologies, and advocacy of ideological criticism,[43] Kellner notes cultural studies' greater focus on the working class as agents of social change and youth cultures as sites of resistance. A pertinent divergence related to the study of media is that "British cultural studies would valorize resistant moments in media culture and audience interpretations and use of media artifacts, while the Frankfurt School tended, with some exceptions, to see mass culture as a homogeneous and potent form of ideological domination—a difference that would seriously divide the two traditions."[44] Against the background of Kellner's intellectual history, we might understand screen as a metaphor that both proceeds with its own commitments and interrogates, if not resolves, significant differences in approaches to critical media analysis.

To be sure, there are reasons to quibble with DeLuca and Peeples's rendering of screen. Cara Finnegan and Jiyeon Kang, for instance, claim that this rendering ignores and thus misses an opportunity to engage the later works on aesthetics of that durable theorist and frequent straw figure, Jürgen Habermas.[45] More substantively, they claim that the theorists' efforts to place screen and sphere, each with its distinct set of ontologies and axiologies, into a supplemental or dialectical relationship, in fact, reproduces a dichotomous relation. In our own view, we find peculiar the authors' inclusion of several titles, including *The Black Public Sphere* and *The Public Sphere in Muslim Societies,* in a list of recent works that purportedly exemplify uncritical acceptance of the public sphere. Even a cursory read of, for example, the latter edited collection produces evidence of critical and limited acceptance of sphere, as Shmuel Eisenstadt remarks in his conclusion: "The use of such concepts as public sphere, civil society, and collective identity is helpful as long as we do not assume that the way in which these components were put together in Europe constitutes an evaluative yardstick for other modernizing societies."[46] Although we contest certain features of DeLuca and Peeples's specific introduction of screen, we support their larger goal of prompting—or better, remembering and re-engaging—efforts to take media seriously in studies of publics. Attending to the convergences and divergences between public sphere theory and cultural studies on the issue of media demonstrates both the need and the challenge of goading theories of publics to better account for media.

Culture

The metaphor of *culture* foregrounds the active crafting of artifacts and the active crafting of codes and norms. Further, it expands our understanding of how social space is constituted. Scholarship interested in culture as it relates to publics proceeds in general terms as well as in specifically named lines of inquiry, such as "the cultural public sphere," "public culture," and "cultures in public."[47] As illustrations of the culture metaphor, we discuss the cultural public sphere and one version of public culture.[48]

Galvanized in large part by the Center for Transcultural Studies and its launching of the journal *Public Culture* in 1988 and later the Public Worlds and Public Planet book series, "public culture" scholarship emphasizes transnationality and globalization and the effects of those forces on the constitution of publics.[49] Nearly a decade into the metaphor's launch, Arjun Appadurai and Carol Breckenridge sustain its viability by calling for and enacting a loosening of the meaning of public and by carefully distinguishing the goals and interests of public culture studies from public sphere and popular culture studies.[50] While their description of public culture as a "zone of cultural debate" is expansive and similar to public sphere, their added insistence on transnationality distinguishes the concept. Gayatri Gopinath demonstrates the virtues of a transnational public culture approach. Arguing for a simultaneous queer and feminist reading of transnational movements of South Asian diasporic texts, she claims that such a reading dramatizes the specific ways in which South Asians constitute zones of cultural debate about popular films, novels, and other artifacts as those artifacts circulate through the diaspora.[51] Such a reading also challenges powerful ideologies of "home" that commonly circulate in transnational imaginaries—home as a place of purity and authenticity of principles and practices and home as a total or near total zone of oppression from which marginalized subjects must escape to achieve liberation.[52]

Semantically, efforts that proceed under the heading of "the cultural public sphere" perform both a retention and a rehabilitation of the public sphere. Specifically, the cultural public sphere attends to the communication of identities and the significance of affective (versus exclusively cognitive) communication. The results of this enterprise have been mixed. Taking care to distinguish the cultural public sphere from counterpublics, John Hartley and Joshua Green claim, "Displayed via private pursuits such as music, sport, domestic life and leisure or entertainment venues . . . , the cultural public sphere develops more or less out of sight of 'the' public sphere, and its 'citizens' communicate using media that are equally invisible to the mainstream."[53] We find Hartley and Green's conceptualization of the cultural public sphere to be unnecessarily anemic. In fact, it commits precisely the kinds of offenses that we argue against here and elsewhere.[54] Specifically, it retains clear distinctions between private and public (treating them as settled categories), it conflates and thus reduces the private sphere to culture (and vice versa), and it discerns the cultural public sphere only in moments of "spectacular public visibility."[55]

We find a more felicitous rendering of the cultural public sphere in McGuigan's work. For McGuigan, who explicitly extrapolates the concept from Habermas's account of the literary public sphere, the concept "refers to the articulation of politics, public and personal, as a contested terrain through affective (aesthetic and emotional) modes of communication."[56] Such a rehabilitation permits greater consideration of the work of affective communication in the modes of melodrama, sentimentality, and humor, for example, and in popular culture as well as political culture. Yet even as the assertion of culture in the study of publics marks an advancement, we caution against the potential risk of using culture to replace or ignore the significance of official, overtly political modes of constituting publics. If it is reductive to accord public significance solely or primarily to official discourses, it is equally reductive to accord culture (conceived as "high" aesthetics, popular culture, or however) such primacy.

On a broader scale, culture contests certain versions of public sphere theory's origins within and preoccupations with Western—especially statist and national—formations. These origins and preoccupations compel myriad entry points for scholarly interrogation, including Gayatri Gopinath's prompting that historical accounts of the emergence of public spheres in European countries may fail to narrate how those countries' "evolution" toward the public sphere was dependent upon forced labor of colonial subjects or slaves and the exploitation of natural resources in colonized or conquered territories.[57] Additionally, and more broadly, if there is legitimate wonder about the fitness of European historical concepts for the U.S. situation,[58] then we can imagine that there is legitimate wonder about the fit—more, the incongruity—of Western concepts to non-Western contexts. That is, the further that one travels geographically from western Europe, the further one may simultaneously travel from the relevance of western Europe's conceptual resources. In short, culture asks, What relevance or salience do the concepts of publics, publicity, and the public sphere have in non-Western, postcolonial, or transnational contexts? More starkly, do *public*, *publicity*, and *public sphere*, with their presumption of democratic conditions and more, even make sense in non-Western, postcolonial, or transnational contexts?

Generally, and perhaps surprisingly, many scholars focusing on non-Western and transnational contexts have found certain features of publics and the public sphere to be fruitful and illuminating even as they have conducted such work with reservations about publics and the public sphere. Expression and elaboration of these reservations exposes the limits of public sphere theory even as this scholarship retains certain of its features and insights. Sociologist Shmuel Eisenstadt, for example, recognizes the unavoidability of Western concepts in studies of political, economic, and religious characteristics of the Muslim world, although he insists that scholars must "make them more flexible . . . through differentiation and contextualization."[59] Yet even this project of extending the theoretical reach and capacity of public sphere theory raises the specter of conceptual neo-colonialism, a not inconsequential specter given the historical facts and continued legacies of conceptual impositions and misreadings of non-Western and colonial contexts which, as Edward Said and others have shown, enable and are in turn enabled by other forms of degradation such as genocide, forced labor, political rule, and restricted ownership.[60] More circumspect about the cultural fungibility of publics and the public sphere is Klaus Eder, who calls for much sharper precision in the telling of stories about the public sphere. "For three centuries," he deadpans, "a small portion of the world's population have had to reckon with a collective experience that divided their world into a private sphere of household existence and a public sphere of political and economic action."[61] Eder calls for comparative analyses that explore the specific cultural forms through which collectives forge social bonds and social space. In this vein, Tatsuro Hanada elaborates a Japanese version of something like the public sphere but one that employs the "indigenous historical concepts" of *Kugai* (public authority), *muen* (being unconnected or unbound), and *raku* (pleasure, comfort, or ease).[62]

Modalities

As the title of this volume and this introduction suggest, our arrival at the metaphor of *modalities* is hardly disinterested. We both recognize modalities as its own metaphor and value its identification of the rhetoricity of metaphors. The metaphors we have enumerated illuminate public life variously, enabling insights even as they exhibit blind spots. In our explications of these prevailing metaphors, we have indicated that sphere invites critical attention to forums for public discourse, network draws scholars toward connections among publics, publicity suggests that we elevate phenomena and data over received concepts and theories, screen encourages us to appreciate the visual qualities of public activity, and culture asks scholars to consider the influence of socializing norms and practices. Invoking modality, then, raises the question of what we hope to highlight in studying public life. In this light, we regard modality as a metaphor that foregrounds productive arts of crafting publicity.

These metaphorical attributes become clearer when we consider that the *Oxford English Dictionary* defines *mode* as, among other meanings, "a way or manner in which something is done or takes place; a method of proceeding in any activity."[63] Modality's "manner" implicates practice and theory, referring both to ways that social actors engage others publicly and to ways that scholars study processes of public engagement. With respect to practice, modality illuminates the diverse range of processes through which individuals and groups engage each other, institutions, and their environment in creating, reformulating, and understanding social worlds. Public engagement may utilize verbal and visual symbols, statistical evidence, narrative testimony, formal argumentation, tactical consumerism, humor, sentimentality, corporeality, and more. In terms of theory, as the pesky appearance of "method" in the *OED* definition intimates, modality calls attention to the constitutive power of our language use in relation to the subjects we study. Although method sometimes has been invoked to discipline critical scholarship by insisting that such work adhere to narrowly conceived and ostensibly neutral norms and procedures, modality indicates instead the ways that scholars write and talk about public matters. To be sure, scholars do not simply impose their values on processes of publicity, but judging values discerned through inquiry in light of one's critical commitments constitutes an important aspect of the critical work of modalities.

Even as metaphors illuminate public life variously, they sometimes shine light in similar directions and together cast a complementary glow. In this way, neither modality nor any of the other metaphors discussed in this introduction presents an utterly idiosyncratic view of public life. For instance, both publicity and modality draw critical attention to movement and process, and a networked public sphere facilitates the multiform engagement conveyed by modality. Rather than revealing limitations of public metaphors, these resonances foster metaphoric collaboration. For example, the work of Sheller and Urry foregrounds transnational systems of movement that offer a contemporary global context for the productive knowledge we ascribe to modality. To this, we may add a networked public sphere to represent the sites of discourse implicated in these processes of publicity. Together, these metaphors (and other combinations) promise a more complex understanding of public life. Moreover, metaphoric complementarity underscores our desire to offer modality as a displacement, not replacement, of sphere and other metaphors. Our earlier coedited collection, *Counterpublics and the State,* performed an explicit defense of instrumental political publics. There we argued for the continuing relevance of the state as an interlocutor with and mediator of publics and public spheres. We continue to support those views. With *Public Modalities,* we forward a different, but not contrary, project.

Even as we announce our arrival at modality as decidedly interested, we also recognize this arrival as potentially curious, for at first glance modality may seem like a "dead metaphor." We (over)heard this assessment at a U.S. conference where we first publicized our interest in modalities during a roundtable discussion. This is a legitimate concern, since scholars in many disciplines sometimes mobilize modality for overtly taxonomical or mechanistic purposes. In grammar studies, for example, modality is frequently used to categorize and distinguish types of words and sentences.[64] For many years, social scientists studying communication generally treated modality as a synonym for the type or channel of communication (e.g., television, radio, print, interpersonal, public address, etc.) that bore an insignificant relationship to the content or meaning of a message. In his assessment of the field of communication studies through the 1980s, Michael Pfau, one of the leading social scientists of communication modalities, discerns that modality "has been treated as a 'neutral' conduit of message content."[65] More recently, social scientific approaches to communication modalities have replaced this deadening neutrality with the recognition that communication modalities—manners, processes, ways of communicating—matter. Along these lines, Andrew Rancer and colleagues have encouraged researchers to account for the ways in which modalities influence the variables that are being studied.[66] Elsewhere, Pfau and colleagues explore the relationships between modalities (video versus print) and cognitive processes relating to resistance to persuasion, finding small but significant differences in, for example, the timing of the inoculation effect from video versus print.[67] Yet even as these and other recent efforts render modality more robustly, the specter of the dead metaphor of modality lingers. We attribute this to more than ignorance of these recent advancements.

Indeed, we discern a clash of scholarly paradigms: Evaluating social scientific approaches to modalities against criteria from a critical perspective can prompt a deadening assessment of the former's accomplishments. Asserting that critical theory "is not a single school, philosophy, or point of view but an arena of debate," Della Pollock and Robert Cox explain that critical theory "offers a stance of engaged skepticism in which its own suppositions may be exposed and questioned."[68] Understood in these terms, a critical approach may be leveraged to expose and question the scope of the social science enterprise and the manners by which it crafts its knowledge claims. With regard to modalities, social scientific efforts have largely focused on the effects of different modalities on cognitive processes in interpersonal relationships. As an exemplar, Rancer and colleagues assess modalities in terms of perceptions, estimations, and attitudes about interpersonal conflict, using "accuracy" and "errors" as standards for their assessments.[69] A critical perspective would invest in a different semantic and ontological register and would interrogate the constructedness of rationality as a standard for disputation rather than positing it self-evidently. The interpersonal and cognitive scope of much social scientific deployments of modality seems not nearly robust enough to help us account for the grander themes of inclusion, participation, marginality, and more that are perennial interests of many critical scholars of publics.

Broadening the scope of inquiry to the realm of political communication and making explicit reference to the work of Marshall McLuhan, Pfau and colleagues nevertheless eschew the critical implications of this linkage between McLuhan and the political. The critical media ecology approach often traced through Harold Innis, McLuhan, and James Carey famously theorized media *bias* not in terms of the political partisanship (e.g., conservative versus liberal) that characterizes institutional politics but in terms of the ontological partisanship (including *space* and *time*) that distinguishes types of media. That is, the scope of McLuhan's political was expansive, interrogating relations among culture, knowledge, power, forms of social organization, and more. While Pfau and colleagues excel in attending to the specific ways in which modalities matter in the conduct of institutional party politics, they do not attend to the broader critical questions prompted by McLuhan. To be clear, in the face of this limitation and the limitations of Rancer and colleagues' work discussed above, one need not—and we do not—indict the social science enterprise in toto. We seek merely to account for that overheard skepticism and to open up conceptual space for the critical potential of modality.

Recovering a more critical, robust—indeed, metaphoric—understanding of modality demands recognition that processes are neither neutral nor value-free. Modifying our initial *OED* definition of *mode,* we must appreciate that how we proceed in an activity shapes the activity itself. Toward this end, we find the resources for a critical recovery of modality in the classical rhetorical tradition of technē, which emerges from within the field of communication studies but animates our participation in a larger critical project.[70] Technē typically has been translated as "art" or "craft." David Roochnik explains that the original meaning of the term likely meant the communal building of a house by weaving together trunks and twigs.[71] However, the term's meaning steadily expanded to include other productive arts, including the verbal art of rhetoric. In this way, technē came to signify a process of productive knowledge. Drawing on the traditions of Protagoras, Isocrates, and Aristotle, Janet Atwill identifies three characteristics of technē as a productive knowledge: "A technē is never a static normative body of knowledge"; "A technē resists identification with a normative subject"; "Technē marks a domain of intervention and invention."[72] These characteristics underscore technē's processual constitution and its connection to ameliorative social action. Further, the rhetorical tradition frequently has associated technē with cunning reason and good timing to indicate a distinct mode of timely intelligence. Atwill explains that "knowing how" and "knowing when" help distinguish technē from "rule-governed activities that are less constrained by temporal conditions."[73] Emphasizing process and timing, technē stands against compulsion, force, necessity, and fate. In various ways, these latter terms all insist on predetermined outcomes to human affairs, thereby removing the productive contingency of public life.

Our explication of technē offers several benefits for a critical recovery of modality. The tradition of technē demonstrates that public engagement is an active, purposeful process. Public agents seek to pursue their needs and interests and influence others in light of identifiable and potentially changing values and aims. Technē guarantees neither success nor failure, but it recognizes the roles of individuals and groups in crafting their lives, even as people act amid constraints. Further, technē indicates a social, transformative process. A technē is learned and practiced among others, which reminds us that engagement has an epistemic value: we may learn when we engage others publicly, even in cases of conflict and disagreement. As a productive art, technē transforms the material it uses—as wood serves as material to build a house, words can construct an inspiring vision of the future. Karlyn Kohrs Campbell has written that technē thus "opens up possibilities for resistance" by enacting cultural "performances that repeat with a different, altering meaning."[74] Were technē wedded to a particular subject domain, such differential repetition might not be possible. At the least, technē's capacity to cross and connect subjects and knowledge facilitates its capacity for productive innovation.

Technē also demonstrates that processes of public engagement are value-laden. Considering technē as "craft," we revisit Celeste Condit's case for the resonance of this term for discussions of public morality.[75] Condit holds that thinking of morality as a craft recognizes the mutually informative participation of individuals and collectives. In a related manner, the fluid and transformative qualities of a craft suggest that engaged groups and individuals may revise public norms and values. Unlike "high" arts, crafts retain an everyday quality, illuminating the lives of their practitioners and audiences. Approaching public morality in this fashion resists viewing it as a transcendent realm that stands over (and against) the lives of the people morality supposedly guides. Rather than existing in an awesome, untouchable realm, public morality as craft rightly persists as a process in our world, which we may know, create, and question. Part of the value of processes of public engagement arises from their execution, and technē draws attention to issues of eloquence, creativity, coordination, and determination. From presidents to protestors, individuals and groups that have crafted their rhetoric in innovative and imaginative ways have engaged their audiences more fully than their less rhetorically adroit interlocutors. Jon Stewart often covers the same political ground as many network news and talk shows, but his humorous style attracts the coveted younger viewership sought by networks. And, as researchers have discovered, the *Daily Show*'s satire taps into an impressive knowledge of public affairs among its viewers.[76]

Even as we have sketched a potentially empowering vision of technē, another classical tradition suggests a less democratic and potentially disempowering version: technē as a specialized type of knowledge. This tradition attaches a specific subject matter to technē, reducing competence in public discourse to memorizing a set of rules and precepts. To be sure, this version is unsuitable for our purposes, but it serves an illuminating function nevertheless because considering empowering and disempowering versions of technē adumbrates the tasks attendant on scholars pursuing modalities as a critical project.

A familiar villain stands as a prominent proponent of technē as a specialized type of knowledge—Plato, who, in the figure of Socrates, often dismissed rhetoric as not an art at all. In the *Protagoras*, Socrates outlined a technē of practical deliberation by reordering this fluid practice according to the science of weighing, counting, and measuring. This project depended crucially on the presumption that different values were commensurate on a single scale, which Socrates identified as the singular end of pleasure. Only by deferring to this asserted value framework could deliberators assure a rational outcome to their interactions. Considering difference—and accepting that the ends of life may be plural—simply courted trouble. As Martha Nussbaum explains, "recognition of heterogeneity, the dialogue tells us, is a necessary condition for the development of irrational motivations."[77] In this way, Plato's vision of a deliberative technē was hostile to difference, and it appeared oblivious to the role of force and unequal power relations in making incommensurable values (e.g., justice and profit) commensurate. Technē, then, signifies neither an inherently emancipatory process nor a reactionary process. Its productive knowledge may be inclusive and exclusive, enabling and constraining, democratic and dictatorial.

So, too, modalities. The critical character of this project does not arise from an inherent quality of a modality per se, since processes of public engagement may advance praiseworthy or censurable ends. Rather, the critical character of public modalities arises from the intervention and judgment of the scholar, who discerns the values implicated in particular engagements and judges their progressive or regressive qualities. When investigating progressively democratic engagement, the scholar may elucidate its potential to bolster public life in terms of inclusiveness, diversity, economic justice, and other criteria. When analyzing regressive engagement, the scholar may explicate its potential to harm public life, including imposed silences, threatened or actual coercion, and exacerbated inequality, as well as other baneful implications. Put differently, in recognizing processes as value-laden, we recognize that these values may be good or bad; and in attending to modalities we should not artificially confine our interest only to sympathetic cases. This position carries a risk—in situating our critical project this way, we risk losing the secure normative ground that would come with placing our project at a specific point along an ideological continuum. Yet we regard this risk as necessary to retain the processual character of modalities and to avoid hypostatizing our metaphor by linking modality to a specific subject matter.

Moreover, in highlighting the critical intervention of the scholar, our project resonates powerfully with the tradition of critical theory itself. In his famous essay "Traditional and Critical Theory," Max Horkheimer explicated differences among these two modes of inquiry. Whereas traditional theory accepted as given received norms and concepts and adhered to a strict separation of knowledge and action, critical theory recognized its embedment in society and oriented itself toward ameliorative social change. Horkheimer explained that "every part of the [critical] theory presupposes the critique of the existing order and the struggle against it along the lines determined by the theory itself."[78] In this distinction, we may discern that a crucial element lies in the approach of the scholar, who may accept or question received norms and practices. Of course, Horkheimer and other first-generation Frankfurt School theorists operated out of a Marxist paradigm. Our public modalities project retains the critical orientation advocated by Horkheimer while adopting the more expansive, pluralistic rendering of critical theory by Pollock and Cox as an "arena of debate," which affirms that a variety of perspectives and methods may produce trenchant critique. Indeed, our critical orientation resonates with Elyse Pineau's account of the range of commitments that fund critical approaches to pedagogy: "While critical educators do not always agree on the appropriate form of activism nor even the most salient forms of oppression (i.e., ethnicity, class, gender, etc.), they share a common vision of a more egalitarian society in which all members have the opportunity and skills necessary for full participation, and where public policy is motivated by a deep sense of social responsibility."[79] In foregrounding the scholar's critical intervention in the direction of a more egalitarian society, the metaphor of modalities sustains the mediation of practice and theory implied in the definition of a "method of proceeding in any activity."

Illustrating the pluralism of a critical approach to modalities, Radhika Parameswaran animates postcolonial theory to highlight the "Othering modalities of European colonial discourses" in *National Geographic* magazine, while Biman Basu attends to Foucauldean "modalities of power, punishment and discipline" in an analysis of African American subjectivity.[80] By design, the chapters in *Public Modalities* mobilize an array of theories and concepts from psychoanalysis, cultural studies, media studies, rhetorical studies, and elsewhere; and, by design, they assess a wide range of communicative activities that dramatize that material political, social, and cultural change occurs in myriad settings and myriad ways. Indeed, in this collection, analyses of official or institutional politics in national and transnational contexts stand alongside analyses of popular culture, poetry, and everyday life to dramatize different *manners* or *ways* of constituting publics matter.

Contributions of Chapters to a Public Modalities Framework

Broadly, the first four chapters of the volume constitute case studies of publics or publicity in the United States. Beyond that general characterization, however, these chapters animate modality in significantly different ways. Eric King Watts's chapter, "Pragmatist Publicity: W.E.B. Du Bois and the New Negro Movement," reads W.E.B. Du Bois's writings and speeches about aesthetics and publics alongside those of John Dewey. In doing so, Watts dramatizes the particular challenges that Du Bois faced during the 1920s in crafting a "New Negro" aesthetic. Acutely troubled by white people's often uncritical consumption of black aesthetics, Du Bois worked to refigure the primitive/savage trope of aesthetic consumption. Watts's account of New Negro publicity as a distinct aesthetic modality recasts Dewey's notion of experience to account for white supremacist systems. Decades later, in the 1950s, the San Francisco Bay area poet Jack Spicer confronted a similar aesthetic crisis. As a queer poet located within an overwhelmingly heteronormative civic culture, Spicer retheorized agency and publicity in confounding ways. In their chapter, "'VIII. Lowghost Publicity, or, My Vocabulary Did This To Me,'" Dale Smith and Joshua Gunn demonstrate the ways in which Spicer's accounts of poetic agency and poetic function offer substantial challenges to theories of publics as zones that constitute citizenship. Importantly, Smith and Gunn's routing of their reading through Jacques Lacan and Slavoj Žižek introduces psychoanalysis as a powerful (and uncommon) way of theorizing publics. Yet the authors also animate modality in a third way not anticipated in our discussion above—modalities as ways of performing one's scholarship. Claiming to have endured serial possession by the spirit of Jack Spicer, Smith and Gunn craft their chapter as an annotated transcription of these possessions, their conspicuous use of footnotes—rather than the endnotes used in the other chapters within this volume—prompting a trilogic encounter among readers, authors, and Spicer that enacts and extends Spicer's account of poetic agency.

In their chapter, "Everyday Life and Death in a Nuclear World: Stories from Fernald," Phaedra C. Pezzullo and Stephen P. Depoe examine the dynamics of an environmental mishap in Ohio in the 1980s, one characterized by the slow accumulation of evidence leading to the eventual discovery of malignant neglect and resulting in community organizing and social controversy. These contours of environmental controversy may be familiar, but Pezzullo and Depoe excel in recuperating the everyday, or the mundane, as an illuminating vantage point from which to explore nuclear culture, for which the tendency is to think in terms of disaster or catastrophe. Indeed, Pezzullo and Depoe draw upon archived interviews with people directly affected by the nuclear contamination at Fernald, weaving together these narratives to show provocatively how atypical events are made familiar in the everyday. Further, these authors keenly demonstrate how a modalities framework helps us to see how nuclear issues reconfigure commonly held notions of space and time. Robert Asen's chapter, "The Ownership Society, or Bourgeois Publicity Revisited," fruitfully draws our attention to the theme of home and the relationship between home ownership and citizenship. Ownership of property figured prominently in Habermas's account of the emergence of public spheres in Europe, but subsequent critiques and extensions of his work have diminished ownership as a criterion for citizenship. Yet, as Asen notes, ownership as an index of and prerequisite for citizenship resounded in the official pronouncements of U.S. President George W. Bush. In his chapter, Asen carefully charts the ways in which Bush centers markets as sites of soul building and links ownership to compassion. Further, Asen adroitly notes the tensions engendered by capitalism's ambivalence toward mobility, tensions that give rise to a contradictory presidential rhetoric.

Home literally refers to the physical structure of a domicile—the sort of thing that George W. Bush wants you to own. Yet home also functions as a powerful metaphor of affective space. In her essay, "(In)Hospitable Publics: Theorizing Modalities of Access to U.S. Publics," Sara McKinnon examines asylum cases involving gender, sex, and sexuality by imagining, via Derrida, the nation as home and asylum seekers as potential guests. Importantly, McKinnon's focus on asylum cases draws our attention to dynamics of publicity and publics *across*, rather than the more commonly attended to *within*, nations. She argues persuasively that theorizing the public aspects of asylum cases cannot proceed without reference to theories of globalization, transnationality, and neoliberalism. Complicating both the reasons why people may seek asylum and the criteria upon which asylum decisions are made, McKinnon challenges naïve renderings of asylum in the United States as a primarily *humane* or *political* issue. Also attending to transnational mobilities, contributor Radha S. Hegde examines the 2006 controversy in Britain occasioned by then–prime minister Tony Blair and senior British politician Jack Straw's remarks about the visibility of Islam. In her chapter, "Eyeing New Publics: Veiling and the Performance of Civic Visibility," Hegdé uses Blair's self-congratulatory proclamation about Britain's courteous extension of access to immigrants and Straw's vexed account of not being able to see fully a veiled constituent as prompts to interrogate that country's strained efforts to map transnational Muslims onto its rubric of citizenship. In doing so, Hegde powerfully insists upon a historical reading that calls out Britain's configuration of ideal political bonds as particular and specific against their universalist presumptions.

Together, the four remaining chapters foreground media as distinct modalities or examine particular modalities deployed through various media. The first entry here is authored by Helene A. Shugart. In her chapter, "Mediating Modalities: Practicing Popular Politics," Shugart takes up the enduring problematic of audience agency in critical media studies. Against a rigid text/audience dichotomy that she discerns even in contemporary cultural studies scholarship and against a certain tendency in media analysis to always discover hegemonic complicity in seemingly liberating texts, Shugart advocates a modalities framework. To illustrate the utility of this framework, she foregrounds pastiche and parody as intersecting tropes of media reading and employs these tropes in a reading of sexual alterity in contemporary televisual texts. John M. Sloop charts the intersections of new media and automobility in his chapter, "Citizenship, Freedom, and the Family: Public Access through Private Modalities." In current debates about the integration of digital video disc (DVD) players in cars, Sloop discerns persistent ideologies of gender, publicity, and safety even as the "floating screen" has become an ostensibly uncomplicated part of the heteronormative family road trip. Sloop discusses three themes in the debate—physical safety, friction-free citizenship, and healthy families—and charts the various modalities of ideal citizenship constituted by the various positions in the debate. Ultimately, Sloop argues that a capitalist, consumerist framing of freedom has won the day in this debate, and he calls for recuperation of a more deliberative version of freedom.

Invested more in wit than deliberation, Daniel C. Brouwer explores deployments of camp humor in the second decade of the HIV/AIDS epidemic in the United States in his chapter, "Risibility Politics: Camp Humor in HIV/AIDS Zines." Brouwer argues that camp humor is fruitfully understood as a counterpublic modality that generated oppositional understandings of infection. Exploring a series of print-based zines, he charts the multiple functions of *glamour* for zine writers and readers; additionally, he interrogates the frequent activity of *writing in drag,* or using *noms de plume*, describing it as an ironic rejection of the ostensible self-abstraction that such an act promises. Further, Brouwer essays to describe the relationship between camp humor's symbolic politics and a much graver material politics of HIV/AIDS. The final chapter, by Robert Glenn Howard, addresses the constitution of publics and publicity through online political activity. In his chapter, "The Vernacular Mode: Locating the Non-institutional in the Practice of Citizenship," Howard characterizes blogs through divergent theories of vernacular discourse, theories with competing views on the relationship between institutional and non-institutional discourses. Highlighting a controversy sparked by the delinking of the John Kerry–John Edwards 2004 U.S. presidential campaign blog from the *Daily Kos* blog because of the latter's critical comments about the campaign, Howard argues that the naming of the Kerry-Edwards site as a blog activated a particular notion of *non-institutional* vernacular and a corollary set of assumptions about what would take place there.

Notes

1. Clive Thompson, "Sex, Drugs, and Updating Your Blog," *New York Times Magazine*, May 13, 2007, 47.

2. I. A. Richards, *The Philosophy of Rhetoric* (1936; repr., New York: Oxford University Press, 1965), 90. Here, Richards follows the spirit if not the full ontological letter of Nietzsche's famous metaphorizing of truth in "On Truth and Lies in a Nonmoral Sense" and one of Derrida's important offerings in his assertion of the *différance* that characterizes all language. See Friedrich Wilhelm Nietzsche, "On Truth and Lies in a Nonmoral Sense," in *Philosophy and Truth: Selections from Nietzsche's Notebooks of the Early 1870's*, ed. and trans., with an introduction and notes, by Daniel Breazeale, foreword by Walter Kaufmann (Atlantic Highlands, NJ: Humanities Press, 1979); Jacques Derrida, "Signature Event Context," in *Limited Inc.*, ed. Gerald Graff (Evanston, IL: Northwestern University Press, 1988).

3. Investigating the rhetoric of economics, Deirdre McCloskey writes that "each step in economic reasoning, even the reasoning of the official rhetoric, is metaphoric." Deirdre N. McCloskey, *The Rhetoric of Economics*, 2nd ed. (Madison: University of Wisconsin Press, 1998), 40. For an exploration of metaphor in public policy, see Mark Schlesinger and Richard R. Lau, "The Meaning and Measure of Policy Metaphors," *American Political Science Review* 94 (2000): 611–26.

4. See George Lakoff and Mark Johnson, *Metaphors We Live By* (1980; repr., Chicago: University of Chicago Press, 2003), 7–13.

5. It bears noting that even as we emphasize variation in metaphors for the study of public, we recognize the extraordinary variability in the very meaning of public (and publics, and publicity, and so forth) itself. Michael Warner's brief but trenchant list of prominent meanings of *public* illustrates this great variability. See Michael Warner, "Public and Private," in *Publics and Counterpublics* (New York: Zone Books, 2002), 29–30. One of the implications of our discussion in this introduction is that metaphors function implicitly and explicitly to shape definitions and understandings of public; this is in part what we mean by our assertion of the mutual implication of theory and practice that modality delivers by asking how any particular public is achieved or constituted.

6. Jürgen Habermas, *Between Facts and Norms: Contributions to a Discourse Theory of Law and Democracy*, trans. William Rehg (1992; repr., Cambridge: Massachusetts Institute of Technology, 1996), 360.

7. Rita Felski, *Beyond Feminist Aesthetics: Feminist Literature and Social Change* (Cambridge, MA: Harvard University Press, 1989); Nancy Fraser, "Rethinking the Public Sphere: A Contribution to the Critique of Actually Existing Democracy," in *Habermas and the Public Sphere*, ed. Craig Calhoun (Cambridge: Massachusetts Institute of Technology Press, 1992), 109–42.

8. Valeria Fabj and Matthew J. Sobnosky, "AIDS Activism and the Rejuvenation of the Public Sphere," *Argumentation and Advocacy* 31 (1995): 163–84; Catherine Helen Palczewski, "Argument in an Off Key: Playing with the Productive Limits of Argument," in *Arguing Communication and Culture*, ed. G. Thomas Goodnight (Washington, DC: National Communication Association, 2002), 1–23.

9. We thank Catherine H. Palczewski for the lava lamp image.

10. Robert Hariman and John Lucaites, *No Caption Needed: Iconic Photographs, Public Culture, and Liberal Democracy* (Chicago: University of Chicago Press, 2007), 317n4.

11. For an account of the implications of an overly spatialized take on Habermas's *The Structural Transformation of the Public Sphere* by contemporary historians, see Harold Mah, "Phantasies of the Public Sphere: Rethinking the Habermas of Historians," *Journal of Modern History* 72 (2000): 156–68.

12. G. Thomas Goodnight, "The Personal, Technical, and Public Spheres of Argument: A Speculative Inquiry into the Art of Public Deliberation," *Journal of the American Forensic Association* 18 (1982): 216.

13. See, e.g., Kendall Phillips, "The Spaces of Public Dissension: Reconsidering the Public Sphere," *Communication Monographs* 63 (1996): 231–47.

14. Thomas Burger, translator's note to *The Structural Transformation of the Public Sphere: An Inquiry into a Category of Bourgeois Society*, by Jürgen Habermas (1962; repr., Cambridge: Massachusetts Institute of Technology Press, 1989), xv.

15. Habermas, *Between Facts and Norms*, 314.

16. Gerard A. Hauser, *Vernacular Voices: The Rhetoric of Publics and Public Spheres* (Columbia: University of South Carolina Press, 1999), 71–72.

17. Catherine R. Squires, "Rethinking the Black Public Sphere: An Alternative Vocabulary for Multiple Public Spheres," *Communication Theory* 12 (2002): 449.

18. Research on the Internet and the public sphere has considered both the range and quality of engagement online. See, e.g., Steffen Albrecht, "Whose Voice Is Heard in Online Deliberation? A Study of Participation and Representation in Political Debates on the Internet," *Information, Communication & Society* 9 (2006): 62–82; Yeslam Al-Saggaf, "The Online Public Sphere in the Arab World: The War in Iraq on the Al Arabiya Website," *Journal of Computer-Mediated Communication* 12 (2006): 311–34; Bart Cammaerts, "Critiques on the Participatory Potentials of Web 2.0," *Communication, Culture & Critique* 1 (2008): 358–77; Lincoln Dahlberg, "The Internet, Deliberative Democracy, and Power: Radicalizing the Public Sphere," *International Journal of Media and Cultural Politics* 3 (2007): 47–64; Ananda Mitra, "Marginal Voices in Cyberspace," *New Media & Society* 3 (2001): 29–48.

19. Michael Warner, *Publics and Counterpublics*, 90–91.

20. Henry A. Giroux, "The Politics of Emergency Versus Public Time: Terrorism and the Culture of Fear," *Culture Machine*, April 2002, http://www.culturemachine.net/index.php/cm/article/view/240/221 (accessed January 15, 2009). In his analysis of the conditions for deliberation post-September 11, 2001, Giroux relies upon Cornelius Castoriadis and Jerome Binde, who offer, respectively, conceptualizations of "public time" and "emergency time."

21. We recognize publicity as a vigorously treated topic in media, public relations, and journalism scholarship, but we do not treat that version of publicity here.

22. One early effort by Gerard Hauser and Carole Blair mined the classical Greek rhetorical tradition to emphasize the uniquely *rhetorical* dimensions of the public sphere. See Gerard A. Hauser and Carole Blair, "Rhetorical Antecedents to the Public," *Pre/Text* 3 (1982): 139–67.

23. Hauser, *Vernacular Voices*, 77–78.

24. Erik Doxtader, "In the Name of Reconciliation: The Faith and Works of Counterpublicity," in *Counterpublics and the State*, ed. Robert Asen and Daniel C. Brouwer (Albany: State University of New York Press, 2001), 65–66.

25. Rosa Eberly has been a prominent advocate. See, e.g., Rosa A. Eberly, *Citizen Critics: Literary Public Spheres* (Urbana: University of Illinois Press, 2000).

26. For a recent elaboration of this position, see Janet Newman, "Re-Mapping the Public: Public Libraries and the Public Sphere," *Cultural Studies* 21 (2007): 887–909.

27. Mimi Sheller and John Urry, "Mobile Transformations of 'Public' and 'Private' Life," *Theory, Culture & Society* 20 (2003): 114.

28. Ibid., 122.

29. To be precise, our specific objection to Sheller and Urry concerns their call for an eradication of the categories of public and private. Elsewhere, one of us has endorsed and employed their ideological framework for understanding mobility. See Daniel C.

Brouwer, "From San Francisco to Atlanta and Back Again: Ideologies of Mobility in the AIDS Quilt's Search for a Homeland," *Rhetoric & Public Affairs* 10 (2007): 701–21.

30. Robert Asen and Daniel C. Brouwer, "Introduction: Reconfigurations of the Public Sphere," in Asen and Brouwer, *Counterpublics and the State,* 1–34.

31. Richard Sennett, *Flesh and Stone: The Body and the City in Western Civilization* (New York: W. W. Norton & Company, 1994), 353.

32. Raka Shome, "Space Matters: The Power and Practice of Space," *Communication Theory* 13 (2003): 41.

33. Judith Butler, *Undoing Gender* (New York: Routledge, 2004), 1.

34. See Gunther Kress and Theo van Leeuwen, *Multimodal Discourse: The Modes and Media of Contemporary Communication* (London: Arnold, 2001); and Gunther Kress, "Gains and Losses: New Forms of Texts, Knowledge, and Learning," *Computers and Composition* 22 (2005): 5–22. We would like to thank Cara Finnegan for drawing our attention to Kress's scholarship.

35. See Kevin M. DeLuca and Jennifer Peeples, "From Public Sphere to Public Screen: Democracy, Activism, and the 'Violence' of Seattle," *Critical Studies in Media Communication* 19 (2003): 125–51; and Cara A. Finnegan and Jiyeon Kang, "'Sighting' the Public: Iconoclasm and Public Sphere Theory," *Quarterly Journal of Speech* 90 (2004): 377–402.

36. Jim McGuigan, "Cultural Policy Studies," in *Culture and the Public Sphere* (London: Routledge, 1996), 27. We would like to thank Jason Zingsheim for drawing our attention to McGuigan's scholarship.

37. Max Horkheimer and Theodor W. Adorno, *Dialectic of Enlightenment,* trans. John Cumming (1944; repr., New York: Continuum, 1993), 120–67.

38. See John Durham Peters, "Distrust of Representation: Habermas on the Public Sphere," *Media, Culture & Society* 15 (1993): 541–71.

39. DeLuca and Peeples, "From Public Sphere to Public Screen," 125.

40. Ibid., 131.

41. Other scholars have endorsed the public screen in their analyses for offering better criteria than sphere for assessing popular culture texts and for prompting focus on social movement actors' engagements with and interpretations of dominant media rather than their representations in dominant media. See Emily West, "Scolding *John Q.*: Articulating a Normative Relationship between Politics and Entertainment," *Communication Review* 8 (2005): 79–104; and Julie Kalil Schutten, "Invoking *Practical Magic*: New Social Movements, Hidden Populations, and the Public Screen," *Western Journal of Communication* 70 (2006): 331–54.

42. DeLuca and Peeples, "From Public Sphere to Public Screen," 132.

43. See Douglas Kellner, "The Frankfurt School and British Cultural Studies: The Missed Articulation," *Illuminations: The Critical Theory Web Site,* http://www.uta.edu/huma/illuminations/kel116.htm (accessed September 20, 2006).

44. Ibid.

45. Finnegan and Kang, "'Sighting' the Public," 391.

46. Shmuel N. Eisenstadt, "Concluding Remarks: Public Sphere, Civil Society, and Political Dynamics in Islamic Societies," in *The Public Sphere in Muslim Societies*, ed. Miriam Hoexter, Shmuel N. Eisenstadt, and Nehemia Levtzion (Albany: State University of New York Press, 2002), 159.

47. We would like to thank Christina Colp-Hansbury for bringing the "cultures in public" literature to our attention.

48. Complementary but distinct trajectories have emerged under the heading of "public culture." Characteristic of one trajectory is historian Thomas Bender's definition of public culture as "a forum where power in its various forms, including meaning and aesthetics, is elaborated and made authoritative." While in our view, Bender's rendering of public culture is not much different from feminist (especially Rita Felski's) and other critiques of the bourgeois public sphere that have pluralized not only fora but also modes of communication and topics of inquiry, we welcome Bender's call for scholars to attend carefully to aesthetic modes of public engagement. Bender quoted in Hariman and Lucaites, "Public Culture, Icons and Iconoclasts," *No Caption Needed*, 316n2. Cf., Rita Felski, *Beyond Feminist Aesthetics: Feminist Literature and Social Change* (Cambridge, MA: Harvard University Press, 1989).

49. For further discussions of transnationalization and globalization, as well as strategies of resistance, see, e.g., Bart Cammaerts and Leo Van Audenhove, "Online Political Debate, Unbounded Citizenship, and the Problem of a Transnational Public Sphere," *Political Communication* 22 (2005): 179–96; Nick Couldry and Tanja Drehere, "Globalization and the Public Sphere," *Global Media and Communication* 3 (2007): 79–100; Nahed Eltantawy, "Pots, Pans, & Protests: Women's Strategies for Resisting Globalization in Argentina," *Communication and Critical/Cultural Studies* 5 (2008): 46–63; Nancy Fraser, "Transnationalizing the Public Sphere: On the Legitimacy and Efficacy of Public Opinion in a Post-Westphalian World," *Theory, Culture & Society* 24 (2007): 7–30; Phyllis Mentzell Ryder, "In(ter)ventions of Global Democracy: An Analysis of the Rhetorics of the A-16 World Bank/IMF Protests in Washington, DC," *Rhetoric Review* 25 (2006): 408–26.

50. Arjun Appadurai and Carol A. Breckenridge, "Public Modernity in India," in *Consuming Modernity: Public Culture in a South Asian World*, ed. Carol A. Breckenridge (Minneapolis: University of Minnesota Press, 1995), 3–5.

51. Gayatri Gopinath, *Impossible Desires: Queer Diasporas and South Asian Public Cultures* (Durham, NC: Duke University Press, 2005), 1–28.

52. Ibid., 14–15.

53. John Hartley and Joshua Green, "The Public Sphere on the Beach," *European Journal of Cultural Studies* 9 (2006): 341–42. According to these authors, activism "does not amount to a cultural public sphere until it intersects with society-wide media and culture" (345). In this rendering, they replicate Kristy Maddux's reduction of counterpublicity to spaces and practices of internal communication. These renderings violate the spirit of Rita Felski's, Nancy Fraser's, and Jame Mansbridge's accounts of

counterpublicity as both inwardly and outwardly directed. See Kristy Maddux, "When Patriots Protest: The Anti-Suffrage Discursive Transformation of 1917," *Rhetoric & Public Affairs* 7 (2004): 303–305.

54. The elsewhere to which we refer is Asen and Brouwer, "Introduction: Reconfigurations of the Public Sphere," 10–13.

55. Hartley and Green, "The Public Sphere on the Beach," 344.

56. Jim McGuigan, "The Cultural Public Sphere," *European Journal of Cultural Studies* 8 (2005): 435.

57. Gopinath, *Impossible Desires*.

58. G. Thomas Goodnight and David B. Hingstman, "Studies in the Public Sphere," *Quarterly Journal of Speech* 83 (1997): 351–70.

59. Eisenstadt, "Concluding Remarks," 159.

60. Edward W. Said, *Orientalism* (New York: Pantheon Books, 1978).

61. Klaus Eder, "The Public Sphere," *Theory, Culture & Society* 23 (2006): 607.

62. Tatsuro Hanada, "The Japanese 'Public Sphere': The *Kugai*," *Theory, Culture & Society* 23 (2006): 613–14.

63. "Mode," *Oxford English Dictionary*, http://www.dictionary.oed.com/entrance.dtl (accessed September 2, 2006).

64. For a discussion of pragmatic and semantic/logical definitions of *modality* in linguistics, see Galia Hatav, "The Deictic Nature of the Directives in Biblical Hebrew," *Studies in Language* 30 (2006): 733–55.

65. See Michael Pfau, "A Channel Approach to Television Influence," *Journal of Broadcasting & Electronic Media* 34 (1990): 195.

66. Andrew S. Rancer, Felecia F. Jordan-Jackson, and Dominic A. Infante, "Observers' Perceptions of an Interpersonal Dispute as a Function of Mode of Presentation," *Communication Reports* 16 (2003): 35–38.

67. Michael Pfau, R. Lance Holbert, Stephen J. Zubric, Nilofer H. Pasha, and Wei-Kuo Lin, "Role and Influence of Communication Modality in the Process of Resistance to Persuasion," *Media Psychology* 2 (2000): 1–33.

68. Della Pollock and J. Robert Cox, "Historicizing 'Reason': Critical Theory, Practice, and Postmodernity," *Communication Monographs* 58 (1991): 172.

69. Rancer, Jordan-Jackson, and Infante, "Observers' Perceptions of an Interpersonal Dispute."

70. For an activation of technē to rejuvenate dialogue in the public sphere, see Nola J. Heidlebaugh, "Invention and Public Dialogue: Lessons from Rhetorical Theories," *Communication Theory* 18 (2008): 27–50.

71. David Roochnik, *Of Art and Wisdom: Plato's Understanding of Techne* (University Park: Pennsylvania State University Press, 1990), 19.

72. Janet Atwill, *Rhetoric Reclaimed: Aristotle and the Liberal Arts Tradition* (Ithaca, NY: Cornell University Press, 1998), 48. See also Joseph Dunne, *Back to the Rough Ground: 'Phronesis' and 'Techne' in Modern Philosophy and in Aristotle* (Notre Dame, IN: University of Notre Dame Press, 1993).

73. Atwill, *Rhetoric Reclaimed*, 59.

74. Karlyn Kohrs Campbell, "Agency: Promiscuous and Protean," *Communication and Critical/Cultural Studies* 2 (2005): 7.

75. Celeste Michelle Condit, "Crafting Virtue: The Rhetorical Construction of Public Morality," *Quarterly Journal of Speech* 73 (1987): 94–95.

76. See Dannagal G. Young and Russell M. Tisinger, "Dispelling Late-Night Myths: News Consumption among Late-Night Comedy Viewers and the Predictors of Exposure to Various Late-Night Shows," *Harvard International Journal of Press/Politics* 11 (2006): 113–34.

77. Martha C. Nussbaum, *The Fragility of Goodness: Luck and Ethics in Greek Tragedy and Philosophy* (Cambridge: Cambridge University Press, 1986), 117.

78. Max Horkheimer, "Traditional and Critical Theory," in *Critical Theory: Selected Essays*, trans. Matthew J. O'Connell (New York: Continuum, 1992), 229.

79. Elyse Lamm Pineau, "Critical Performative Pedagogy: Fleshing out the Politics of Liberatory Education," in *Teaching Performance Studies*, ed. Nathan Stucky and Cynthia Wimmer (Carbondale: Southern Illinois University Press, 2002), 43.

80. See, respectively, Radhika Parameswaran, "Local Culture in Global Media: Excavating Colonial and Material Discourses in *National Geographic*," *Communication Theory* 12 (2002): 287; and Biman Basu, "The Genuflected Body of the Masochist in Richard Wright," *Public Culture* 16 (2004): 241–42.

1

Pragmatist Publicity

W.E.B. Du Bois and the New Negro Movement

Eric King Watts

W.E.B. Du Bois may have been seated comfortably in his high-back leather chair in the offices of *The Crisis* as he perused the morning mail in August 1925, but he must have felt like the captain of a ship trying to put down a full-scale mutiny. After enjoying the rank of "prime mover" of the Negro Renaissance and navigating the NAACP's journal onto uncharted racial waters,[1] Du Bois was hit full in the face by an insurgency from within his organization and was being out-maneuvered by rival imprimaturs of the budding black arts. A year earlier, Mary White Ovington and Joel Spingarn, long-time NAACP board members, produced a study of the editorial and financial strength of *The Crisis*. The motive and timing of the study rankled the editor greatly, for Ovington and Spingarn had been trying to get their prickly friend to be more responsive to the views of the trustees with little success. Now, however, they were armed with evidence that *The Crisis* was weakening. Their report was scathing: subscriptions were down by nearly 50 percent from all-time highs, the editorial direction seemed muddled, and much of the reporting was redundant. But the real dagger thrust at Du Bois was the opinion that the National Urban League's upstart journal, *Opportunity*, had offered to date the finest intellectual assessment of black artistry of any " 'colored magazine.' "[2]

The morning of August 3 promised no relief for the beleaguered editor. A letter from one of the more prominent black judges of the literature contest sponsored by *The Crisis*, respected novelist Charles W. Chesnutt, raised the hotly contested issue of how and when blackness should be a topic in African American literature. After dutifully spelling out for Du Bois the key elements in good storytelling—theme, plot, language style, and reader impact—Chesnutt stressed that "the most important of all is the effect upon the reader." Since a good story must "ring true" by exhibiting fidelity to the reader, the submission entitled "Three Dogs and a Rabbit" failed to persuade the late-Victorian writer of its sincerity due to the revelation of a "race motive" that violated "dramatic necessity." Chesnutt's critique sharpened its focus: "The story would have been, from any standpoint *but that of a colored reader*, equally dramatic and effective without that disclosure. So the story is not convincing." Du Bois would have surely bristled at the core presumption underlying this opinion; that the standpoint of the "colored" reader should not be used to shape aesthetic practices like writing; that the colored standpoint signals distortion of and deviation from the "truth." The question of when and where blackness enters is answered, according to Chesnutt, by appealing to objectivity—a universal audience. For everyone knows, Chesnutt continued to lecture Du Bois, that Negro dialect, while wonderfully funny and popular, is "merely mispronunciation . . . a local corruption of good English."[3]

Chesnutt's opinion was hardly peculiar. William Stanley Braithwaite, a black educator and critic and a frequent contributor to *The Crisis*, "refused to write political propaganda and generally avoided the theme of race."[4] It was not from the colored reader that these black intellectuals sought approval. From their perspective, the colored reader needed to be taught how to transcend "racial motives" even when, as Chesnutt himself demonstrated in one of his most widely read books, *Conjure Woman*, the black writer writes about colored characters. The key to understanding Chesnutt's remonstration lies in the commonplace perspective on "dramatic necessity." The phrase invokes the logic of analytic aesthetics, which seeks to uncover the a priori conditions regarding the achievement of beauty. Reflecting the grasp of Kantian aesthetics, the reader must experience pleasure from the storytelling through disinterested engagement—by attaining a state of mind where the cognitive faculties can enjoy free play, can be released from any particular use-value or moral purpose while contemplating the aesthetic object.[5] To Chesnutt, then, the necessary conditions for the free play of the reader's imagination were foreclosed by the introduction of a racial motive—a motive that presumably constrains rather than liberates.

Du Bois had long ago dedicated himself to promoting just this kind of racial motive. To him, the colored reader was not merely an audience, a group of subscribers to *The Crisis;* the colored reader stood for the "problem" of the color line as well as the project necessary for its remedy. The colored reader made up the "thinking Negro," the black folk who could be pulled together to spearhead the fight for civil rights and social justice. The colored readers were neither passive nor disinterested; their standpoint was situated in time and space, where vague memories of African genius could be cultivated and ushered through to the present and to Harlem. The colored reader, therefore, could be moved from sharing common feelings about racial oppression to sharing common specific interests about social change through collective action. This consciousness raising required strategic rhetorical invention and modes of publicity; and, as we will see later, Du Bois believed he could not count on folks like Chesnutt or Braithwaite to perform this sort of race labor. In this chapter, I examine Du Bois's attempt to produce an African American public by imagining a pragmatist aesthetics as a conceptual schema for New Negro artistic works. Du Bois makes critical appropriations and alterations to American pragmatic philosophy in order to theorize black aesthetic experiences and practices. To Du Bois, the value of black art lies in its capacity to transform the basic character of black life and American civic culture. In order to bring about such a transformation, Du Bois sought to grasp, shape, and channel the aesthetic practices of the New Negro movement as public modalities for the constitution of black voice.

In so doing, Du Bois anticipates the problems of publicity that occupy his contemporaries like John Dewey. American pragmatism displays a nostalgic imagination regarding the Great Community, a vibrant organism capable of democratic governance of just relations among diverse people and groups. By reading Du Bois beside Dewey, I intend to address the American pragmatic "evasion" of African American intellectualism. As Du Bois's rhetoric generates black publicity, we may better apprehend how he treats black aesthetic practices as constitutive of the artful communication for which Dewey longs to reanimate the Great Community. Also, by putting Du Bois in dialogue with Dewey, we may appreciate another echo of Du Bois's voice—the endowment that is achieved when we mediate across time and space Dewey's acknowledgment of Du Bois. I first provide a discussion of pragmatist aesthetics, paying particular attention to the relations among aesthetic experience, aesthetic practice, and the potential for publicity. Pragmatism asserts that aesthetic experiences stimulate one's senses toward one's environment, provoking new forms of understanding one's relations with others. Aesthetic experiences may also inspire novel aesthetic practices—conceived as communicative—that alert persons to the character of their shared interests, constituting publics. I will demonstrate how Du Bois argues that New Negro artistry should be generative of black aesthetic experiences of racial strife and African cultural memory. Du Bois exploits the pragmatist's yearning for forms of naturalism by reinterpreting primitivism as a modern and ancient source of aesthetic experiences and practices. Black pragmatist aesthetics mediates "savagery" as a public modality. In closing, I will contemplate the constraints on black voice and publicity introduced and modified by Du Bois's rhetoric.

Toward a Pragmatist Aesthetics

John Dewey, in *Art as Experience,* responds to a form of bodily suffering brought about by existing in the machine age. The rise of the factory as the engine of the industrial revolution helped to create wealth and leisure for the owners of capital while dominating the everyday work life of labor. It is easy to see why Dewey would be concerned about how mechanical reproduction would affect the working body; one goes about one's day regimented by the tempo of automatic processes. The muscles in the arms, legs, and back stretch and strain in time with the cadence of making of things seen only in fragments. The assembly line nearly perfected the orchestration of human collective movement, training the worker to do the same series of behaviors over and over as fast or as slow as automation dictated. Dewey laments three forms of separation produced, along with all those commercial objects, in the machine age: the imagination from the body, the worker from the overall means of production, and everyday life from aesthetic experience. Although this description of self-alienation is of the laborer's life, we shall see that virtually everyone in the modern era endures "esthetic hunger."[6]

At the heart of pragmatism is naturalism, which "is dedicated to rooting aesthetics in the natural needs, constitution, and activities of the human organism."[7] The human body requires interaction with its environment and with other creatures to survive and thrive. As living beings, our bodies mediate our surroundings: we process nourishments; we encounter heat and cold and adjust to each; we measure the distance between objects with our eyes and hands; we hear the buzz of bees and the song of birds; and we flee in fear of beasts and delight at the sight of children playing. Human life itself is made up of these encounters with our times and spaces, and death marks our departure from them. "Here in germ are balance and harmony attained through rhythm. Equilibrium comes about not mechanically and inertly but out of, and because of, tension."[8] Communion and confrontation define the porous membrane between us and everything else, and the mediation that occurs (always already occurring) is constitutive of change that comes momentarily to rest and then changes again. This transaction, this passage between states of being, marks our experience of our humanity. Essential to this experience are the emotions that are stirred, awakened, and coordinated by the body's construal of the encounter. Dewey explains the relational character of affect in this manner: "But, in fact, an emotion is *to* or *from* or *about* something objective, whether in fact or in idea. An emotion is implicated in a situation, the issue of which is in suspense and in which the self that is moved in the emotion is vitally concerned."[9] What we sometimes obliquely refer to as "normal" life *is* experience. But this reference occludes an important insight. Dewey bemoans the fact that the normal in the machine age is regimented and routinized; the normal is the same as always and, thus, experience risks becoming a programmed joylessness.[10]

In Weberian terms, this over-rationalization of social life is accompanied by various forms of segmentation that deceive us into feeling that unhappiness is normal. In this apportionment, religion loses spirituality, education misplaces imagination, and government forgets the people. Artists, too, are victimized. Once integrated into the social life of the community, artists now are separated out. Pushed aside by mass production of fetishized objects, they produce art for the sake of personal expression. Moreover, in order to be noticed, artists "often feel obliged to exaggerate their separateness to the point of eccentricity."[11] These individualistic works of art become identified with prized personal possessions of art collectors and museum curators, further discoloring normal life. Once fooled into believing that it takes high-minded leisure to appreciate art works in order to be brought back to life, we accept the premise that the ordinary citizen should not expect to enjoy aesthetic experiences—that one's mundane state of affairs is inevitable, perhaps even right. Still, we crave and seek stimulation, turning to "the cheap and the vulgar."[12] In this fashion, Dewey asserts, high art is believed to foster aesthetic experiences, while popular culture is considered to be mere entertainment. Importantly, as Richard Shusterman notes, this misunderstanding about the nature of aesthetic experience dampens the capacity of so-called low art to be transformative: "The idea of art and the aesthetic as a separate realm distinguished by its freedom, imagination, and pleasure has as its underlying correlative the dismal assumption that ordinary life is necessarily one of joyless, unimaginative coercion."[13] We have arrived at Dewey's central concern: to make aesthetic experiences more readily available to normal people. If "art would be richer and more satisfying to more people,"[14] aesthetic experiences might provide the "impulsion" for folks to dream otherwise.[15] But what does a pragmatist really mean by aesthetic experience?

When we speak of aesthetics broadly, we refer to a philosophy of sense-making that occurs through our organic experience of our surroundings. Alan Goldman calls the resultant understanding "sensuous knowledge."[16] The intellect is critically engaged here as well. We ask ourselves, What does this feeling mean? How is it different from previous affects? And what should I do now? These questions, however, do not fully amount to inquiries into aesthetic experience as a special kind of experience because they characterize our daily, unavoidable negotiations with life. As noted before, we must ask them in order to survive, to get along with others. There is a notable difference between asking these sorts of questions robotically—like we may do at large gatherings when we are met with a faceless crowd with which we must interact—and doing so with enthusiasm. The former is unenergetic and, perhaps, insincere. It may be performed through the instigation of previous manners and mechanisms; we pay attention, but it is a dull sort of consideration. We learn from these questions, but they do not offer aesthetic value because they do not awaken us to the possibilities for living and being outside of the scope of behaviors and attitudes routinely recalled by the faceless crowd. They do not pull us intellectually, spiritually, and emotionally toward new ground. What is required is a unified response that literally changes our perception of the faceless crowd into a sparkling vision of fascinating faces. In a sense, we must (for a short time) surrender our balance: "The live being recurrently loses and reestablishes equilibrium with his surroundings. The moment of passage from disturbance into harmony is that of intensest life."[17] Richard Shusterman describes an aesthetic experience as a temporary disjuncture in time and space that "invigorates and vitalizes us, thus aiding our achievement of whatever further ends we pursue."[18] American pragmatism owes much to the historicism and holism of Hegelian dialectics, a debt implicated in Shusterman's continued account: "Aesthetic experience is differentiated not by its unique possession of a particular element but by its consummate and zestful integration of all the elements of ordinary experience."[19] Standing idly in the midst of the faceless crowd, what happens to bring about such an intense interest in faces?

Aesthetic experiences can be provoked from within and from without: a raspy voice when one expects velvet; a soft kiss on the cheek when a firm handshake is the norm; a strong guttural laugh that breaks through the white noise of hushed conversations. Or, the shade on an idea recedes to reveal cognition more clearly as one looks upon a political campaign button worn on a colleague's lapel. In any event, Dewey asserts that this happening "stirs up a store of attitudes and meanings derived from prior experience. As they are aroused into activity they become conscious thoughts and emotions, emotionalized images. To be set on fire by a thought or scene is to be inspired."[20] Inspiration, like heat applied to any object, excites the being through and through. Once inspired, one cannot sit still. "Yet what is evoked is not just quantitative, or just more energy, but is qualitative, a transformation of energy into thoughtful action, through assimilation of meanings from the background of past experiences."[21] In skillful hands, an aesthetic experience can become an aesthetic practice that "reaches out tentacles for that which is cognate, for things that feed it and carry it to completion."[22] Indeed, pragmatist aesthetics insists that aesthetic experiences find meaningful expression. Inspiration sets off aesthetic experiences, but they are achieved "because they are shared."[23] A personal transformation can become a collective one under the right circumstances and with the right expression. This is, of course, why Plato feared poetics and disparaged rhetoric. And since pragmatism seeks to level the kind of distinctions erected by Platonism, "Art's role (like philosophy) is not to criticize reality but to change it; and little change can be effected if art remains a cloistered domain."[24] Far from sequestering art, Dewey seeks for aesthetic experiences to inhabit everyday life so as to revitalize the psychical and material conditions obliged for a Public.

In *The Public and Its Problems*, Dewey sets an idealized Great Community against the Leviathan he calls the Great Society. There are competing senses of "Great" working here: the former indexes the civic good while the latter indicates immense complexity. These notions of greatness also arise and are sustained by distinct "theories of the state."[25] Dewey contends that prominent conceptualizations of government start from a false premise; that is, they assume that there is an inherent and immutable "instinct" in humanity to construct specific forms of political systems. Theorists beginning with this instinct in mind rationalize current state-formations as "natural" reflections of the idea of the state with which we are born. This thinking also leads to the tendency to make corrections in state policy to better yield the a priori instinct. Great men, who know much better than the *hoi polloi*, shape the growth and maturation of society "in terms of authorship."[26] Yet everyone—not just great men—enters into transactions and exchanges with interested others to promote our well-being. When those exchanges and contracts produce consequences that ripple (or flood) outward, away from the private citizens directly involved and toward others who are indirectly impacted by them, we have the making of a public. "The characteristic of the public as a state springs from the fact that all modes of associated behavior may have extensive and enduring consequences which involve others beyond those directly engaged in them."[27] Dewey contends that if we wish to constitute better government, we must dispense with the notion of authorship, principally determined by a collection of individuals, and reclaim the notion of authority granted by citizens. "Those indirectly and seriously affected for good or for evil form a group distinct enough to require recognition and a name. The name selected is The Public."[28] How is such a group formed? What process secures acknowledgment of shared interest?

The problem with the public is precisely the gathering force required to allow persons to perceive clearly how they are impacted by the associated behaviors of others and to act collectively to regulate and control the consequences of human action. To be sensitive to their shared plight as a community, people must be awakened from slumber. Here, Dewey takes what we have come to call a "linguistic turn." While critiquing social theory for presupposing a pre-individuated subject who must then be reconciled with society, Dewey claims, "The essential need . . . is the improvement of the methods and conditions of debate, discussion and persuasion" for persons to more fully recognize the power that resides in coordinated action.[29] Individuals, Dewey says, are not striving for freedom *from* the domination of society, but desiring new forms of social relations: "They may think they are clamoring for a purely personal liberty, but what they are doing is to bring into being a greater liberty to share in other associations, so that more of their individual potentialities will be released and their personal experiences enriched."[30] Such enrichment is constitutive of aesthetic experiences that serve as the inspiration for aesthetic practices in the form of communication arts.[31] What I have just described is *the process of publicity*. The public is not waiting for us "out there," it must be born through aesthetic experiences and communicative action functioning as modalities making known the shared interests of a group.

Dewey is at once realistic regarding the innumerable ways that the Great Society impedes aesthetic experiences and idealistic about recovering this experience. Rapid technological advancement accelerated the transformation of the city-state into the nation-state by establishing political economic connections among localities through the telegraph, telephone, railways, and highways. Given the racially diverse make up of these localities, Dewey marvels at how successfully a form of "unity" was manufactured. He also sees the shadow of an "eclipse" of the public: "In many respects, the consolidation has occurred so rapidly and ruthlessly that much of value has been lost which different peoples might have contributed."[32] We need to keep in mind that at the time Dewey was fashioning his critique of the public, American rhetoric of "race" conceived eastern and southern European immigrants as having distinctive "racial" characteristics from Anglo Americans. These racial differences needed to be "ruthlessly" subjected to forms of "consolidation" to yield "unity." My point here is to note two competing implications of such ruthless consolidation: first, processes of Americanization, made popular and inexorable by Theodore Roosevelt, worked arduously to homogenize cultural practices, contributing to everyday non-aesthetic experiences and practices. Early twentieth-century immigrants from Europe were compelled to adopt as many Americanisms as possible, changing their names, religions, and languages. David Roediger contends that new arrivals to New York harbor learned from the start a rhetoric of "race" that located their bodies in relation to other "raced" persons and the political economy of the nation. One may be a "wop," a "greaser," or a "guinea"—each term pregnant with meanings and values that constrain and promote specific bodily and collective movements. Folks subjected to this rhetoric of Americanization quickly learned how to negotiate it, making the terms fluid or coherent so as to constitute shared interests. In short, this American racial rhetoric shaped aesthetic experiences and aesthetic practices of race constitutive of segregation, discrimination, and violence.[33]

Even though mechanisms of Americanization dulled experience in keeping with the logic of the machine age, the rhetoric of race animated aesthetic experience due to the associated demand to navigate tense "racial" demarcations and occasionally enter into sensitive "inter-racial" exchange. To Dewey, these competing forces are responsible for the "eclipse" of the public and might also serve as the source of its recovery. Recall the remarkable technological network responsible for producing even a tenuous unity among diverse groups. Dewey outlines an ever-complex political economic system required to regulate and order exchange relations: the party system, the big business lobby, and the operations of caucuses. How can a public be constituted through the perception of shared interests regarding the consequences of actions by political agents if we only vaguely sense the agents and cannot fully understand the consequences? In response to such complexity, the circumference of shared interests shrinks. "It is not that there is no public," Dewey laments. "There is too much public, a public too diffused and scattered and too intricate in composition. And there are too many publics . . . with little to hold these different publics together in an integrated whole."[34] Dewey warns against a fragmentation of the Public into distinct and uncommon publics, and I share his concern. But we must be wary of the mechanisms for consolidation, for they can squeeze the life out of us. We rightfully regenerate ourselves in enclaves where we can specify and ritualize norms, customs, values, and beliefs made of shared understanding. Dewey comprehends this, too, appreciating that sources of aesthetic experience are available in art. "Artists have always been the real purveyors of news, for it is not the outward happening in itself which is new, but the kindling by it of emotion, perception and appreciation."[35]

The chief problem with "too many publics," for Dewey, is the fact that they are mainly derived from complicated governmental agencies that may lose touch with democratic daily life. Once established, forms of political democracy are treated as sacred symbols of democracy and may resist change. But the conditions of everyday life are dynamic and vital. When the agencies and bureaucracies ostensibly set up to serve our daily needs fail, they must be revised and such reform must be humanistically—not mechanistically—guided by public interest.[36] Somehow publics must be able to identify themselves with a Public that hears and responds to their differing needs and desires without melting them into one, and this sort of identification has to precede political reform so that the transformed relations among the Public and its publics may structure it. "The highest and most difficult kind of inquiry and a subtle, delicate, vivid and responsive art of communication must take possession of the machinery of transmission and circulation and breathe life into it."[37] But Dewey's work gestures unconsciously toward the practical problem of the "color line." The Great Community only has a chance for life if it is generative of a "close neighborhood experience. . . . How well do we understand our neighbors? . . . Democracy must begin at home, and home is the neighborly community."[38] New Negro movement leaders resided in Dewey's intellectual neighborhood—and he knew it.[39] *The Public and Its Problems* emerged out of a series of lectures delivered in January 1926, at the height of the New Negro movement. Dewey draws from the critical thinking of an impressive array of minds—from Aristotle to Walt Whitman. And yet, the work is disquieting because it seeks "the reconstruction of face-to-face communities" without acknowledging any black face or community.[40] I am not merely pointing out the raced presupposition that black intellectualism is non-existent. Dewey's project is doomed if it does not, from the beginning, become sensitized to the aesthetic experiences of race. At the heart of Du Bois's rhetorical activity—before, during, and after the production of *The Public and Its Problems*—is a critical inquiry into how aesthetic experiences of blackness may function as public modalities constitutive of black voice.

Pragmatist Aesthetics, Voice, and Publicity in the New Negro Movement

It is no exaggeration to assert that the audience gathered at New York's Civic Club on the evening of March 21, 1924, entered into a covenant goaded on by aesthetic experiences of what would soon be referred to as a Negro Renaissance. Organized by Charles S. Johnson, editor of *Opportunity*, the affair was advertised as a celebration of Jessie Fauset's novel *There Is Confusion*. The promotion of the evening's events as recognition of the accomplishment by the literary editor for *The Crisis* could easily be considered as "bait-and-switch." Fauset received kind applause as she was introduced, but Master of Ceremonies Alain LeRoy Locke of Howard University had no intention of dwelling on her for very long. There were many more distinguished black writers to be presented, some in absentia. Langston Hughes, the handsome young poet from many parts of the world, was traveling abroad while his name was uttered with great enthusiasm. Also present in spirit only were Claude McKay and Jean Toomer. Countee Cullen, Harlem's very own favorite son, was in attendance and his upcoming book of verse, *Color*, was announced. Fauset would sit stewing while Georgia Douglas Johnson, Rudolph Fisher, Gwendolyn Bennett, and Eric Walrond were thrust into her spotlight.

Du Bois undoubtedly felt a little uneasy about the rapid displacement of his compatriot from the center ring but sensed something grander percolating among the participants. There was a heightened awareness of the convergence of diverse energies around the bodies of these young black hopefuls. New York City had rarely before seen such an array of interracial power brokers seated elbow-to-elbow, standing together in ovation of black nascent stars. There was an impressive array of black intelligentsia not only from Harlem, but also railed in from Philadelphia and Washington, D.C. Moreover, playwright Eugene O'Neill, satirist H. L. Mencken, editor Carl Van Doren, and the first female editor of *The Nation*, Freda Kirchwey, were only a few of the white illuminati contributing to the vigor and verve of the evening's proceedings. Everyone at the "coming out party" seemed electrified by the awesome spectacle of wealth and race made strangely palpable by the rupture the event exhibited of class and racial convention. If this was an aesthetic experience of the New Negro, it did not occur accidentally. Charles S. Johnson, a well-respected Chicago-trained sociologist, arrived in New York in 1922 with the express intention of joining the fight for civil rights. After becoming editor and watching *The Crisis* become the key forum for black artistic expression, *Opportunity* "switched . . . from being a forum for the cutting-edge articles of distinguished social scientists and educators to become the premiere review for the literary and artistic effusions of the so-called New Negro." Du Bois was already enacting a strategy that could perhaps transform the racial landscape by producing "exemplary racial images in collaboration with liberal white philanthropy, the culture industry centered in Manhattan, and artists from white bohemia."[41]

The Civic Club affair was a kiln that fired these persons and groups into a near unified whole dedicated to cultivating keener and more powerful New Negro aesthetic experiences and practices. Indeed, we might be tempted with perfectly good reason to say that the shared interests in New Negro art—in directing its thematic structure, its editorial oversight, and the terms for its publication and distribution—amounted to the emergence of a New Negro public. The Civic Club hosted a strategic discursive act, "the first act of the Harlem Renaissance,"[42] and this rhetorical performance was a public modality. As black and white folks rose to pay tribute to this public and movement, persons testified to two complementary and competing conceptions of aesthetic understanding. Du Bois, Locke, Charles Johnson, and James Weldon Johnson had been waiting for many years to have a high-level acknowledgment of the emotional and ethical dimensions of black speech—to be endowed with voice. Each wasted no time proclaiming that the New Negro heralded a "generation-skipping" force of nature; black folk had leapt forward in time, talent, industry, and temperament and were now ready for social equality.[43] Others took the podium and expressed a quiet angst regarding the modern human condition and revealed that their aesthetic experience of the evening was, in part, sparked by a craving for relief from the mechanics of society. For example, Carl Van Doren argued that the American literary scene had become monotonous, bland, and listless. These New Negroes bring gifts like the ancients to the modern world: the New Negro ushers in "'color, music, gusto, the free expression of gay or desperate moods.'"[44] It is easy to imagine thunderstorm clouds gathering in Du Bois's mind upon hearing a prescription for black cultural performance written on checks and publishing contracts. But on this night, he joined in the applause for Van Doren while planning to appropriate the desire for a vibrant blackness as a topic for rhetorical invention and as a schema for New Negro aesthetic practices.

There were several problems facing any definition of black art: black cultural performance was already being thought of as imitative, primitive, or needing to rise above the theme of race. As Sterling Brown argued in 1933, black writers had to contend with a long legacy of racist Southern literature that sought to heal a psychic trauma in the minds of white supremacists regarding a loss of prestige.[45] To some observers, the very idea of serious black writing was absurd. For the remainder of this chapter, we shall see how Du Bois enacts a rhetorical strategy that defines black aesthetic practices as fundamentally informed by aesthetic experiences of black collective endurance of racist oppression. Du Bois argues that the practices emerging in the New Negro are ineluctably conditioned by African cultural habits. This connection allows him to re-imagine the figure of the "primitive" in ways that make the "savage" a co-equal in the re-making of the modern world. It is here that Du Bois takes up Dewey's concerns over the Great Society, offering the African village as an ancient and contemporary architecture for the future. The aesthetic practices Du Bois enacts and recommends function as public modalities for the endowment of New Negro voice and, perhaps, for Dewey's Great Community as well.

During 1925, Du Bois seemed to dedicate much of his considerable energies to harvesting the crop that was planted at the Civic Club.[46] As I mentioned previously, Du Bois viewed the effort as a noble form of race labor, and he could be downright peevish toward folks he viewed as threats to the well-being of the race. Lewis describes Du Bois's temperament thusly: "Seeing his people's predicament as that of an undermanned fire brigade facing an inferno, the editor came to regard uncoordinated and freelance undertakings within the race as nothing less than reprehensible."[47] In "The Social Origins of American Negro Art," Du Bois's topical sentence is a question meant to be a fulcrum for shifting the weight of the public conversation from discussing black writers to deliberating on the *ethos* of black art. "Is there any body of artistic expression which can be fairly called American Negro art?" he asks.[48] Let us note two implications here: first, his answer posits collective aesthetic experiences as the ground for this body of artistic expression. Second, Du Bois can draw a troubling but effective distinction between "American artists of Negro descent" and black art. He was not always interested in making such a demarcation. In "The Contribution of the Negro to American Life and Culture," published in 1921, Du Bois took up "American literature by Negroes" as his subject.[49] In "Social Origins," Du Bois claims that "Charles W. Chesnutt and William Stanley Braithwaite are both American Negroes who have done fine artistic work in the novel and poetry, but they could hardly be classed as contributing to any particular group expression."[50] In 1921, Du Bois heaped high praise on Chesnutt and Braithwaite, but in "Social Origins" he pushes them aside.

To be fair, Du Bois is remarkably consistent in his treatment of both men. Whereas the earlier essay presumes that "Negroes" produce "Negro art," the latter essay is more sensitive to the role of aesthetic experience in art and arises in the midst of conflict over the basic (and essential) "truth" of black art. Chesnutt and Braithwaite held fast to the belief that aesthetic experiences of blackness defiled art and crippled the artist. By 1925, it was time for Du Bois to cut them loose. Du Bois proclaims, "On the other hand, there is without doubt a certain group expression of art which can be called American Negro. It consists of biographies written by former slaves and colored men of achievement, of poetry portraying Negro life and aspirations and activities, of essays on the 'Negro problem' and novels about the 'Color Line.' There are pictures and sculptures meant to portray Negro features and characteristics, plays to dramatize the tremendous situation of the Negro in America, and of course, above all, the group has expressed itself in music."[51] Du Bois gathers a wide assortment of cultural expression under the rubric of art and bonds them into a unified aesthetic practice through an appeal to history and emotion, realism and racism. These folks scattered across time and space in this passage responded to their individual life experiences in various ways, but there was also "a certain group compulsion . . . meaning that the wishes, thoughts and experiences of thousands of individuals influence consciously and unconsciously the message of the one who speaks for all."[52] Two years earlier, in *Theatre Magazine*, Du Bois noted that the black dramatic instinct is not so much a biological trait as it is "a heritage, with common memories and experiences."[53] And, in an unpublished essay titled "Culture through Literature in Terms of Sociological Foundations," Du Bois, this time including Chesnutt in what is most likely an early work, specifies common experiences of "work and human contact and organization" as the unifying principle for black culture.[54]

Why consider these common experiences aesthetic? In "Introduction to Folk Songs," a fragment apparently composed as a preface to another work, Du Bois explores the manner in which the black folk body mediates the transformation of pain and pleasure to constitute aesthetic experience: "They have known life with all its depths of sorrow and degradation and they have also experienced its finer and higher compensations in sunshine and love, sacrifice and toil."[55] Du Bois tests the body's durability by widening the expanse between pain and pleasure, chaos and equilibrium. In this treacherous transformation, regaining one's footing means being pulled back from the brink of disaster. Du Bois thus makes the black body in America the site of "intensely human" aesthetic experiences. Not only is the individual body subject to the torture of sadness and the elation of coming out on the other side, but the "group compulsion," so important to pragmatist aesthetics, becomes profound because it "was built on the sorrow and strain inherent in American slavery, on the difficulties that sprung from Emancipation, on the feelings of revenge, despair, aspiration and hatred which arose as the Negro struggled and fought his way upward."[56] Du Bois exposes a tension between a furtive aesthetic experience shared by "a great mass of millions of men" and the white supremacist system that sought to make forms of black subjugation permanent through slave codes, black codes, and Jim Crow.[57] On the one hand, the near-complete domination of black bodies throughout American history amplifies Du Bois's assertion of collective, conscious and unconscious, aesthetic experiences. Each of the forms of black art outlined above calls out the name of a specific degradation, and many hearers will shudder in response. Du Bois published numerous photos of mutilated bodies and descriptions of what he referred to as "deadly amusements," the spectacular ritual of cutting, stabbing, shooting, and burning black men and women to death in the South. These atrocities preserve Du Bois's outrage and relay to us the terror inspired by lynching. Through Richard Wright, Grace Elizabeth Hale is able to convey the unimaginable: "Hearing that 'the white folks' quietly shot his classmate's brother, Richard Wright recalled the impact all 'white death' had on young African American men: 'the white brutality that I had not seen was a more effective control of my behavior than that which I knew. The actual experience would have let me see the realistic outlines of what was really happening, but as long as it remained something terrible and yet remote, something whose horror and blood might descend upon me at any moment, I was compelled to give my entire imagination over to it.'"[58] We hear how one can be seized by the awful anticipation of an aesthetic experience and how the mind works to keep the experience afar and yet lively. Terror is an aperture to aesthetic experience and it shapes aesthetic practices. "The Negro has given the world new music, new rhythm, new melody and poignant, even terrible expression of joy, sorrow and despair. The world dances and weeps at the beating of the black man's baton."[59]

Let us recall that there are complementary and competing aesthetic understandings implicated in Du Bois's rhetorical construction of black pragmatist aesthetics. Du Bois attempts to constitute the idea that black folk widely share aesthetic experiences and these have and should condition the New Negro's aesthetic practices. These practices perform as public modalities if they move folks to acknowledge the ethical and emotional dimensions of speech, endowing the artists with voice. But lynching stimulates appetites in white onlookers and participants quite different from Wright's description of terror. For whites, the mutilation and consumption of black bodies ramified the aesthetic experience of white mastery, an experience bordering on the sublime as it "purifies" and makes whole the white self.[60] In the context of the more refined Civic Club affair, the primary duty of the New Negro was to satiate white modern aesthetic "hunger." New Negro artistry was commended by folks like Van Doren as a fountain of youthful naturalism to be consumed by those who can no longer drink directly from the spring. Dewey described the world view in this way:

> There is much in the life of the savage that is sodden. But, when the savage is most alive, he is most observant of the world about him and most taut with energy. As he watches what stirs about him, he, too, is stirred. His observation is both action in preparation and foresight of the future. He is as active through his whole being when he looks and listens as when he stalks his quarry or stealthily retreats from a foe. His senses are sentinels of immediate thought and outposts of action, and not, *as they so often are with us*, mere pathways along which material is gathered to be stored away for a delayed and remote possibility.[61]

Dewey's "savage" exudes energy, vitality, and intensity—these are the forces Van Doren craves. Dewey describes a life unmediated by system, society, and mechanical regulation and thus "most alive." Although his savage is spared the social death endured by "us," there is nothing in his description that would safeguard savages' lifeblood if they were suddenly transplanted to the modern world. Taking advantage of both Van Doren's appetite and Dewey's conceptualization of the value of the "primitive" and his native habitat, Du Bois steeps the New Negro's pragmatist aesthetics into the eternal life force of African soil.

For Du Bois, the origins of New Negro artistry are nearly infinite. When describing the impact of slavery on Negro cultural expression, Du Bois pays tribute to the spirit of the slave: "Art expression in the day of slavery had to be very limited, a matter of wild strains of music with still wilder laughter and dancing."[62] This wildness soothed the soul and made New Negroes possible. However, when we juxtapose the capaciousness of Africa with the "very limited" slave compound, we begin to understand the "still wilder" expression as a peculiar practice energized by aesthetic experiences of slavery rather than, as was commonly held at the time, an essential characteristic of blackness. African culture inhabited the bodies of persons who were stolen and cramped aboard ships, whipped and beaten and raped. It should not be surprising that black expression gushed forth like a raging river in "wild strains of music." To understand the origins and to reinterpret them, Du Bois takes us back to Africa, for the first time, where we get our initial view of a village: "It was a thing of clay colored cream and purple, clean, quiet, small with perhaps a dozen or more homes. Authority was here and religion, industry and trade, education and art. It was not a complete thing from a modern point of view. It had little or no machinery, it lay almost defenseless against surrounding malaria. News service with the greater world, there was none."[63] Originally titled "The Essence of African Culture," this article romances and reinterprets African village life as the birthplace of the New Negro and as an alternative modernity. There is no hint of wildness in Du Bois's vision; there is order, peace, work, commerce, and faith. The village rolls into the surrounding world like water trickling into a stream. Since the village encounters and struggles with its natural environment, it is always changing. But its "beginning stretched back in time thousands and thousands of years and yet gathered to itself traditions and customs springing almost from the birth of the world." Timeless and changing, the village embodies the basic principles of pragmatist aesthetics. The whole village experience integrates art, religion, and education. Persons living here are socialized "completely" without destroying their humanity, without producing "esthetic hunger." Sounding like Dewey, Du Bois laments that "when the nation attempts to socialize the modern man the result is often a soulless Leviathan."[64] Since it is a small, organically organized system, the village treats children individually, catering to their differing needs, cultivating their special talents. What emerges is a human being with self-respect and reverence for the village.

The figure of Dewey's "savage" materializes before us as well, transfigured into a worshiper of Africa's natural wonders: "The climate, the flora and fauna of Africa. . . . The sunshine of its central zones cloaks you like a golden blanket; it hangs heavy about your shoulders; it envelops you; it smothers you in soft but mighty embrace. The rain of Africa is a consuming flood, a river pouring out of heaven." The African must be keenly aware of these rapid and ferocious climate changes and behave accordingly. "In Africa the swift, the energetic are the Dead. In Africa the lazy survive and live. . . . [I]t is hiding from the fierce sunlight; it is shelter from the penetrating rain; it is defense from malaria."[65] It is the body's violent confrontation with harshness and splendor, arriving at equilibrium through rest. It is African pragmatism. It is rational and contingent. The rhythm of the Africans' arbitration with their environment sires their aesthetic experience and draws out a suitable practice that reconciles their body, mind, and community with the world that inhabits them: "It is this sort of thing that has given Africa beauty in exchange for slavery and disease; in exchange for that isolated provincialism which men call primitive culture. Deep in forest pictures and by the banks of low, vast rivers; in the deep tense quiet of the endless jungle, the human soul whispered its folk tale, carved its pictures, sang its rhythmic songs and danced and danced."[66]

There remains in Du Bois a partial investment in essentializing the *ethos* of black aesthetics: "The sense of beauty which is the last and best gift of Africa to the world and the true essence of the black man's soul."[67] The last and best of Africa is also the "true" essence of its humanity. Such rhetoric may seem mystic, but Du Bois's aim is to constitute a black pragmatist aesthetics that supplies a method for a critical intervention in American social life. Shamoon Zamir argues that Du Bois seeks to develop a "pragmatist sociology" that would force a "return of philosophical speculation to the realm of material existence."[68] Adolph Reed agrees with this assessment, noting that Du Bois's brand of pragmatism "can be construed as a 'humanized' positivism that invigorated the latter's notion of progress by emphasizing the importance of human action—an emphasis which, more likely than not, was rendered in practical terms to mean social engineering."[69] For both Du Bois and Dewey, a humanized positivism would insist on inspecting up close the concrete practices inspired by aesthetic experiences and subjecting them to reasoned theoretical inquiry regarding their impact on social life. Shusterman sees Dewey as striving to conceptualize theory so that its value is as an intervention in practice, "as a critical, imaginative reflection on practice, emerging from practice and the second-order problems that practice always generates . . . [and] what constitutes proper practice, and . . . how the practice should be continued or modified."[70]

The Public and its modalities have been eclipsed by complicated mechanized processes that keep persons who are impacted by them from clearly perceiving the consequences of the processes. Common experience of the consequences of political action is not sufficient for the generation of public modalities; groups must have an aesthetic experience that is fulfilled through the expression of the shared interests that are clarified by the experience. If we comprehend the machinery that Dewey describes as constituting forms of automated practices, we can treat Du Bois's rhetoric as offering critical, imaginative reflections on those practices. By folding temporality, Du Bois invents a conduit through which primordial customs of Africa get announced at the gate of modern culture as methods for critical intervention in what Dewey and Du Bois each called "habits" of living. A habit is composed of the patterned accumulation of practices and experiences that result from training and make up the process of educating others. Quoting Du Bois's Harvard mentor, William James, Dewey suggests its most harmful effects: "'It dooms us all to fight out the battle of life upon the lines of our nurture or our early choice, and to make the best of a pursuit that disagrees, because there is no other for which we are fitted and it is too late to begin again. It keeps different social strata from mixing.'"[71] Habits are "orderly and established ways of action."[72] They may be "intelligent," but they are stubborn.[73] Dewey observes that "habits of opinion are the toughest of all habits; when they have become second nature, and are supposedly thrown out of the door, they creep in again as stealthily and surely as does first nature."[74] Du Bois is in full agreement when he describes race hate as "a vicious habit of mind."[75] So, what sort of intervention can alter such "brute training and drill"?[76]

In what amounts to a public confession of his own tremendous transformation while encountering the sorrow songs in rural Tennessee as a college student at Fisk University, Du Bois dramatizes the kind of aesthetic experience necessary for the intercession of vicious habits:

> And there rolling down across the valley came music. It was as the Voice of Angels upon the Halls of God. It was the sorrow of riven souls suddenly articulate; it was the tears of slaves, the sobs of raped daughters, the quiver of murdered bodies, the defiance of deathless hope. I shivered and ran. I hurried along the stony creek, and up hard hills and through the grey and twinkling village. And ever as I ran the music, the terrible, beautiful music swept nearer. It became more human, louder, pulsating with life and vigor and yet more poignantly sweet. There was a building. . . . There within swayed and danced a people mad with song. It was the demoniac possession of infinite music. . . . O, it was bizarre. . . . I sat down cold with terror and hot with new ecstasy.[77]

Shocked and terrified, Du Bois is pulled along by the gravitational forces of something originating from an inner and outer compulsion. His daily routine—teaching black kids in a dilapidated school house—is forever altered for he cannot look upon their faces as he did before. Du Bois's transformation is recounted in many of his writings and marks the moment when he dedicates himself to social justice for black folk and wholly identifies with blackness. The artistry of the New Negro has similar power because it feeds off mother Africa's milk. Du Bois admits in many writings that slavery dismantled African culture, amounting to "the entire break of millions of Negroes with their past: their language, their memories, their ideals and dreams, their habits of eating, bathing, playing, and even thinking"; however, "this break was not complete."[78] African art has "circled the world" and in the hands of black Americans has been made "new."[79] We have journeyed to Africa and back and are now prepared to hear—to acknowledge—the emotional and ethical dimensions of black cultural performance, at once constituting a public modality and endowing the New Negro with voice: "Have you heard the tom-tom in [Eugene] O'Neill's 'Emperor Jones'? Below this, this ecstasy of Fear, runs that rhythmic obbligato—low, somber, fateful, tremendous, full of deep expression and infinite meaning; have you danced in your soul and have you heard a Negro orchestra playing Jazz? Your head may revolt, your ancient conventions scream in protest but your heart and body leaps [*sic*] to rhythm."[80]

Du Bois is taking advantage of the presumed "primitive" power of black art, which Van Doren longed for and which might have satisfied Dewey's "esthetic hunger." But we should also recognize Du Bois's critical alteration in the temperament of the "savage." In "The Primitive Black Man," published in *The Nation*, Du Bois reiterates the reasonableness of "laziness," but insists that African-inspired habits are not backward. "Primitive men are not following us afar, frantically waving and seeking our goals; primitive men are not behind us in some swift foot-race. Primitive men have arrived. They are abreast, and in places *ahead of us*; in others behind. But all their curving advance line is *contemporary, not prehistoric*."[81] Du Bois reinvents the primitive as an alternative form of modernity, not by distinguishing it as an essentially different racial being, but rather by emphasizing its capacity to generate differing aesthetic experiences and practices. The Great Society is in such disrepair that Dewey fancies that, in order to instigate the Public, citizens may need to dream up "a new race of human beings to escape in the use made of political forms, from the influence of deeply ingrained habits . . . with their inwrought limitations of expectation, desire and demand."[82] Dewey seems to have a very limited imagination in terms of racial characteristics, but he is clear that a new race may bring new speech forms. "Communication can alone create a great community. Our

Babel is not one of tongues but of the signs and symbols without which shared experience is impossible."[83]

Du Bois proposes a marriage of sorts between the "civilized" and the "primitive," emphasizing that one of the chief benefits of the village system is its capacity to nurture richly efficient communicative practices: "Even the African city as it rose time and time again was a city of villages. Ancient Jenne, whence comes our modern word Guinea, 'had seven thousand villages so near to one another that the chief of Jenne had no need of messengers,' but cried his message from gate to gate and village to village until within a few moments it had gone a hundred miles to Lake Dibo."[84] If Dewey could put aside the hyperbole of Du Bois's sentiments, he might be inspired by the possibilities for New Negro pragmatist aesthetics to bring about the "perfecting of the means and ways of communication of meanings so that genuinely shared interest in the consequences . . . may inform desire and effort and thereby direct action."[85] New Negro aesthetic experiences and practices promise to provide a rupture in the Babel of the Great Society. For Du Bois, the aspiration is for black folk to constitute a black public composed of folks who "feed themselves upon a mass of literature which deals with themselves and their experiences in a particular way."[86] Shusterman understands this consumption as precipitating cultural transformation that provides "new nourishment and alternative orientations."[87] The Great Community is conceived and begotten through "full publicity" of shared interests constitutive of "artful communication."[88] New Negro artistry offers fresh topoi for the invention of creative expressions that interrupt the hum of the machine. Dewey sensed this possibility while writing *The Public and Its Problems*. Dedicated to Albert C. Barnes, one of the white illuminati signing the covenant with Harlem's black intellectuals, this work was informed by, even if largely unacknowledged by Dewey, the vigorous interactions white patrons and critics had with New Negroes. It would seem that at the heart of the solution to the Public's problems resides black pragmatist aesthetics. And it is precisely the habit of disregard that Dewey displays for African American pragmatic thought that I wish to repair.

Conclusion: There Is No Public without Publics

The New Negro movement made great strides during 1925, and Du Bois was strutting, too. He had imagined how black aesthetic practices could be enjoyed as aesthetic experiences, producing publicity and voice. His rhetorical performances dramatized the manner in which folks should be inhabited by black aesthetics, be remade by them. In constituting a black public, the "truth" of black life is also altered from the "sordid facts" regarding sex and violence scattered across the pages of newspapers. This is so because if a characteristic of living can be "beautifully expressed and transformed . . . into art, it becomes, from its very origin, new, unusual, splendid."[89] It is not the facts that change, but their meaning and value, their shape and comportment with our changed perspective. Black publicity leads to black folk caring about the diverse needs of black folk: "The new Negro business man caters to colored trade. So far has this gone that today in every city of the United States with a considerable Negro population, the colored group is serving itself with religious ministration, medical care, legal advice, and education of children."[90] This self-interest arises through aesthetic experiences of blackness in New Negro art and life. "In drawing, painting, and sculpture the modern Negro artist is beginning rather late and half shamefacedly to paint himself and find himself not simply humanly beautiful but tremendously interesting in the dark and infinitely varied new types of this much mixed American Negro race."[91] For Du Bois, black pragmatist aesthetics yield black self-love and care, being open to all the unknowable possibilities for black beauty. But we have all along been sensitive here to the complementary and competing aesthetic understanding of white audiences.

Writing in support of black social equality with whites, essayist Sarah N. Cleghorn exposes us to a troubling phenomenon drawn from aesthetic experiences of artifacts of otherness: "Often when I take children to the Museum of Natural History, and note how they shriek and run away from the painted Indian masks exhibited there, I think of our characteristic American reaction to the question of social equality with Negroes. The children are at the same time fascinated and frightened; they are fascinated by their own fright. They are not intellectually, but emotionally deceived; their judgment is stampeded; they are mesmerized."[92] In the concluding chapter of *The Public and Its Problems*, Dewey explores the value of the pragmatic method as "experimental"; that is, as a way of testing and evaluating ways of social life and adjusting the fluid interests of groups with one another.[93] But in the American mind—including Dewey's—aesthetic experience of blackness always threatens to "stampede" judgment. Or, conversely, the habit of conceiving of aesthetic experiences as positive value leads one away from the negative space of race. Either way, the free play of experimentalism is itself eclipsed by the "characteristic American reaction to the question of social equality" with New (or old) Negroes.[94] Du Bois conceived of these limitations to pragmatism much like Cleghorn—comprehensible in terms of the way children shrink from blackness. Here the children are encountering the cloistered effects of the museum, where otherness is preserved, made to stand still, to pose for white gazes. During the New Negro movement, the space for such encounters is Harlem. But is this desire for the vitality projected into the soul of the other *necessary* for the constitution of the Public? Citizens must have a source of aesthetic nourishment that allows for all other pursuits to be heightened. However, if the New Negro is a conspirator in the constitution of the Public, if her or his aesthetic practices *must* stimulate the senses, can she or he also be a "normal" citizen? Or, does this "savage" always have to be peculiar and strange? The tension is tremendous because the desire for the naturalism of the savage scars the subject of pragmatist aesthetics. One's *ethos* as American citizen is phantasmal—an imaginary concept that takes form as one performs the "primitive" in service to the Public.[95] The terms of one's integration are predetermined; one's aesthetic practices must open worm holes to sacred times and utopist places.

We have now reached a silent space between Du Bois and Dewey. Du Bois insists on a black public and invests nearly his entire oeuvre to bringing it into being. Without such black publicity, there can be no culturally distinct aesthetic practice to invigorate the Public. But Dewey is neglectful of black pragmatic thought. In his own terms, if black pragmatism goes unheeded by the Public, there is no social knowledge of it. The Public is hampered by this omission and is in constant danger of stiffening itself against an aesthetic understanding of black life. Such rigidity hardens the outlines of "savagery," deepening its recession into lifeless myth—weakening whatever power it once held to generate aesthetic experience. Without an artistic language for the production of modalities of publicity, publics risk reifying their distinct interests. This dilemma still haunts us today as the American Public seeks to solve its immigration "problem" in a presumably humane and healthy manner. There are, of course, stark disagreements as to what healthy means and whose (public) health matters most. Pragmatism offers itself as a method, not of resolution, but of mediation—as a way to test and judge the ethical and emotional character of practices meant to improve our lives. Dewey thus must acknowledge Du Bois (and other black pragmatists of the era, like Alain Locke) if the Public is to hear his voice. For if we learn anything from this episode of New Negro publicity and its black pragmatist aesthetics, we should glean the notion that no matter how disturbing and unsettling the fact may be, there is no Public without publics.

Notes

1. Arnold Rampersad, *The Art and Imagination of W.E.B. Du Bois* (Cambridge, MA: Harvard University Press, 1976), 190.

2. David Levering Lewis, *W.E.B. Du Bois: The Fight for Equality and the American Century, 1919–1963* (New York: Henry Holt, 2000), 155.

3. *The Correspondence of W.E.B. Du Bois, vol. 1, 1877–1934*, ed. Herbert Aptheker (Boston: University of Massachusetts Press, 1973), 316.

4. Rampersad, *Art and Imagination*, 186.

5. Immanuel Kant, *The Critique of Judgment*, trans. J. H. Bernard (Amherst, NY: Prometheus Books, 2000), 45–53, 67–72.

6. John Dewey, *Art as Experience* (New York: Minton, Balch, 1934), 6–10.

7. Richard Shusterman, *Pragmatist Aesthetics: Living Beauty, Rethinking Art*, 2nd ed. (New York: Rowan & Littlefield, 2000), 6.

8. Dewey, *Art*, 14.

9. Ibid., 67.

10. Ibid., 67.

11. Ibid., 9.

12. Ibid., 6.

13. Shusterman, *Pragmatist*, 20.

14. Ibid., 19.

15. Dewey, *Art*, 58.

16. Alan Goldman, *Aesthetic Value* (Boulder, CO: Westview Press, 1995).

17. Dewey, *Art*, 17.

18. Shusterman, *Pragmatist*, 9.

19. Ibid., 15.

20. Dewey, *Art*, 65.

21. Ibid., 58.

22. Ibid., 67–68.

23. Shusterman, *Pragmatist*, 28.

24. Ibid., 20.

25. John Dewey, *The Public and Its Problems* (New York: Henry Holt, 1927), 17.

26. Dewey, *Public*, 18.

27. Ibid., 27.

28. Ibid., 35.

29. Ibid., 208.

30. Ibid., 194.

31. Ibid., 184.

32. Ibid., 115.

33. David R. Roediger, *Working toward Whiteness: How America's Immigrants Became White* (New York: Basic Books, 2005); see also Gary Gerstle, *American Crucible: Race and Nation in the Twentieth Century* (Princeton, NJ: Princeton University Press, 2001), 14–43.

34. Dewey, *Public*, 137.

35. Ibid., 184.

36. Ibid., 145–46.

37. Ibid., 184.

38. Ibid., 213.

39. Dewey made more than one excursion into Harlem for research purposes during the movement. In May 1927, he served as master of ceremonies for the *Opportunity*'s literary contest award dinner. See George Hutchinson, *In Search of Nella Larsen: A Biography of the Color Line* (Cambridge, MA: Harvard University Press, 2006), 248.

40. Hutchinson, *In Search of Nella Larsen*, 213.

41. Lewis, *Du Bois*, 156.

42. Ibid., 153.

43. Ibid., 156.

44. Carl Van Doren quoted in Lewis, *Du Bois*, 158.

45. Sterling A. Brown, "Negro Characters as Seen by White Authors," *Journal of Negro Education* 2 (1933): 179–203.

46. Amy Helene Kirschke, *Art in Crisis: W.E.B. Du Bois and the Struggle for African American Identity and Memory* (Bloomington: Indiana University Press, 2007).

47. Lewis, *Du Bois*, 512.

48. W.E.B. Du Bois, "The Social Origins of American Negro Art," *Modern Quarterly* 3 (1925): 53–56.

49. W.E.B. Du Bois, "The Contribution of the Negro to American Life and Culture," *Pacific Review*, June 1921, University of Massachusetts W.E.B. Du Bois Collection.

50. Du Bois, "Social Origins," 53.

51. Ibid.

52. Ibid.

53. W.E.B. Du Bois, "The Ethiopian Art Theatre," *Theatre Magazine* 38 (July 1923), University of Massachusetts W.E.B. Du Bois Collection.

54. W.E.B. Du Bois, "Culture through Literature in Terms of Sociological Foundations," not dated, University of Massachusetts W.E.B. Du Bois Collection.

55. W.E.B. Du Bois, "Introduction to Folk Songs," not dated, University of Massachusetts W.E.B. Du Bois Collection.

56. Du Bois, "Social Origins," 53.

57. See, for example, William E. Weithoff, *The Insolent Slave* (Columbia: University of South Carolina Press, 2002).

58. Richard Wright quoted in Grace Elizabeth Hale, *Making Whiteness: The Culture of Segregation in the South, 1890–1940* (New York: Vintage Books, 1998), 204.

59. Du Bois, "Social Origins," 54.

60. Hale argues that post-Reconstruction stress on Southern power fragmented white classes and exacerbated growing tensions between white men and women. The grand and awful spectacle of lynching and the consumption of black bodies helped heal these fractures because they re-established white paternalism as necessary to safeguard white "purity" and minimized class conflict through the shared "tasting" of black flesh and white power. See Hale, *Making Whiteness*.

61. Dewey, *Art*, 19 (emphasis added).

62. Du Bois, "Social Origins," 54.

63. W.E.B. Du Bois, "What Is Civilization: Africa's Answer," *Forum* (February 1925), University of Massachusetts W.E.B. Du Bois Collection.

64. Ibid.

65. Ibid.

66. Ibid.

67. Ibid.

68. Shamoon Zamir, *Dark Voices: W.E.B. Du Bois and American Thought, 1888–1903* (Chicago: University of Chicago Press, 1995), 150, 151.

69. Adolph Reed Jr., *W.E.B. Du Bois and American Political Thought: Fabianism and the Color Line* (New York: Oxford University Press, 1997), 46.

70. Shusterman, *Pragmatist*, 59.

71. William James quoted in Dewey, *Public*, 159.

72. Dewey, *Public*, 160.

73. Shusterman, *Pragmatist*, 124.

74. Dewey, *Public*, 162.

75. W.E.B Du Bois, *Darkwater: Voices from Within the Veil* (1921; repr., New York: Washington Square Press, 2004), 55.

76. Shusterman, *Pragmatist*, 126.

77. Du Bois, "What Is Civilization."

78. W.E.B. Du Bois, "Negro Culture," not dated, University of Massachusetts W.E.B. Du Bois Collection.

79. Du Bois, "What Is Civilization."

80. Ibid.

81. W.E.B. Du Bois, "The Primitive Black Man," *The Nation*, December 17, 1925, 675–76 (emphasis added).

82. Dewey, *Public*, 160–61.

83. Ibid., 142.

84. Du Bois, "What Is Civilization."

85. Dewey, *Public*, 155.

86. Du Bois, "Social Origins," 5.

87. Shusterman, *Pragmatist*, 61.

88. Dewey, *Public*, 167, 184.

89. Du Bois, "Social Origins," 56.

90. W.E.B. Du Bois, "The Segregated Negro World," *The World Tomorrow* (May 1923): 136–37.

91. Du Bois, "Social Origins," 56.

92. Sarah N. Cleghorn, "But of Course No Social Equality!" *The World Tomorrow* (March 1922): 84.

93. Dewey, *Public*, 202.

94. Cleghorn, "But of Course No Social Equality!" 84.

95. See Elizabeth Povinelli, "Settler Modernity and the Quest for an Indigenous Tradition," in *Alternative Modernities*, ed. Dilip Gaonkar (Durham, NC: Duke University Press, 2001), 24–57.

2

"VIII. Lowghost Publicity, or, My Vocabulary Did This To Me"

An Excerpt from The Seminar of Jack Spicer, Book III: On Dead Letters, Freakish Noises, Necropolitics, Fire-Engines, and the Missing Couch

As Channeled by and Dictated to Dale Smith and Joshua Gunn

Dictation and the Resurrection of Poetics
Yeats, A Great-Rooted Blossomer
No Kid, Don't Enter Here
The Public Does Not Exist

I

As we have been doing these past few days, I am going to read more of my work-in-progress in order to look at some of the problems of poetic dictation, which you will recall Blake and Yeats were the first to take all that seriously.[1] To them, the force of words comes from the Outside. You might recall I said

1. The "I" of this sentence is occupied, of course, by Jack Spicer. Born in Los Angeles, 1925, Spicer is best known as the leading poet of the San Francisco Renaissance, which included West Coast Beat-inspired writers and artists such as Robert Duncan, Robin Blaser, Joanne Kyger, David Meltzer, and others who, in the 1950s, met in San Francisco's thriving North Beach district to participate in that city's vibrant literary culture. His reputation since his death in 1965 has grown considerably, and his work continues to exert significant influence on contemporary American avant-garde poetry. Over the last decade, for instance, there has been an increasing interest by scholars in his work, with the appearance of new print editions of his poetry and lectures, along with a biography and numerous articles. Most recently, after the writing of this chapter, a new volume of his collected poetry was published by Wesleyan University Press, indicating

this once in a living room in Vancouver.[2] It's worth repeating it here, however, since I'm not at all sure how you, my dear fleshy vehicles, understand this phenomenon, the transmission of the outside inward.[3] Bear with me: remember, "instead of the poet being a beautiful machine which manufactured the current for itself, did everything for itself—almost a perpetual motion machine of emotion until the poet's heart broke or it was burned on the beach like Shelley's—instead there was something from the Outside coming in."[4] The poet cannot force the word into existence. It must be resurrected through the living body, yet poetic language remains in the possession of the Lowghost.[5] No one controls home plate, to put it in baseball-*ese*, you only pass over

---

an ongoing interest among scholars and readers in his writing. See Peter Gizzi and Kevin Killian, eds., *My Vocabulary Did This to Me: The Collected Poetry of Jack Spicer* (Middleton, CT: Wesleyan, 2008); Lewis Ellingham and Kevin Killian, *Poet Be Like God: Jack Spicer and the San Francisco Renaissance* (Middletown, CT: Wesleyan University Press, 1998); and Michael Davidson, *The San Francisco Renaissance: Poetics and Community at Mid-Century* (Cambridge: Cambridge University Press, 1991). This excerpt is from Jack Spicer, *The Seminar of Jack Spicer, Book III: On Dead Letters, Freakish Noises, Necropolitics, Fire-Engines, and the Missing Couch*, eds. Dale Smith and Joshua Gunn (San Francisco: Persona Press, 2008).

2. Spicer here refers to "Vancouver Lecture 1: Dictation and 'A Textbook of Poetry,'" delivered on the hundredth anniversary of William Butler Yeats's birth. Spicer introduced "Yeats as his poetic precursor—his ghost father—and his poetics perform a kind of serious play (like *Hamlet*) in which the living are responsible for carrying out the desires of the dead." See Peter Gizzi, ed., *The House That Jack Built: The Collected Lectures of Jack Spicer* (Middleton, CT: Wesleyan University Press, 1998), 1.

3. According to the authors, although Jack Spicer died August 17, 1965, he routinely continues to visit (signaled by overwhelming wafts of scotch and sweat) and to awaken in others a more complete understanding of the transmission and reception of language. During a series of Enochian evocation rituals that occurred March 11–18, 2007, in the appropriately drunken state, we, Dale Smith and Joshua Gunn, channeled his thoughts and will, the results of which are the present seminar. We edited Spicer's remarks sober, however, and the text has been corrected only for continuity of style, punctuation, and tone. Copies of the handwritten notes that were dictated to us during the rituals are available upon request. In what follows we are careful to comment on a number of Spicer's more cryptic references.

4. Spicer in Gizzi, *House*, 5.

5. "Lowghost" is Spicer's pun for logos. Other metaphoric vehicles for the transmission of logos include "Martians," "Spooks," and "the dead," all sources of the "Outside" for poets. See also Gizzi, *House*, 99: "As a charlatan and dissembler Spicer also seems to delight in creating the drama of an Event, like a magician who shows the audience the daggers that are about to pierce the box with the body in it. The daggers are real but the scene is accomplished with one of Spicer's most impacted metaphors for composition: the composite mirror that reflects the poem back at him through its readers."

it or through it or take what's provided on it for nourishment. But we cannot forget the power of the dead that accumulates in us, fusing to our own wishes to apprehend more than we alone can see.[6] This is how we discover a world for the dead and contribute to its disclosure.[7]

Let us take a banal convenience of modern technology: "the telephone is empty / now I realize the time."[8] It's only a matter of time for communication (and therefore dictation), of course—and I'm much better off on the Other side.[9] Consider that ghostwritten tale by W. Hartenau, "The Resurrection Co.," when the entire necropolitan area is wired for telephonic feedback.[10] After an unfortunate bout with premature burials, the city of Necropolis, Dakota, contracts with a company that installs telephones in caskets, just in case Auntie Bob was really just (and only) asleep. Well, wouldn't you know it was no time until the dead started calling back, pulling legs, talking the varnish off coffins now that there's somebody to pick up. We should not think of the poet outside of the telephonic field, if only because taking the line short circuits the ability to visualize in favor of an iconoclastic ESP.[11] The dead have

6. Compare to Jacques Lacan, "Seminar on 'The Purloined Letter,'" trans. Jeffrey Mehlman, *Yale French Studies* 48 (1972): 38–72.

7. Another way to confront Spicer's radical poetics is to use Slavoj Žižek's model of the parallax to understand how words evoke particular patterns of our experience that otherwise are not registered through other perceptive modalities. In order to confront the public values of the Cold War, Spicer turned on himself through alcoholism to remove the physical ease of being in the world and to heighten the spectral modalities of other voices speaking through him. By removing the culturally scripted self (the one, say, of his Berkeley education in philology), he was able to apprehend other perspectives that he received. Spicer should not be read as a poet of transcendence, but more along the lines of a materialist whose absorption of the words of the dead restored to his alcohol-soaked body a proper position in the world of the Real. See Slavoj Žižek, *The Parallax View* (Cambridge: Massachusetts Institute of Technology Press, 2006).

8. Spicer is referencing a little-known song by the band Love and Rockets. See "Earth, Sun, Moon" performed by Love and Rockets, *Beggars Banquet*, 1987, compact disc.

9. "The telephone," Larry Rickels reminds us, "occupies the place of the unconscious: whatever the unconscious may be, as regards its role in psychoanalysis it might as well be the phone or on the phone." We suppose for Spicer poetry also occupies this place of transference (the poet is but a switchboard for the dead). See Laurence A. Rickels, *Aberrations of Mourning: Writing on German Crypts* (Detroit: Wayne State University Press, 1988), 279–93; see also Avital Ronell, *The Telephone Book: Technology, Schizophrenia, Electric Speech* (Lincoln: University of Nebraska Press, 1989).

10. Walter Hartenau, "Die Resurrection Co.," trans. Louis Kaplan, *New German Critique* 62 (1994): 63–69.

11. The point is also made by Marshall McLuhan, in Rickels, *Aberrations*, 280.

always been calling to the world through us (before the telephone, there were disembodied voices and dreams).[12] "Hello, hello. Yes, hello." And here I am suddenly overcome by their presence. What am I supposed to do? Let me tell you: get out of the way. Really, like scram and in a hurry.

The poet is not important; only the poet's ability to be used up completely matters. The poet is a fiction just like the audience.[13] It's what's coming through that gets interesting. The poet is a tool, an open window, a switchboard—pick a metaphor—something as pliable and useful as a hammer.[14] Who sends these telegraphic signals? Who receives the final glyphs of image cognitions from this craggy, broken-down world of power-hungry shits?

This reminds me of a letter I wrote in 1957 for the great Spanish poet Federico García Lorca. In it I said, "The imagination pictures the real. I would like to point to the real, disclose it, to make a poem that has no sound in it but the pointing of a finger."[15] In this conversation with the dead I was learning how to listen to what it was in me that was trying to get out. That disclosure of the real is a kind of publicity for the world, making it more apparent to the reader of a poem. I am disappearing, locked in embrace with the cold arms of Lorca running through me like rooted vines defoliated by winter cold. Only through the living, the flesh and blood of the poet, do we now see what we were to each other in me in 1957. The world is recomposed for the dead in the composition of the living poet. Again, looking back to my letter to Lorca: "How difficult to take a boy in a blue bathing suit that I have watched as casually as a tree and to make him visible in a poem as a tree is visible, not as an image or a picture but as something alive—caught forever in the structure of words. Live moons, live lemons, olive boys in bathing suits. The poem

12. See John Durham Peters, *Speaking into the Air: A History of the Idea of Communication* (Chicago: University of Chicago Press, 1999), 137–255; Jeffrey Sconce, *Haunted Media: Electronic Presence from Telegraphy to Television* (Durham, NC: Duke University Press, 2000), 1–91.

13. See also John Hartley, "Invisible Fictions: Television Audiences, Paedocracy, Pleasure," *Textual Practice* 1 (1987): 121–38; John Hartley, "'Text' and 'Audience': One and the Same? Methodological Tensions in Media Research," *Textual Practice* 13 (1999): 487–508; see also Bonnie Dow, "Response: Criticism and Authority in the Artistic Mode," *Western Journal of Communication* 65 (2001): 336–48.

14. Read aloud Avital Ronell, "The Walking Switchboard," *SubStance* 19 (1990): 75–94.

15. Jack Spicer, "After Lorca," in *The Collected Books of Jack Spicer*, ed. Robin Blaser (Santa Rosa: Black Sparrow, 1999), 33–34. Compare to Jacques Lacan, *The Seminar of Jacques Lacan, Book II: The Ego in Freud's Theory and in the Technique of Psychoanalysis, 1954–1955*, trans. Sylvana Tomaselli (New York: W. W. Norton, 1988), 97.

is a collage of the real."[16] This "collage" excites me and I thrill to the fact that "things do not connect; they correspond." I take part in this correspondence to the extent that I can make way for the spooks to come and arrange the images streaming through my eyeballs and through the vast portal of imagination. Look, I don't know what's going on when I'm writing except that I am not in it. "I" is a fiction as far as the poem cares. Who wants to wait around with that glob of personal motives and histories of broken hearts and wild obsessions? Attention goes to things, to composing a world for whatever it is that can be registered in that composition. "Even the objects change. The seagulls, the greenness of the ocean, the fish—they become things to be traded for a smile or the sound of conversation—counters rather than objects. Nothing matters except the big lie of the personal—the lie in which these objects do not believe."[17] The publicity of the world is at stake. It arrives out of nowhere to shock us out of our personal stupor of emotions and dreams. It doesn't do *me* any good. "Me is memory. . . . [T]ake me out, take me out," a good friend said.[18] Who needs that memory of "me"? Move it and then something happens. Others become apparent in their otherness. Only the dead can listen through us, though. They riot with envy for what we can see, but also it is the case that we don't know how to see without them. They complete the circuit of the physical sensations we apply to phenomena. The poem publicizes the world. The dead read everything we might miss. They force me out of the way to apprehend the experience of every day.

2

We have been discussing a special kind of communication.[19] Rather, this communion with the dead, a communion of the dead through us, opens the world a little bit. There goes the traffic this morning: a young woman in a black

16. Spicer, "After Lorca," 34.

17. Ibid., 48.

18. Joanne Kyger, "Energy on the Page: Joanne Kyger in Conversation with Dale Smith," *Jacket Magazine*, April 2000, http://jacketmagazine.com/11/kyger-iv-dale-smith.html (accessed April 11, 2007).

19. This "special kind of communication" can be read in a number of ways. Primarily, it expresses a modality of communal expression that seeks to include the perspectives of the dead—an otherness beyond the immediate sensory realm. As an artist, this provides Spicer with a way to use language in poetry that does not originate with his specific intents for the poem. The point he stressed frequently was to remove what interested him in the poem to allow intrusions of nov-

scarf and sweatshirt; the mechanic, gruffly aware, chewing cold tamales over his computer keyboard; the extravagant figure of a man in a cape, of a type last seen in the nineteenth century; a bespectacled linguist squinting into the fine print of his lexicons.[20] O forlorn images bereft of the identifying markers of time, moving like flies in a skull. The poem publicizes the significance of the unnoticed random images that occupy the peripheries of the poet's existence. My identification crashes upon entering the field of the poem. The most familiar becomes strange and the poem is realized as an entity that communicates across time between actors who violate the host's body. The geographic and temporal occasions of composition provide a kind of rich flavoring for the gumbo of the poem. San Francisco 1957. Ireland 1916. Austin 2007. Vancouver 1965. What is common for these places and dates arrives through the attention and ability of participants in a process of writing that proposes to reveal something other than the limited subjectivities of said participants. This therefore is the secret of the enfolding, the rushing forward of all secrecy to penetrate the membranes of the mundane: evagination again.[21]

A train rushes against the night in California—land of greedy spectacle. An Old World couple cling to each other in the darkness of America, 1918. One William Butler Yeats observes with boredom the gloom of orange groves. His new bride scolds him playfully, knitting her brows. "Come here, sexy Tiger," she says, spreading a Tarot deck on the dining table. Reluctantly he goes to her. She closes her eyes and picks up a pen.

Georgie's voices enter the corridor of the passenger car, filling his head with a tale from Hell.[22] Listen as if the mouth of a woman should transmit signals

---

elty and unexpected visitations of image and voice. This operates in opposition to traditional lyric poetry, wherein the singular perspective of the self is magnified in the poem to reveal a special insight. Spicer resists this value placed on self-perspective, seeking instead to create a space in his work where multiple perspectives emerge, oriented by the expressive purpose of "the poem."

20. This "linguist" could indeed be a reference to none other than Spicer himself, who completed course work, but no dissertation, toward a PhD in Anglo-Saxon and Old Norse at U. C. Berkeley in the early 1950s. Spicer's only professional publication comes from this period in *Language: The Journal of the Linguistic Society of America*. His essay, "Correlation Methods of Comparing Idiolects in a Transition Area," was coauthored with David Reed. See Michael Davidson, *The San Francisco Renaissance: Poetics and Community at Mid-Century* (Cambridge: Cambridge University Press, 1989), 157.

21. We are not sure, but for Dante, perhaps? "Abandon all hope." We wrote it as he spoke it.

22. Spicer associates his literary lineage with the Irish modernist William Butler Yeats. He introduces his first Vancouver lecture (1965) and his concern for poetic dictation in the form of the serial poem by describing a scene from Yeat's biography: "He was on a train back in, I guess it

from that inhuman geography. She writes words and the poet steps back with delight. She filters the energy of the train through her. The poet apprehends the presence of his wife. She is a voice, a hand moving over paper. The words pump out of her as an organ grinds sounds to delight an audience of children. Outside the dark passage of California penetrates her husband's mind.[23]

"Like, wow," says Yeats.

Eyes on his wife. She is not his wife speaking. Those words—"The signs escape you."[24] They are little appendages arriving through her fingers.

"Like, yeah, okay," he says. "Poetry channeled from Hell."

What do you do when the spooks arrive? Georgie's calm, even voice projected images to her husband, the poet, and in this union there was a circuit—a common exchange. In this unique communication process,[25] both man and woman possess energies together that coax the dead to speak, whereas

---

was 1918. The train was, oddly enough, going through San Bernardino to Los Angeles when his wife Georgie suddenly began to have trances, and spooks came to her. . . . Georgie was in the tradition of the Psychic Research Society and all of that, and so naturally they would come in the form that the Psychic Research Society would think spooks would come in. And she started automatic writing as they were going through the orange groves between San Berdoo and Los Angeles." Yeats, observing his wife's trance, spoke to the "spooks": "He asked, 'What are you here for?' And the spooks replied, 'We're here to give metaphors for your poetry.'" See Jack Spicer, "Vancouver Lecture 1: Dictation and 'A Textbook of Poetry,'" in *The House That Jack Built: The Collected Lectures of Jack Spicer*, ed. Peter Gizzi (Middletown, CT: Wesleyan University Press, 1998), 4–5.

23. We note the complicated gender politics of Spicer's illustration, which is in keeping with the long, Western association of women with voice and men with speech (*logos*). The muses inspire, but the male poet is venerated. This association is compounded by the belief that women are closer to the spiritual domain than are men, which is one of the principle ways in which women claimed public authority during the Spiritualism movement in the United States. Despite the sexism these remarks may betoken, Spicer consistently advocated what some would term a feminine disposition of openness toward possession. See Ann Braude, *Radical Spirits: Spiritualism and Women's Rights in Nineteenth-Century America* (Bloomington: University of Indiana Press, 2001). For a careful critique of the association of masculinity with logos and femininity with voice, see Adriana Cavarero, *For More Than One Voice: Toward a Philosophy of Vocal Expression*, trans. Paul A. Kottman (Stanford, CA: Stanford University Press, 2005).

24. Spicer in Blaser, *Collected*, 103.

25. Again, this "unique communication process" mirrored Spicer's own practice. He wanted to disrupt traditional notions of poetic inspiration, wisdom, and claims of authority and authorship in the poem in order to stress the significance of other modalities of psychic force, or trauma, on language in the midst of composition. For Spicer, it is misleading for a poet to claim possession of language when, in fact, it is the poet who is possessed by it. Since the practice of poetry, as Spicer theorizes it, requires particular attention to the limits and boundaries of language, he

in sexual isolation the words fail to arrive as communicable utterances. That union of two, the Ur-Pair of mystery, the *heiros gamos*—or whatever you want to call it—those forces in the self join in the communication process to receive these far-out signals.[26] For in each man there is a woman, and in each woman a man reaches through her flesh and voice to provide a balance to nature's chaotic singularity. The outer garments of our flesh reveal a limitation marked by genitalia. These are social markings and mean nothing to the dead who apply force to force; they set in motion the essential drama of the self's division to acquire access through this struggle to see into the singular force of the poet. They make use of the war within a poet to limit self-interest in writing. Those interests are coveted and revealed in the dynamic union of forces known as man and woman, constant expressions of energies possessed by all.

This war of sexual difference cannot be easily discussed because you have to live with it while the dead are pushing through to understand what a challenge it is.[27] I don't mean to be obscure here; it's all quite simple, but it's also impos-

---

wants to bring attention to something that we usually don't think about. We might pause to consider here for a moment, however, what it would mean to our understanding of public speech and its modalities if we thought of language in diverse instances as also being in a sense aerated by otherness. Of course, practical daily life must go on, and this is Spicer's unique situation both as a witness to the outer limits of language usage and as a public figure attuned to the specific cultures it inhabits.

26. Spiritual fucking is Jung's life's work; see C. G. Jung, *Alchemical Studies:* Vol. 13 of the *Collected Works* (Princeton, NJ: Princeton University Press, 1967), 122–24, 180–85; C. G. Jung, *Psychology and Alchemy:* Vol. 12 of the *Collected Works* (London: Routledge/Kegan Paul, 1953), 36–37; and Nathan Schwartz-Salant, *Jung on Alchemy* (Princeton, NJ: Princeton University Press, 1995).

27. Compare Spicer's views here to those of Lacan on "sexuation." Spicer seems to be suggesting that sexual difference cannot be discussed because it would be like studying the body of a moving car while driving it. Lacan argues that when we are introduced to the social world, *the* most fundamental public modality is that of sex: either you are a male or a female, and once that choice is made for you, you will apprehend the world from that determination alone. There is no way to "merge" or "meld" these fundamental subject positions for something called empathy. Consequently, Lacan suggests a sexual relationship does not exist, because relationships presume knowledge of another, and we can know nothing of the difference that makes identity possible. Such knowledge would, in fact, presume a thirdness, a divine, meta-perspective that is impossible. Similarly, Spicer seems to suggest here that "the dead" represents that third, impossible perspective that would mediate sexual difference—or rather, the figure of the impossibility of that meditation. Fittingly, we are uncertain. See Jacques Lacan, *Encore: The Seminar of Jacques Lacan, Book XX: On Feminine Sexuality, the Limits of Love and Knowledge, 1972–1973*, trans. Bruce Fink (New York: W. W. Norton, 1998), 1–13, 64–89.

sible, especially since it is in our nature to be divided and torn to pieces and always hopeful for that transcendent figure of perfection who can reassemble our limbs and retrieve us from the dead.[28] Another way to illustrate this is through the films of Jean Cocteau, especially his Orphic Trilogy.[29] The poet falls in love with Death and becomes her (she is gendered) lens. What looks through is a mystery. Suddenly this world appears as if seen against a great field of vision. We establish relations. A woman vanishes. We seek her at the bottomless heart of ourselves torn asunder. Our words lose their other half without her. Our harp gets a flat. The road turns bumpy and the walls melt. This is not an Aeolian harp. Something specific turns us on: the phone rings, the radio tunes in on some wild transmission. The poet receives special training in the operations of otherness. A rift signals this in the speech and written word that cannot be controlled.[30] These haunted auditors gather over the body of the poet to feast on words and images that relate the real. And the dead like a pack of rats devour that body buoyant in booze or disorient the personal medium that receives value only in so far as it is capable of inhering to a public force that is dead and extensive through time all the way back toward a rotary moment of no-time.

28. "There is no third position," argues Alain Badiou. "The idea of a third position engages an imaginary function: the angel. The discussion regarding the sex of angels is so important because its stakes are to pronounce on the disjunction [between male and female]." Again, as we mentioned in the previous note, it may be helpful to compare the angel here to Spicer's dead. See Alain Badiou, "What Is Love?" in *SIC 3: Sexuation*, ed. Renata Salecl (Durham, NC: Duke University Press, 2000), 267. See also Garth Ennis and Steve Dillion, *Preacher: Gone to Texas*, bk. 1 (New York: DC Comics, 1996), 42–43.

29. French poet, playwright, and filmmaker Jean Cocteau's Orphic Trilogy consists of *Blood of a Poet* (1930), *Orphée* (1950), and *Testament of Orpheus* (1959). Spicer refers to Cocteau in his lectures and in the serial poem "Homage to Creeley." "And here the analogy of the medium comes in," said Spicer in the first Vancouver lecture, "which Yeats started out, and which Cocteau in his *Orphée,* both the play and the picture, used a car radio for, but which is essentially the same thing. That essentially you are something which is being transmitted into, and the more that you clear your mind away from yourself, and the more also that you do some censoring—because there will be all sorts of things coming from your mind, from the depths of your mind, from things that you want, which will foul up the poem." See Spicer in Gizzi, *House,* 7.

30. Here Spicer's comments suggest that the experience of the poet as both private and public artist becomes the property of "others." The dead, in Spicer's view, rely on the perceptive life of the poet, and through him they arrange a poetic modality suitable to them. We might rightly ask what they hope to achieve and to whom they write through the living host of the poet. Perhaps, indeed, they (through the poet) write to no one, which poses a unique problem. What constitutes this "no one"? See Avital Ronell, *Dictations: On Haunted Writing* (Champaign: University of Illinois Press, 2006).

Goddammit!

In this intermittence we find the *real*.[31] Film captures images from the totality of what might appear to the eye. The negative space isolating the image separates it from each successive transformation of the frame. We don't see the black space that lies between the individual frames, but that metaphoric intrusion of darkness into the light gives life to the image. The dead interfere in life much like this, the self and no-self threaded in irresolution and completion. Existence is permeated with non-existence.[32] Words drag the dead through them to where we are. By *we* I mean the poet—the poet alive to certain mystery. The Lowghost intrudes on the poet's calm and is *logos*. We, who are all poets in our subjectivity, have the random fact of the dead in us. "I do not remember the poem well but I know that beauty / Will always become fuzzy / And love fuzzy / And the fact of death itself fuzzy / Like a big tree."[33] We shall hereafter acknowledge the perfection of such fuzziness over any claims for beauty. The train is here; now it's not. That's how it goes. The full force of the actual devours our calm. Enter the detaining perspectives of the dead who are just beyond us and held in us. They shall see what we did to apprehend their views.[34]

3

A kind of magic is involved with this process of writing. I'm not talking about the hocus-pocus spooks of hell spark. I am curious about our orientation to the world, and magic provides a way to aid in that orientation. The movement away from convention and from the false demands of the public sphere requires

31. See Jacques Lacan, *The Seminar of Jacques Lacan, Book XI: The Four Fundamental Concepts of Psychoanalysis*, trans. Alan Sheridan (New York: W. W. Norton, 1978), 167.

32. For more on Dorsky's theory of non-existence intermittently woven into existence, see Nathaniel Dorsky, *Devotional Cinema* (Berkeley, CA: Tuumba Press, 2003).

33. Spicer in Blaser, *Collected*, 91.

34. At this juncture it is perhaps helpful to note that we think the transcript of these visits useful as a poetics for understanding the secretive nature of world apprehension through the concentrated efforts of an individual in conflict with others. Indeed, the experience of the public is very much of that between the subject and its otherness in conflict with its coming into being under the watchful eyes of others. For Spicer, however, this is complicated through a notion of poetry regarded as a field of energy in words for which the subject is only partially responsible. The poet, according to Spicer, prepares herself for participation in secret communications that others do not hear. The poem's charge to the poet becomes essentially one of ethics. To what degree am I responsible to the other? How far through me does the other reach? What advantage does the otherness of the living have over the otherness of the dead, and vice versa?

a self-generating magic of renewal, optimism, and spunk. This isn't to hide the obvious fact of the public sphere's dreadful influence over the world, itself a kind of magic projection that eliminates all but the most manufactured consent.[35] I would rather smoke myself into nothingness, hacking up lung snot on my shirt and wheezing a last breath to find an identification with the world. This other thing—this vivid, news-hungry, Habermasian Haze—is the magical overflow of an evil genius and alien, a flower-like force. It is an evil flower and I sink my butts in its filthy soil. This black flower seduces the citizens of our country into thinking democracy is alive and well, represented by the talking heads whose mimetic performances as democratic citizens generate faux debates, phony issues, and disingenuous social affect. Yet still off we march to war in Mesopotamia, Vietnam, Korea—wherever their evil magic is required. We are possessed of this dead thing, which is quite different from the *dead* out there. The corpse-like forms we inhabit here beguile our attentions and mock the living presence of men and women. Those others, those abundant ones—damned to otherness in the silence of eternity—slip in quietly through the dark to practice magic in their tool—the poet—an instrument of perception. In this anti-aesthetic realm our magic makes messages for the damned.

In San Francisco—many years ago before I drank myself to death—I envisioned the study of poetry as a kind of magic workshop. I developed a questionnaire that was designed to inform the participants of the seriousness and flexibility such study would demand.[36] But why focus on magic? What does poetry have to do with magic?

35. Spicer's remarks here recall the work of Jodi Dean, who argues that the public sphere is party to an ideology of publicity first discerned by Habermas as a principle of rationality. The public sphere is a construct that continues demands for revelation and legitimizes surveillance in a manner that encourages invasion and (poetic) depletion. "Magic," in this respect, resists the ideology of publicity in secret operations. See Jodi Dean, *Publicity's Secret: How Technoculture Capitalizes on Democracy* (Ithaca, NY: Cornell University Press, 2002); Jürgen Habermas, *The Structural Transformation of the Public Sphere: An Inquiry into a Category of Bourgeois Society*, trans. Thomas Burger and Frederick Lawrence (Cambridge: Massachusetts Institute of Technology Press, 1989). For other work done on poetics and publics, see Joseph Harrington, *Poetry and the Public: The Social Form of Modern U.S. Poetics* (Middleton, CT: Wesleyan University Press, 2002); Charles Bernstein, ed., *The Politics of Poetic Form: Poetry and Public Policy* (New York: Roof Books, 1990).

36. See the appendix to this chapter. Spicer's questionnaire offers a map toward a kind of aesthetic modality wherein potential students are asked to confront what they know—and do not—as potential values in a poem. Spicer here, as elsewhere, wants to subvert the priority of the self in traditional lyric poetry in order to bring participants into a fuller understanding of their relationship to poetry as a public document that spans history. Instead of a public located in a par-

Well, in anticipating your objections here, I just want to say that poetry and magic share the same chemical properties, so to say. The poem, like a spell or talisman, provides a compositional space for the psyche of the observer, and through this unique projective moment, the poem gathers "the news" to relate its narrative. Now in the current sense of the poem as a kind of precious object of bourgeois consumption, it exists as an object with no meaningful relation to other things. Poets like Robert Pinsky, who praise the "social voice," or Dana Gioia or Charles Bernstein,[37] who want to put poets on the radio, fail to engage the poem as a more profound instrument of communication. By flattening the complex expressive range of the poem to fictional social and public spheres, they make the poem into an impotent reflection of the interests that compose those realities. Their understanding of democracy lives according to the force of the personal as he or she is subjected to social forces that essentially demand that you behave and believe in it as a totality—which it most definitely is not. Pinsky and Gioia offer a poetics of behaviorism, and it stinks because the full potential of the poem is hidden under this social and economic force. The dead can't do anything with that. No, they need a person who is capable of shitting on the force of the social and who refuses to participate in the phony public sphere by resisting its appeal for an easy identification with the self as a kind, decent, concerned, freedom-loving human being of a particular race or class, and etcetera *ad nauseam*. The dead want men and women who can suspend their entangled positions in the social in order to be possessed of vaster regions of intelligence.[38]

---

ticular cultural moment and geographic location, Spicer's cosmic and trans-historical sense of it offers a more expansive modal range. The goal of the questionnaire is to expand the capacities of his potential students and prepare them for the sublime realization of poetry as a kind of ritualistic experience wherein the poet is responsible to a history that reaches far beyond the present locations of the self. In some ways, Spicer can be seen following in a modernist adaptation of the sublime first theorized by Ralph Waldo Emerson. For a discussion of adaptations of Longinus's notion of the sublime in modernist American poetry, see Jeffrey Walker, *Bardic Ethos and the American Epic Poem: Whitman, Pound, Crane, Williams, Olson* (Baton Rouge: Louisiana State University Press, 1989).

37. Robert Pinsky, *Democracy, Culture, and the Voice of Poetry* (Princeton, NJ: Princeton University Press, 2002); Dana Gioia, "Can Poetry Matter?" *Atlantic Monthly*, May 1991, http://www.danagioia.net/essays/ecpm.htm (accessed April 9, 2007); Charles Bernstein, "Warning—Poetry Area: Publics Under Construction," *My Way: Speeches and Poems* (Chicago: University of Chicago Press, 1999), 304–11.

38. Spicer's remarks are, obviously, intended as hyperbolically reductive. There are alternative conceptions of publics and counter-publics that Spicer might have appreciated. See, for example, Michael Warner, *Publics and Counterpublics* (New York: Zone Books, 2002).

Trees offer a kind of intelligent opposition to the lumped force of the social, for instance.[39] I remember, when alive, staring for hours over the Golden Gate, watching clouds form and ships roll in. I would take off my shoes, roll up my pant legs, and dip my feet into sudsy surf, accepting that cold tidal force, skin turning pink until the sharp pins started poking so tight with the cold water and the soft sandy bottom received the weight of me. Physical and imaginative environments enter the poet, and the dead use those experiences to read the real as it is made manifest to this individual loon—the poet. But to write for the public sphere, to believe in that social totality, is to beef up a personal system that relies on the self not as gate but as a "decider," to use the term of your recent piggish president.[40]

The poetic decider makes pretty word choices, creates interesting allusions, justifies banal concerns with greedy pathos, and safely inspects the limitations of a subjected audience—a fictional gathering of relaxed figures who could just as well be (and would probably prefer being) at a backyard barbecue in Texas (or daydreaming in a Sunday school classroom or otherwise destroying the world somehow). The decider runs the show. The decider makes every bad decision there is to make. The decider assumes an understanding

39. "So I was in the park just now," writes Sartre as Roquentin. "The roots of the chestnut tree were sunk in the ground just under my bench. I couldn't remember it was a root any more. The words had vanished and with them the significance of things, their methods of use, and the feeble points of reference which men have traced on their surface. I was sitting, stooping forward, head bowed, alone in front of this black, knotty mass, entirely beastly, which frightened me. . . . If anyone had asked me what existence was, I would have answered, in good faith, that it was nothing, simply an empty form which was added to external things without changing anything in their nature. And then all of a sudden, there it was, clear as day: existence had suddenly unveiled itself. It had lost the harmless look of an abstract category: it was the very paste of things, this root was kneaded into existence. . . . This veneer had melted, leaving soft, monstrous masses, all in disorder—naked, in a frightful, obscene nakedness. The chestnut tree pressed itself against my eyes. Green rust covered it half-way up; the bark, black and swollen, looked like boiled leather." Jean-Paul Sartre, *Nausea*, trans. Lloyd Alexander (New York: New Directions Publishing, 1964), 126–35.

40. Spicer is referring to George Walker Bush, the forty-third president of the United States of America. He also is objecting to uses of poetry based on the singular perspective of the individual. He argues, instead, that one's perspective requires constant subversion in order to arrive at a more accurate view. While democracies function on the decisions of people working at different levels of private and public governance, Spicer seems to argue that democracies focus on the public act or decision more than on the ethical complexities involved at arriving, in private, at a point of decision. Poetry offers strategies of delaying judgment, preparing readers to reflect more carefully on the possibilities available to them as public participants in a democracy.

of audience, presuming to know these participants in a public consumption of words. Therefore the decider adjusts a message that "may offer ways to inspect characteristic dramas of our national life."[41] But what makes a "characteristic drama"? Whose "national life" is at stake? Why inspect it with the snooping, grinding effort of the behaviorist sniffing for dirty underwear in the locker room? The decider is confident with an understanding of our "nature," whereas it is her nature that should be scrutinized within a context of excruciating uncertainty. For the decider, "the art of poetry by its nature operates on a level as profoundly individual as a human voice."[42] But "a human voice" is not individual; it is multiple ("I am Multitudes," Whitman yawped).[43] And in that multitude plenty enters the illusive bodily presence that is most definitely not human as we know it. Otherness is profoundly other. And at least under the terms of that otherness the real has a chance of arrival. It is manipulative to blubber on about some "solitary voice" when such solitude is a hangover of a romanticism that was always sick at its black little heart with fear of the masses of democracy.[44] The romantics fled the scene, running off to the lake or into opium—whatever it took to survive their changing world. But to revive that slop as national tradition in the solitary figure of a twenty-first centurion is a registration of extraordinary failure. The dramatic failures of two world wars revealed the stench of literature as national tradition. The Cold War and the recent Desert Wars have shown how the traditions of "freedom-loving" people leave them enslaved and numb to the administered wills of corporate leaders and the fantasy of publicity. The decider. This figure, confident in "the nature of human solitude and the human voice, invokes a social presence."[45] But this "social presence" is oppressive too. It violently restricts radical forms of expression, denying the validity of the private and dispossessed while fabricating a

41. Pinsky, *Democracy*, 16. Here, Spicer objects to the use of the adjective "characteristic" as it is applied to "dramas of national life." The moment a drama is made characteristic, it becomes contained and ordered. It is absorbed into the ideological narrative—interpreted in advance for a willing audience. Moreover, dramas we might not identify as characteristic do reflect a dramatic subtopic in American social life. Consider, for instance, the types of drama that might be seen on any given episode of the reality-based television show, *Cops*. More importantly, the dramatic is not something that can be characterized for Spicer. It arrives fully unexpected and unmediated. It confronts the habits and consciously scripted terms of democracy.

42. Pinsky, *Democracy*, 18.

43. See also Michael Hardt and Antonio Negri, *Multitude: War and Democracy in the Age of Empire* (New York: Penguin Books, 2005).

44. Pinsky, *Democracy*, 18.

45. Ibid.

public imagined by the decider to be as humanly bankrupt as the individual solitude the decider clings to as a kind of mantra for poetic solutionism. This is not communication; it is right-wing propaganda—an insidious form of propaganda that pre-determines the spiritual capacity of the auditor by defining the terms of the soul's constitution. This too is a form of magic.

In 1957, against this black force I devised an approach to the poem through a series of magic workshops that would prepare a poet to be flexible and versatile as a communicator in the restrictive cultural context of the Cold War. Remember back then everything was frowned upon and considered subversive. Queers were bad. Drugs were bad. Up all night reciting poems with bottomless bottles of Dewars was bad. It was a time of war. War on the American mind. War on voices, speech, action. The public sphere functioned to squeeze the individual into its little molds. So my workshop was created to make things happen—to restore possibility for words and to recognize them in us as the wild organisms they are.

My friend George Stanley remembers those workshops and their compositional exercises:

1. Write a blasphemy
2. Create a Universe
3. Become a flesh-eating beast
4. Choose a character from the *Wizard of Oz* who wants something and impersonate him in a poem.[46]

The writers in my workshop were to be responsible for various topics: politics, religion, history, poetry, personal insights, and their practice. These criteria were necessary so as to prepare the writer for understanding the situation they encountered with words in the making of poems. Yeats could hear the voices in Georgie because he was immensely prepared as a poet to apprehend those messages she channeled. A writer must be responsible to a broad range of experience through a number of special modalities and reflexes of thought and action. To understand politically that the public sphere exists to manipulate agendas that ensure those in power get their way is essential. The poem works against those interests by making secret public modalities that are composed of the diverse voices of the dead and dispossessed. "The Authors are

46. Spicer in Gizzi and Killian, *Vocabulary*, 353.

in Eternity," Blake said, and so is the audience. We, here, composed of flesh and blood, act as circuits between these disembodied forces. And the power of these forces is immense, scaring the bejesus out of those technicians of the public sphere and the manufactured designs that prey on the fragile psyches of a gone people.

My workshop therefore provided a way for poets to open themselves to possessions of words in them that gave not one tight turd for American cultural life. My questionnaire deflated the seriousness many poets bring to their writing by forcing them to reinvent their art with a sense of humor and self-doubt—cracking the tedious artifice of the head. The questions were designed to open the writer to another set of relations that exist outside the public sphere, and in this shared secret, the initiates into my workshop had a platform from which to begin to create something meaningful and through which the real could impose itself. I also wanted to show how great works and ideas are not generated aesthetically, despite all the damaging slop Kant spits to the contrary. The world is fuzzy. That's all. The poet tries to make it less so, in part, to let in some vision of this place for anyone desperate enough to look out through these organs we possess.

4

You will remember, too, how once upon a time being queer was complicated by the utter rejection of homosexuality from the public sphere.[47] There were threats from all directions. But this made me strong and reaffirmed my disgust with a public sphere that manufactures appropriate responses to sexuality through its many reinforcing narratives of this obsession on the parts of our capitalist owners. What I envisioned instead was a ritual search for the chalice—the Holy Grail. This spiritual quest for some understanding of myself you might say was inspired perhaps by this other problem of sexuality—the woven threads of spirit and body in conflict with the Outside. To be in or out matters. Where we side is essential in the ongoing process of self-revelation through the other voices that enter and wrestle *you* down in order to observe our condition with accuracy. With this in mind I ended the "Book of Gawain" thus:

47. See Davin Allen Grindstaff, *Rhetorical Secrets: Mapping Gay Identity and Queer Resistance in Contemporary America* (Tuscaloosa: University of Alabama Press, 2006).

Perverse
Turned against the light
The grail they said
Is achieved by steady compromise.
An unending
The prize is there at the bottom of the rainbow—follow the invisible
markings processwise
I, Gawain, who am no longer human but a legend followed the markings
Did
More or less what they asked
My name is now a symbol for shame
I, Gawain, who once was a knight of the Grail in a dark forest.[48]

I possessed this shame in order to fully retaliate against the mainstream straight culture that would project it over me. Doubly damned by them for poetry and queer sex, I integrated the condition of the Outside into the habits of my life: haunting bars all day and night; seeking the company of beautiful boys; submitting myself to the mercy of the dead the long hours of early morning; smoking unfiltered cigarettes and banging myself against a typewriter trying to hear what was coming in and moving—to get me out of the way.[49] It was

48. Spicer in Blaser, *Collected,* 190.

49. Spicer's shift in cadence is in keeping with his acute attention to the daily. The rhythm establishes a space for his voice to acquire the elements of his surroundings. He might argue that, through song, the world is apprehended as an imagined value reflected in language. His poetics—with other writers of the San Francisco Renaissance—stresses the importance of what's happening rather than lifting the thoughts and feelings of the individual to public inspection. Spicer's poetics, in a sense, publicizes quotidian aspects of experience typically neglected by the officially sanctioned public representations of American democracy. While poetry is only one genre of many epideictic modes of communication in a democratic society, it is, by its very isolation from more popular genres of communication, more capable of disclosures of the complexity and variety of public and private life. Indeed, as Spicer sees it, public and private values are always in collision, and if, in his terms, the "dead" are both authors and audience of the living perspectives of the poem, publics and publicity extend far beyond more practical, deliberative modes of life. One may claim that a conception of a public that includes the dead is impractical and foolish. Spicer might even agree. To his defense, however, one might note how until only relatively recently, the dead preoccupied a large proportion of cultural space, and for many cultures the rituals of attendance to the dead remain a popular aspect of daily life. The benefit of recognizing the dead as contemporaneous with the living is important for many. The daily recognition of the limitations of life and of the labor that took place prior to our own provides a perspective that brings reflection on the acts one proposes in the present. How might the dead be honored by the practices of

a motion, a turning to the light noise of morning traffic, cable cars knocking by, some late-night junkie zoned out in mirth in the hallway, taking in my mouth the full force of that Otherness, the stains on my cot, weeping old queens on Polk Street gnashing their teeth in some gutter. It was a quest for self-possession—and then learning how to give it away once you got it. How you can hold nothing—not even yourself—a lover—some fleeting moment—the seagulls against the horizon of the San Francisco Bay—the shattering cold blue of autumn—this fading life—drunkenness—chaos—reaching for—what comes—the invasion of the body by others—forced into words—spoken—my knuckle-dragging form—ape—ape—that ugliness beheld—a boy—and no other but what you are capable of—the heat rush of sex—cold pause—the window—and trolley—emptied—beer and whiskey—so unsexy—hung over—stained shirts—for love—no—for to clear out me and *not me*—the culture that made me—dead—my death to it—it in me—nothing—a secret—to be new—new words for a new world—the secret place outside—

> Fool-
> Killer lurks between the branches of every tree
> Bird-language.
> Fooled by nature, I
> Accepted the quest gracefully
> Played the fool. Fool-
> Killer in the branches waiting.
> Left home. Fool-killer left home too. Followed me.
> Fool-
> Killer thinks that just before the moment I will find the grail he
>   will catch me. Poor
> Little boy in the forest
> Dancing.[50]

---

the living? Since all die, how might we prepare ourselves for their company with good conscience, leaving behind a world that is properly prepared for future generations? Clearly, with this perspective, one might say that the failure to properly honor the dead in Western societies today has lead to a number of potentially catastrophic problems. A public without access to the dead surely lives with a fatal hubris.

50. In this dramatic narrative sequence, Spicer's struggle to apprehend the "grail" can be seen as a battle in the creative spirit between forces of foolery and wisdom. The fool and the wise man—the fool's assassin—together form a dual creative substance, in Spicer's alchemy, through which greater forms of awareness emerge. See Spicer in Blaser, *Collected*, 191.

Fool for sure. Dancing. Fool-killer. Leaving home. This, from "The Book of Percival," illustrates perhaps most adequately the situation. It is tense with self-battle. You must kill the fool but you hate to. The fool in you too makes you dance. And then some other arrives anyway to do that in. How to keep that poor creature alive? There is nowhere for him. The totalizing culture that surrounds us despises such gestures of foolish "behavior" and hates more the dispossession of the self from its fool, or any other spiritual communion with otherness. The public violates all claims for truth. The public participates in a kind of perpetual onanism. The public reeks of self-important members performing scripts for auditors who willingly misbelieve. Are misled. Are mistaken in a doomed spiritual romance of powerful interests. No otherness penetrates that sphere. The dispossessed languish in oblivion. Those voices vanish to the inner corridors of the nothingness succored by poets.

The public with its election. The public with its wars in the East and Middle East. The public with its surveillance. The public with its idiotic majority. The public with its deciders. The public with its solutions. The public with its violence just under the surface. The public with its straight sex. The public with its leash on language. The public with its impossible spiritual claims. The public with its secular determinism. The public with its hatred and indifference. The public with its careers. The public with what it calls education. The public forever festering and destroying global resources. The public with its crazed ethnic hatreds. The public to be pissed on pissing on you instead for speaking another language. The public and its need for legitimacy from the most illegitimate. The public has failed. Unreal public. Spectacular spectacle. The other public of the real. That audience. Who listens. Who reads through our organs. Those others. Those dead ones. The public does not exist. And if it did, the public is dead.

Appendix
"Poetry as Magic" Workshop

This questionnaire is in no sense designed to indicate whether you can write poetry.[51] Since the workshop is limited to 15 people, I must have some guide as to which of you would most benefit from a workshop of this particular content. Some of the questions will seem bizarre or pointless, but it would be useful if you would answer all of them as precisely as possible.

A list of those selected will be posted on Thursday, February 21, on the main bulletin board of the Library and at the Poetry Center, S. F. State College, Juniper 4-2300, Ext. 251.

I. *POLITICS*

1. What is your favorite political song?

____

2. If you had a chance to eliminate three political figures in the world, which would you choose?

    1. ______________________________________
    2. ______________________________________
    3. ______________________________________

3. What political group, slogan, or idea in the world today has the most to do with Magic? ______________________________
______________________. With Poetry? ______________________
____

4. Who were the Lovestoneites?

51. Jack Spicer's Magic Workshop questionnaire reprinted with the permission of the estate of Jack Spicer (from "'Poetry as Magic' Workshop," in Gizzi and Killian, *Vocabulary*, 354–60.

II. *RELIGION*

1. Which one of these figures had or represented religious views nearest to your own religious views? Which furthest? Jesus, Emperor Julian, Diogenes, Buddha, Confucius, Marcus Aurelius, Lao Tse, Socrates, Dionysus, Apollo, Hermes Trismegistus, Li Po, Heraclitus, Epicurus, Apollonius of Tyana, Simon Magus, Zoroaster, Mohammed, the White Goddess, Cicero.

Nearest ____________________. Furthest ____________________.

2. Classify this set of figures in the same way. Calvin, Kierkegaard, Suzuki, Schweitzer, Marx, Russell, St. Thomas Aquinas, Luther, St. Augustine, Santayana, the Mad Bomber, Marquis de Sade, Yeats, Gandhi, William James, Hitler, C. S. Lewis, Proust.

Nearest ____________________. Furthest ____________________.

3. What is your favorite book of the Bible? ____________________.

III. *HISTORY*

1. Give the approximate date of the following people or events:

Plato _____ Buddha ______ The Battle of Waterloo ______ Dante______
The invention of printing ______ Nero ______ Chaucer ______
The unification of Italy ______ Joan of Arc______

2. Write a paragraph about how the fall of Rome affected modern poetry.

IV. *POETRY*

1. If you were editing a magazine and had an unlimited budget, which poets would you first ask for contributions?

____

____

____

V. *PERSONAL*

1. Name: ____________________ Address: ____________________
Age: ____ Sex: _____ City: ________________ Phone: __________
Height: ________ Weight: ________ Married or unmarried: ________

2. What animal do you most resemble? ____________________

3. What insect do you most resemble? ____________________

4. What star do you most resemble? ____________________

5. What card of the ordinary playing-card deck (or Tarot deck) represents the absolute of your desires? ____________________
the absolute of your fears? ____________________

6. Write the funniest joke that you know.

VI. *PRACTICE*

ANSWER EITHER OR BOTH QUESTION 1 AND 2

1. In any of the three following poems fill in each of the blanks with any number of words you wish (including none), attempting to make a complete and satisfactory poem. Do not alter any of the existing words or punctuation or increase the number of lines.

2. Invent a dream in which you appear as a poet.

I

With the gums gone . . . .
are . . . . . . And though the nose is . . . . . nothing,
the eye . . . . . .

And now the . . . . .
Of the radiator . . . . . floor
is . . . . . , the even row of it
fit to raise
. . . . . children.

You will count . . . . .
You will stay in the midst of them,
You will know . . . . . , you will hear them
in the narrow . . . . . .

II
In . . . . endlessness
Snow, ... salt
He lost his . . . .

The color white. He walks
Over a . . . . carpet made
. . . .

Without eyes or thumbs
He suffers . . . .
But the . . . . quiver

In the . . . . endlessness
How . . . . a wound
His . . . . left.

Snow, ... salt . . . .
In the . . . . endlessness.

III
Blue-rooted heron, ... lake
. . . . song, like me no traveler
Taking . . . . rest, loose-winged water-bird
And dumb with music . . . .

I stand upon the waterfront, like him no traveler
. . . . , dangling on . . . . wings.
Aching for flight, for . . . .
I . . . . and take my rest.

They will not hunt us . . . .
The flesh of the . . . . is . . . . and is dumb.
The sound of an arrow, the sight of a hunter
. . . . life without wings.

So let us die for death alone is motion
And death alone will make these herons fly.
. . . . wingless . . . . ocean
. . . . die.

3
Everyday Life and Death in a Nuclear World
Stories from Fernald

Phaedra C. Pezzullo and Stephen P. Depoe

> He had a lump on his tongue, and it was summer. And he and I both had a problem with acid from tomatoes, so we assumed that's what it was. Well, it didn't get any better, and it didn't get any better, and it didn't get any better, so finally, he went to the doctor, and the doctor decided to operate and take it out and he found out it was cancer. And he did fine after that. And later on, um, maybe nine months, he discovered this lump on his neck. And then he went back to the surgeon, and the surgeon did a very big operation on his neck and took all that out, took some of the lymph glands out, and it was just downhill from then on.
>
> —Nancy Abbott, 1999 interview

After working at the Fernald nuclear weapons production complex eighteen miles northwest of Cincinnati, Ohio, for twenty-six years, Nancy Abbott's husband, Gus Abbott, developed multiple forms of cancer and eventually died at the early age of fifty in 1982. His story is a typical one from Fernald insofar as the workers at the site did not expect occupational health complications, though their jobs generally were perceived as integral to national security.[1] Physical signs of illnesses such as cancer were chalked up to more banal causes, like the acidity of tomatoes. Only reluctantly were doctors consulted and questions asked.

Although these stories eventually sparked a public controversy, we aim to explore the moment in history *before* workers and residents were moved to publicize their struggles about living—and dying—in a nuclear world every day. As Gerard Hauser suggests, we are utilizing a rhetorical perspective that "*reveals rather than conceals the emergence of publics as a process.*"[2] In contrast to an isolated incident of disaster, stories from Fernald depict a tale of the banality of nuclear pollution that continued until the facility stopped production. Cumulatively, these voices tell a story about disaster as everyday life.[3] To illustrate this point, we show how everyday life at Fernald involved silence and deception from the government and the contracted corporations that ran the facility, as well as repetition of toxic exposure to the bodies of those who worked and lived in the vicinity.[4] Despite the ways that accidents and death became a part of their everyday lives, the stories from Fernald show how residents and workers were reluctant to publicize any suspicions or concerns with the facility until their sense of the everyday was interrupted.

To more clearly identify elements constituting everyday life in a nuclear world, we listen to the voices of those most directly impacted by the opening and closing of Fernald. In addition to secondary news sources and archival research, this chapter primarily focuses on interviews from the Fernald Living History Project. Since 1999, a decade after the facility stopped weapons operations, over 125 videotaped oral history interviews have been collected from retired workers and local residents and placed in the public domain.[5] Given the repeated references to "everyday life" by residents and workers, we were reminded of how interviews enable us to hear about emergent practices and marginalized voices in ways that might otherwise be deemed not newsworthy by mainstream media and other common sources of studying publics.[6]

These stories also reveal how *the everyday functions discursively to attenuate crisis:* things that more readily seem irregular and dangerous from an outside perspective may appear as typical to those who live with these signs of crisis on a regular basis. We identify the ways Fernald itself, accidents, and death became a part of workers' and residents' everyday lives, and then, in its most nascent moments, how that sense of the everyday initially became interrupted. By following the lead of the residents and workers in framing the stories of Fernald as everyday, we aim to bring attention to how public engagement—understood as an inventional rhetorical process—does not occur ex nihilo, instantaneously, or inevitably when exposure to disaster occurs.

In addition to this empirical analysis grounded in the specificities of Fernald's history and memories of it, the concept of everyday life also promises a rich heuristic for scholarly research more broadly. Ben Highmore notes the ongoing popularity of "everyday life" as a theoretical concept is due to its powers "to make the invisible visible," especially "the lives of those who have been sidelined by dominant accounts of social life."[7] Indeed, for this chapter, everyday life is a useful frame because it goads us to listen to stories about living near and working with nuclear weapons production for what initially is marked as banal or "invisible," so that we can make those moments "visible" for critique.[8] Listening to stories of people's everyday experiences enables us to historicize the ways such a seemingly extraordinary way of life can become ordinary and the moments when that sense of banality is called into question, if it is. Although theorists such as Michel de Certeau have persuasively argued that practices of everyday life *can* provide opportunities for rhetorical invention and resisting alienation, as Henri Lefebvre points out, theorizing the everyday also requires that we come to terms with the barriers to critique.[9]

Further, for purposes of this volume, we want to highlight what difference it makes to analyze these voices and practices from Fernald *as a study of modalities* rather than spheres. Scholarship addressing public *spheres* has enabled critical inquiry into previously less discussed power dynamics related to physical location (e.g., via salons, Internet communities, or prisons) and identity (e.g., infantile, African American, or feminist). For environmental scholars, this turn has enabled a more robust dialogue about environmental communication, including global discourses of sustainability,[10] the ways the media shape environmental activism,[11] and how counterpublic critiques emerge contextually, often within broader corporate frames and through embodied practices.[12] It also has raised provocative discussions about the idea of a "nuclear public sphere" and how it might become more democratic.[13] Although environmental concerns remain marginalized in the vast majority of scholarship about publics, these inroads suggest hopeful possibilities for some of the most pressing challenges humans face.

Prompting a shift from public spheres to public modalities, therefore, could be perceived as an ambivalent turn for scholars who value a more just and sustainable world. On the one hand, de-centering spheres and, by implication, space or place, risks pushing environmental matters even further back into the margins at a time when just the opposite seems appropriate. On the other hand, this move also offers an opportunity to challenge perceptions of nature and environmental concerns as static, merely place-based, and easily divorced from questions of time, technology, or identity. This chapter was written in the hopes of promoting the latter and deterring moves toward the former.

We begin our analysis by painting a broad picture of nuclear culture within the United States and in relation to Fernald. This context briefly articulates how popular discourses of nuclear weapons and waste challenge many assumptions about time and space in the public imagination. Then, we turn our attention to the interviews in order to examine the stories of one specific nuclear facility. These voices help emphasize the significance of listening to people who are marginalized by dominant culture and the stories they have to tell about everyday life, disaster, and emergent publics.

"Going Nuclear"

Mushroom clouds billowing in the sky from nuclear weapons detonation are iconic images of nuclear culture. Perhaps they have gained such popularity due to the concrete form they offer this unparalleled modern technology or to the symbolic index they provide for the "mind-blowing" significance of such a disastrous moment or to the ways the smoke obscures the atrocities undoubtedly happening on the ground. Whatever is the attraction, public engagement with the nuclear is framed by time and space in ways that challenge our quotidian imaginations. As such, it seems helpful to take note of some of the more significant ways the nuclear exists in popular imaginations as a way of assessing specific limitations and possibilities for connections and disconnections between networks of people and places.

Temporally, the use of nuclear weapons in war tends to be understood as an extreme measure or last resort. Consider, for example, how "the day after" is a phrase often reserved for apocalyptic nuclear tales.[14] The traction of such an expression presumably is infused with the tacit belief that a multisided nuclear war would alter life as we know it to such a significant degree that history would need to start all over again. Hence, some argue that the production of nuclear weapons is undertaken as deterrence from war, rather than with the intention or hope of actually using the products being built.

Beyond the moment of detonation, however, nuclear weapons and energy production also require that we alter our sense of time in an astonishingly broader scale. They require that we ask questions such as, How does one write a message designed to leave a public impression for at least *ten thousand* years?[15] In 1991, the Sandia National Laboratories charged a multidisciplinary group of scholars and practitioners with just such a task: to deter future generations from disturbing the world's first underground nuclear weapons waste repository.[16] After a fascinating debate about which combination of language and symbols could stand the test of nuclear time, their answer, in part, was to suggest the following inscription: "This place is not a place of honor. No highly esteemed deed is commemorated here. Nothing valued is here. This place is a message and part of a system of messages. Pay attention to it. Sending this message was important to us. We considered ourselves to be a powerful culture."[17]

Is this statement enough to convince people three hundred generations into the future not to disrupt what is buried under the surface of the Earth and, therefore, to postpone disaster? Does it balance the need to clarify that the site is important without sparking interest in what it could be? Although such questions may sound dire, this exercise has not yet motivated the U.S. government to cease building more nuclear weapons or creating more nuclear waste. Thus, nuclear production poses the temporal challenge of recognizing the longevity of its physical impact while, one might argue, nihilistically moving forward with faith in its worth for the present.

Spatially, nuclear culture is no less complicated. Given the well-acknowledged chances of everyday risk and devastating meltdowns, nuclear facilities tend to be placed in relatively rural, working-class communities with the assumption that any disasters will impact fewer people and, arguably, people deemed less important by dominant culture. Often, for example, uranium ore mining, production facilities, and aboveground testing have occurred on Native American lands.[18] These relatively isolated communities that bear the brunt of the inevitable environmental injustices of "doing business" ironically become spatially linked with global military relations as they are transformed into sites vital to national defense.[19]

Further, as the environmental justice saying goes, "the wind blows and the water flows." Despite identifying places with relatively smaller populations of people to place at risk, the air, ground, and water pollution from nuclear weapons production complexes creates additional spatial linkages between these sites and surrounding communities. These connections occur through the everyday movement of transportation and laborers in and out of nuclear facilities and through releases from the facilities themselves. Spatially, radioactive waste in the water cycle has endless repercussions as it evaporates, precipitates, flows, and absorbs throughout the environment. More immediately, for example, consider that the Chernobyl meltdown resulted in *high* radiation levels for at least a twenty-mile radius. For Fernald, therefore, such a spatial appreciation of the risks of nuclear production would include the entire city of Cincinnati. Further, as Bryan Taylor and colleagues point out, a 2003 study by the U.S. Center for Disease Control and Prevention found "that radioactive fallout from above-ground nuclear weapons tests conducted between 1951 and 1962 exposed virtually everyone in the United States and contributed to 11,000 excess cancer deaths."[20]

Nuclear weapons facilities such as Fernald, therefore, help remind us that places are never merely static, monolithic, and contained. As what de Certeau calls "space," or a "*practiced place,*" these sites involve literal and metaphorical geographical connections across time.[21] As noted earlier, for example, nuclear weapons facilities bridge space and time through global/local flows from their point of inception as vital to national "defense" in a transnational arena, as sources of local jobs with global impacts, and as modern construction sites that transform rural land into nothing short of small urban centers.

Understanding places and spaces as changing, heterogeneous, and leaky further resonates with the environmental principle of *ecology*, which broadly is the study of the significance of how living things are interconnected with each other and within environments. Again, this permeability and transformability of space is both cultural and material. As is apparent from the stories of workers and residents at Fernald, for example, it does matter that the Fernald site was located on an aquifer (insofar as it then polluted local drinking wells), next door to farms (which raised cattle that was then eaten by humans), and seemingly innocuous (and, therefore, not initially raising any concern among those who passed by or lived nearby).

As Daniel Brouwer and Robert Asen suggest in their introduction, therefore, a move to examining *modalities* of public critique need not jettison or replace questions of space and place. Rather, its aim is to highlight the dynamic space-time relations and activities involved in constituting, constraining, and reinventing public engagement. A public modalities approach to environmental publicity, then, suggests that rather than isolating our sense of publicness within a specific location, we take more seriously the significance of any environment as a consequential nodal point of the fluid networks of human relations.

Everyday Life at Fernald

A signature of the nuclear industry and U.S. military is the nuclear secret.[22] Constitutive of the U.S. nuclear weapons production complex has been a historical pattern of privatizing manufacturing processes, health risks, and relevant decision making in the name of national security.[23] This trend makes any gesture toward publicity all the more risky insofar as the U.S government and its licensed nuclear subcontractors have constructed an undemocratic complex that actively has worked to pre-empt public participation and the formation of nuclear publics. Stories from Fernald mark a significant moment in nuclear history because the successful lawsuits that came out of their concerns signal a hopeful—though admittedly new and undoubtedly tenuous—shift from this anti-democratic model to a more public one.[24]

In 1951, the U.S. Atomic Energy Commission obtained by eminent domain 1,050 acres in northwest Hamilton County, Ohio, to construct a uranium refinery as part of the growing complex of nuclear weapons production facilities spread across the country. The site, known locally as Fernald, was chosen due to its proximity to a willing and able labor market, access to housing and transportation, a nearby source of fresh water in the Great Miami River, and its central location relative to other facilities in the complex.[25] The Fernald site offered the advantages of relative isolation amidst rural farmland and rolling hills as well as proximity to Cincinnati, which lay only eighteen miles away. It was not by accident that the government allowed a dairy farm to operate on the southeast edge of the property throughout the site's production era in order to promote the view in the community that Fernald was an innocuous industrial plant. Although Fernald was small in comparison to many other nuclear weapons complex facilities, it played an important role in the production chain of weapons-grade nuclear materials for bomb-making.[26]

Fernald's Presence as Everyday Life: "It Was Always There"

Part of the routine and repetition of everyday life is what induces us to take for granted many fixtures on the landscapes that surround us.[27] For local residents, Fernald's presence was part of their everyday lives. When asked about her memories of growing up in the neighborhood, Anita Holmes recalls: "I guess to me it was always there. It was a part of my life when I was a child and used to go out and play in the yard, you know, from my yard you could see the sign over there and I never really thought that much about it as a child. It was always there." The physical presence of Fernald seemed ordinary to residents who never lived in the area before it was built. In fact, many residents noted that they thought the facility was a Purina Dog Food plant because one of the towers was painted with red and white checkers and the sign that Holmes mentioned at the entrance declared it was a Feed Materials Production Center. Presumably for security reasons, there was no marker indicating the nuclear processes or military significance of the site.

Further, when something seemingly out of the ordinary occurred, residents' initial reactions were to assume not to worry. Consider the story of resident Nick Schwab, who did know Fernald was a nuclear weapons production facility: "I could see it from the backyard. Uh, I didn't worry much about the plant. I knew somewhat what they did, and felt what they did there was important. So I never had a lot of concerns about it, but early on, I know my wife had concerns when there was people that came in white suits once a day and took a sample out of the creek. And we lived upwind, and 'course they said, well, this was just routine." Knowledge of what Fernald was built to produce, therefore, did not necessarily correlate to critique. Notably, even when residents did ask questions, the institutional response was to assure them that everything was "routine" or everyday and, therefore, not worth further questioning.

This rhetoric of reassurance was even more emphasized inside the Fernald plant itself. Loucetta Rathgens, a site employee of forty-two years and the first female production supervisor, recalls the quotidian atmosphere of Fernald for her both inside and outside the facility: "When you walked in the cafeteria there were all kinds of plaques and awards [about] how safe the place was and, um, I never thought of it as being anything dangerous or unsafe or evil or anything bad that it's been made out to be. I mean, you always seen the cows out in the pasture and, um, it just was—we had a lot of softball teams that played there at the site." Nothing seemed out of the ordinary because practices of everyday life, such as farming and sports, appeared to carry on with their usual rhythms. Further, the facility actively promoted itself as not only safe, but worthy of awards for how safe it was.

Since many of the workers had Q-level security clearance, they also were told not to share their work outside Fernald for fear that publicity about what was happening at the site would risk national security. For some, like Robert Gardner, there was no desire to violate this protocol because work itself felt so banal:

> Mostly the job was pretty boring. You know, I have a, had a pretty good view of the whole thing, uh, later on; but that's over a period of forty years. . . . I worked for years in denitration, suckin' these pots out or whatever. Did the same thing every day. Uh, I just didn't talk about my job with my wife and kids . . . because of the security really, and who knows, it mighta had some effect. We were urged over and over again not to talk about the job. But, . . . I guess I still don't. I guess I'm just not interested in talkin' about it. I always had kind of a habit . . . when I left the job that was the last thing I wanted to think about. . . . I could talk for a week about Fernald. At some point you'd be bored to death.

In stories such as Gardner's, everyday life explicitly frames their memories. Working at Fernald required doing "the same thing every day" for decades. It felt "pretty boring"—and even talking about it habitually seemed like it would make people listening feel, ironically, "bored to death." In this sense, when

Fernald became a part of the everyday for residents and workers, imagining life otherwise became less possible.

Accidents as Everyday Life: "It's Just a Part of the Business, I Think"

Not everyone agreed about the closing of Fernald. Some workers, in particular, were loyal to Fernald because it provided them with a paycheck, a job they liked, and/or a sense of personal significance as vital to national security during the Cold War. Even when accidents occurred, therefore, they were perceived as a part of the cost of having a job, especially one involved in national security. As one retired worker, Peggy Doherty, states: "I liked working there and I felt comfortable that the people that were working there were intelligent. They were a well-educated group of people and they still are now. Uh, I think we've got some of the best workers there in the country. And, uh, I knew that they would get it under control. Ya know, and sometimes things just happen; and, uh, I don't think anything there, or at least while I was there, happened on purpose. So, it's just a part of the business, I think." Imagining accidents as "part of the business" of everyday life was predicated, at least in stories such as Doherty's, on the idea that these accidents were forgivable since the intent seemingly was not to cause harm to the workers by other workers. From this perspective, if the people coming into the plant were presumably good, "well-educated," and "intelligent" people who worked with each other every day, they couldn't help if "sometimes things just happen." Further, Doherty was a secretary who did not work on the floor, meaning she was not exposed to the hazards of many of her co-workers; arguably, this distance and lack of personal illness has made her perspective more supportive of the working conditions at Fernald.

Likewise, Bernard Gessiness, a former chemist for thirty-five and a half years at Fernald, explains the inevitability of accidents from his vantage point:

> On a day in 1984, there was a release, an accidental release of, uh, uranium oxide, black oxide, U3O8, from a dust collector, from a smokestack, uh, in Plant 9. This resulted in black oxide being released into the environment. It was on the roof and . . . the prevailing winds that day may have carried it onto some of the local area. . . . It's impossible to operate a plant that is as difficult to operate technologically as our plant without having some kind of mishap. . . . It was very regrettable. We felt very bad about it. Nobody wants to have an accident. Nobody wants to release material into the atmosphere, but dust bags break, and people

> do make mistakes. People press the wrong button, or do whatever they shouldn't do; all of us are human. And as a result, this kind of incident was inevitable, and it did occur. Uh, it's not the first incident of its kind. There were others over the years.

Like Doherty, Gessiness claims that it was "natural" for some accidents to occur as part of everyday life at Fernald "over the years." Again, this admission that accidents were inevitably part of everyday life in a nuclear world enables him to rationalize the regular occurrence of accidents as typical of human nature, rather than to critique the government or corporations that ran Fernald for a lack of adequate occupational safety standards.

Not all felt as resolutely resigned to Fernald's operations, but their questions were often met with the response that everyday life could not change. For example, according to his widow, Corilla Kelly, Herb Kelly was told in 1984 by his supervisor in response to raising the issue that there was dust leaking on him at the job: "You go on and go back to work. . . . There's no sense in saying anything about it because they won't do nothing about it in the front office."

Even after retirement, some workers remained ambivalent about critiquing accidents at Fernald. Consider this dialogue between Hillman Grubbs, a former chemical operator who also had more direct exposure to hazardous materials, and the interviewer:

> Q: Um, did anything unusual happen when you were working at Fernald?
>
> A: Well, nothing other than normal everyday routine. I mean, we wouldn't go a week, we didn't blow a furnace up probably.
>
> Q: Tell us a little about that.
>
> A: Well, nobody ever got hurt too bad in our plant as far as furnaces blowing up, but at Plant 9 they blew one up and, ah, two fellows died from that. One fellow burned all his privates off him, and the other guy lived 'til the next day and, and he died.

In this exchange, Grubbs begins by stating nothing unusual happened and then clarifies that a furnace blowing up was not unusual because it happened weekly. Then, he goes on to state that although nobody was hurt too severely in his plant, two men died from an explosion, one after the fire "burned all his privates off him" and the other the next day. From Grubbs' perspective, weekly furnace fires and the violent death of two co-workers only arose when probed further. Recalling those events, his telling initial reaction was that "nothing other than normal everyday routine" occurred. Like Gardner's earlier memory of the boredom of working at Fernald, when everyday life frames accidents, they too may appear innocuous—particularly to those who did not witness accidents firsthand.

Of course, Fernald did have some occupational health procedures in place. These measures seemed to add to the sense of accidents as everyday. Every worker on the floor had two mandatory showers a day: one before lunch and one before going home. Eventually, there was a "body counter," which former employee Richard Heatherton explains:

> We had people come in, go through a procedure of shower and changing into their clean coveralls of some type so they could run through the counter without anything on their external person or on their clothing. Go into the counter and stay for a period of about twenty minutes, I think it would be. And, ah, in that time, then you would get the count at the various energy levels. This would divide the whole spectrum of radiation into energy intervals of shorter intervals and, ah, would tell you what the count was in each one of those sections. . . . [The] amount of, ah, radioactivity or the amount of uranium that was there. Ah, everyone who worked in production was supposed to be counted.

This routine practice of checking workers' bodies for excessive radioactivity institutionalized the everydayness of accidents. Not only were a few workers tested, but "everyone who worked in production was supposed to be counted." Testing bodies, therefore, was not an indication for alarm about accidents since it was happening routinely.

These stories of the everyday life of accidents are not limited to laboring at Fernald. Donald Cook was a worker who lived on Paddy's Run, across the railroad tracks and downwind from the K-65 silo, where extremely hazardous radioactive material was dumped. When asked about what it was like to live there, he replied:

> Every morning, you'd get up and have this acid in the air. . . . The dust, every morning when the dew was falling, it'd fall on your skin. You'd have to run to your automobile, which was about fifty feet, or you'd feel that stinging. Oh, it'd fall on your face or your arms—you could feel it was stinging you. Acid, they said it was just acid, uh, you know, droppings from the acid from over there at plants two and three . . . which is

> close to K-65. So, there was always a smell. You could smell that orange oxide. You could see it in the sky. It was colored . . . the sun, you couldn't even see the sun it was so thick at times, and that orange oxide coming out of that acid recovery or acid fumes.

Running to one's car to avoid the physical pain of "just acid" became part of everyday life for residents living as close to the plant as Cook, just as hearing the story of co-workers being burnt to death didn't stop Grubbs from stating that nothing ever happened outside the everyday routine. As Cook explained, "there was always a smell." This sensual observation didn't motivate him to move away or quit his job. These painful corporeal accidents were regular and repeated and, therefore, not enough to provoke workers and residents to feel anything extraordinary was happening.

Death as Everyday Life: "It's Just a Matter of Time"

Although some accidents led to quick deaths, other accidents and continual exposures that bio-accumulated or built up over time in the bodies of workers and residents led to long-term illnesses and disease. As of 2006, the U.S. government has recognized 261 former workers of Fernald with cancer as having an illness due to their jobs.[28] More specifically, according to epidemiology professor Susan Pinney in her interview for the Fernald Living History Project, the Fernald Medical Monitoring Program has found approximately a 70 percent increase in urinary system cancers (i.e., kidney and bladder) as well as in malignant melanoma. Prostate cancer also appeared above the national average.[29]

Accordingly, dying became part of everyday life. One emergency firefighter, Maurice Hornbach, recounts: "I had that twenty-seven years ago, the operation [a colostomy]. . . . Because if it takes a hold to the walls of your organs, it gets into your kidneys, it gets in your bladder, gets in your liver, and you're done. That's all there is to it. It's just a matter of time. I know of too many friends o' mine that's had colostomies, and they're dead. Now they was five people on this project. . . . I'm the only one livin', out o' the five that had these colostomies." When death became a routine part of everyday life, its inevitability began to frame expectations. Further, diseases such as cancer often are slow to develop, though cancer's cumulative impact became "a matter of time."

As she continues to reflect upon the banality of her exposure as a local resident, Anita Holmes's story embodies this sense of resignation and the feeling of helplessness that often accompanies such a perspective: "When I was a child and we farmed, it was like it was in the water, and it was in the food that we ate and the water that we bathed with; and my mother canned, and it was in the canned goods. And, I mean, I just feel that I've been exposed from all directions. . . . And I guess I just feel like eventually it's gonna catch up with me." Beyond accidents, therefore, even as awareness that a linkage between Fernald and cancer mortality arose, the practices of everyday life such as farming, eating, drinking, and bathing accumulate into tales of repeated daily exposures—that, in turn, made a deadly disease such as cancer appear like "eventually it's gonna catch up."

Health impacts were not isolated to cancer. Among some of the more serious public health implications were the many reproductive problems that also resulted, impacting both present and future generations. Resident Charles Young shares the following story about his family's health complications:

> Our children, we had two boys and a girl, born '53, '55, and '59 [who] were in that age of puberty . . . when all the dust and all the problems and all the things were happening. We didn't know it; we didn't think anything of it. . . . We have never, in my wife's family or in my family, have never had any birth problems or birth defects or anything of that nature that would, you know, be genetically followed through. But our children and some of [our] grandchildren all have, just about, high percentage of them have had some type of problem. . . . [O]ne was born with like two or three bones in one of his toes, had to be operated on to be taken out. This, of course, falls back to, if you read some of the things that have happened from radiation fallout, this is one of the things that happened. One of the other grandsons had a bone marrow problem when he was first born, has a lot of allergies connected with it. . . . And, uh, then I have another grandson that has a, what they call, a pierrladow [*sic*][30] syndrome which is very few cases in the world that has this. . . . And it affected the median line of his system; along with part of the defects was . . . that he didn't have any femur bones. In other words his knees are attached to his hip area. They're not in any joint; they're just in the muscles area . . . [and] he doesn't have any shoulder joints. He can't put his arm behind his back, but he can work his arms. . . . [T]hat's all part of that syndrome. . . . He did have a cleft pallet, which they repaired early on. . . . And, uh, one of my sons also has reproductive problems, sperm not being as active as it should be.

As an interview about the past, Young now begins to make connections between the exposure to radiation and his children's—as well as their children's—health. In addition to latent impacts, for one of Young's sons, the exposure from living near Fernald also made life itself impossible to conceive in the first place. Since these impacts took some time to manifest themselves in or on the bodies of residents and workers, connections with Fernald were not obvious.

Interrupting Everyday Life: "You're Doing What You Think You Need to Be Doing"

For some families, the repetition of accidents, illness, and death began to accumulate in a way that interrupted previous assumptions about everyday life. Donald Cook finally quit his job in 1970, after working at Fernald for seventeen years. Although his wife died of cancer in 1962, he couldn't quit right away because Fernald did not pay the hospital bills, and although he eventually remarried, he was raising two children as a single father. For some families, like the Youngs and the Cooks, once family members began to die or to face severe health complications, the costs of living and working at Fernald did start to provoke individuals to take a stand. Yet, even once individual concerns arose, many did not have the resources to move away or to quit their jobs, let alone to launch a critique that would transform everyday life at Fernald.

Others were fired once they became too ill to perform their jobs. Fernald fired Herb Kelly, a father of four, then took away his pension and life insurance when cancer began to make it impossible for him to work. His widow, Corilla, notes: "We did the best that we could for a long time." Since illnesses such as cancer took awhile to manifest themselves, critique even for those paying the highest costs took time.

While these signs of disaster began to accumulate, for most, the connection between Fernald and the growing public health crisis was revealed, eventually, by those who did not live near or work at the facility. As the government began tracking the illnesses and deaths related to Fernald without notifying the workers, seemingly surreal phrases such as "nuclear autopsies" and "body snatching" became part of local vernaculars. When asked about the death of a fellow worker named Joe Carvette, Gene Branham explains he realized the health risks that were to be expected in everyday life when Joe's son spoke up: "And when Joe died, his son, having a legal background, had the foresight that none of us had, to have an autopsy performed and preserve the vital organs. And when litigation came up, as you probably know, Joe's case prevailed because he had that evidence. Uh, the autopsy was a nuclear autopsy, as opposed to a normal autopsy. Because you can't perform a nuclear autopsy on a living person because it calls for core samples of the bone. So just things of that nature. So he's a pretty impressive young man. And from that we learn a lot (laughter)." Without a lawyer literally in the family, nuclear autopsies were not a practice that most families considered. Yet, for Joe's son, who chose a career that took him away from Fernald, accidents and death were not a part of his everyday life as an adult. When his father died, therefore, Joe's son asked questions because he did not assume his father's death was routine. It took a different perspective on everyday life, in other words, to launch a more systemic and public critique.

Branham continues at length to describe how the treatment of the bodies of the dead by the government also eventually provoked some locals to question their own everyday assumptions:

> The government has what they call a federal registry. . . . Well, [what] we called it was "body snatching"; they'd steal your bodies. Nuclear workers. And not only the workers, but the administrative people, and people who owned farms in a general area. . . . Because to do an epidemiology you have to have a comparison factor, so you want someone who is actively in the plant working versus someone that isn't in the plant. Now they would take these bodies without the nearest relatives' knowledge or consent and that is not, uh, a violation of law because it's protected by national defense. . . . We suspect these organs were contaminated because we never saw them again. Therefore, without the organ you had no evidence to prove the origin of sickness or the illness or the death came from the workplace. That's how they avoided liability, government body snatching. Some of the bodies they put back in the graves weren't even the same body. . . . .Mr. Eberts . . . [h]is body was placed in the wrong direction. Ray was about 6' 2", 6' 2½", about 210, 220, ex-marine. The body put back in there was 5' 6" thereabouts, 120 pounds. Had missing fingers. Terrible things happened.

Although the silence on the part of the government regarding its own suspicions about a linkage between the nuclear weapons production complex and public health remained a barrier to publicizing the health risks posed by Fernald, people like Branham began to make connections on their own from government practices. Where did the bodies of their nearest relatives go after they died? Why were they buried in caskets seemingly small for their size? And why were their bodies missing parts when they appeared again? What practices were being excused in the name of national security?

In addition to family members who had moved out of town and signs from the government itself, eventually, the medical community reported cause for concern. Born and raised in the area, Paul Davies recounts the following story of exposure as a pipe fitter at Fernald in 1985:

> I walked through the one wet area at that time, Building 13, not knowing that anything was going on, at the end of the shift, to wash up; and when I got down at the other end of the building, well, there was a construction worker in there that used to be a millwright years ago at the plant there. He asked me if I knew what I just had walked through. I said, "No, what?" He said, "'Cause the building had kind of an odor to it that you couldn't really tell when you walked in there, you know, what you was into." He said, "You just went through some hex, uranium hexafluoride gas."

Although Heatherton (previously) recalled that "everyone" was expected to go through the "body counter," Davies only entered when someone suggested he go to the medical facilities. "The body counter" gauged Davies as 46 percent radioactive. Since he had registered as 14 and 12 percent before, seemingly "normal" amounts of exposure, 46 percent seemed high to Davies, so he went outside of town to the Occupational Health Clinic at Providence Hospital. After discovering the level of exposure he had, his doctor persuaded him to subpoena the company health records on him. Given government silence about the health risks posed by Fernald, it is perhaps unsurprising to learn that it wasn't until then, in 1985, that Davies discovered he had exceeded the standards by ten times in 1966 also, but had not been notified.

While some began to make connections once people from outside the community's everyday routine suggested they should, most workers and residents didn't feel concern until the government itself held a public hearing admitting that there was a problem in 1985. One local resident who soon became one of the most vocal leaders to demand government accountability for Fernald's impact, Lisa Crawford, explains how early stories in the media didn't even catch her attention: "I worked full time. I had a child. I didn't read the newspaper. I didn't watch TV. I didn't watch the news and kind of [was] an uninformed person. Which, you know, doesn't make you proud, but you have a life and you're doing what you think you need to be doing." Like many working-class people who do not make a living from keeping up with the news, there was too much happening in Crawford's everyday life to follow the media. Since the sign on Fernald's entrance didn't say anything *and* her landlord, who owned the property she was renting, didn't mention any notices he received to her family *and* her property was upwind from Fernald (as opposed to the Cooks's experiences downwind), it didn't occur to her that her seemingly idyllic country home was a threat to her family's health.

It wasn't until 1985 that she began to question her everyday life, when her husband, Ken Crawford, received a call from their landlord that the Department of Energy and National Lead of Ohio were about to hold a public meeting at one of the local elementary schools to announce that something was wrong with the water in three local wells. Indeed, most of the community did not question their right to know more about Fernald until after this public hearing occurred.

Conclusion

In the years that ensued after the initial 1985 meeting, Department of Energy officials were forced to open the site to broader inspection and regulation by state and government environmental officials.[31] A landmark controversy erupted at Fernald in the early 1990s, when residents won two lawsuits and national press coverage circulated workers' previously marginalized voices in dominant cultural arenas. From attention given in the national media, including the *Donahue Show*, *60 Minutes*, and a *Time* magazine cover story, it appeared as if an irreversible shift had occurred in the ways the nation would talk about and imagine Fernald.[32] Site production was permanently ended in 1991 when the site's mission changed from production to clean-up. As of the beginning of 2007, the Department of Energy has declared that remediation at Fernald is all but completed.[33]

For scholars who study processes of public engagement, we hope to have illustrated how publics are constituted not merely as isolated "spheres" of rational-critical debate somehow suspended in space and time, but as networks of modalities that are constituted in part by space and time. Publicity at Fernald, for example, was shaped by and shaped transnational relations (including global military policy), labor relations, extended families, and so forth. Further, as its immediate and long-term impacts are catalyzed by human practices across the globe, uranium challenges neat distinctions between nature and culture. This shift to a focus on modalities, therefore, helps us recall how nuclear culture reconfigures commonly held notions of space and time.

Our analysis of these interviews revealed three patterns in relation to everyday life as a barrier to publicity. First, the constant and superficially innocuous presence of the facility, coupled with rhetorics of reassurance, concealed the risky and hazardous materials being processed within the facility. This reminds us that the desire to critically question, let alone critique, an institution is deterred when that institution has a constant presence in our lives and we are told that it is normal. Imagining life other than it is lived is challenging to many of us at times; this is a distinct advantage of hegemony and those who wish to maintain the status quo. Second, the rhetoric of national security—as well as job security—served to deflect attention away from the sacrifices people were making as residents and workers at Fernald. Such a definition of "security" eclipses the costs paid by individuals by framing questions about one's quality of life or rights as insignificant compared to the alleged greater good (here defined by a corporation contracted by a national military). Third, the latency of hazardous materials and imagining the health of our bodies as purely "natural" obscures our recognition of the preventablility of certain environmental causes of illness, death, and reproductive problems.

In order for residents and workers to imagine their lives as worth publicizing, these interviews also reinforce Asen's point that one's position in relation to an act (or series of acts) may influence one's perspective.[34] Perhaps unsurprisingly, some of those who asked questions first were those who witnessed accidents firsthand, lived downwind, and/or had family members become seriously ill or die sooner than others. For them, the costs of Fernald eventually became more visceral and exigent. As opposed to those contaminated by underground wells and less acute exposures, being able to see the contact of dust or chemicals enabled some to make connections between their health and Fernald. Further, the tragedy of losing one's partner or parent transforms one's everyday life in ways that open opportunities to reassess the taken-for-granted. Unfortunately, many interviewees reiterated that even once their priorities and values shifted due to personal disasters, they did not have the resources or institutional support to launch a critique on their own even when they did ask questions.

For many, therefore, finding the resources available for a lawyer, a doctor, and a medical agency outside the Fernald area is what was required to help denaturalize everyday life. In these instances, it also took a different perspective of everyday life to recognize that the dangers of Fernald were remarkable and preventable. However, we do not believe this latter observation should be read out of context. Environmental justice communities have fought hard for recognition of citizens as experts in response to histories of outside, formally trained experts devaluing the voices of those most impacted by environmental decision making.[35] Without the local residents and workers at Fernald eventually taking a stand, the subsequent legal and political landmarks would not have been achieved.

Nevertheless, the liminal position of the lawyer who grew up in Fernald and moved away while his parents stayed offers one poignant example of how scholars of publics should remember not to oversimplify identity or positionality as static or essential. Whereas a public *spheres* approach may lend itself to reifying rigid boundaries—between inside and outside, us and them, dominant and resistant—a public *modalities* perspective aims not only to foreground the fluidity of identities across time and space, but also to recognize how specific contexts of time and space constitute our identities. Although a study of Fernald could begin with the 1985 public hearing as an isolated event that offered a public arena for debate and subsequent publicity, these interviews reveal the significance of appreciating how environmental or public health disasters may develop over time as complicated and multidimensional processes.

A rhetorical approach that recognizes publics as processes must value studies that reveal failed attempts at publicity, blockades to democracy, and marginalized stories of critique. This chapter has illustrated how everyday life can serve as a rhetorical constraint for publicity *because we can become accustomed to anything*. Former workers and residents from Fernald share stories that sound horrific to most of us in most contexts, including the burning off of a worker's private parts, deaths, birth defects, drops in sperm count, acid fumes permeating nostrils and dropping on people's skin, water that has become undrinkable, and so forth. Yet, these stories of disaster long felt acceptable on an everyday basis to those who lived them. As scholars and as citizens, we must ask ourselves what quality of life we desire and identify rhetorical resources for changing the circumstances we find unacceptable. These are normative judgments. Expanding on Karl Marx's theory of capitalist alienation, Lefebvre wrote: "Critique demands the dissolution and the revolutionary metamorphosis of the everyday, by reducing its disparities and time-lags. By demonstrating theoretically that the everyday is not an immutable substance, it has already begun to dissolve it. Finally, it demands a twofold movement within a unitary praxis: that the everyday catch up with what is possible and that the processes which have been distanced from it return and reinvest themselves within it."[36] Identifying the conditions that hegemonic culture "naturalizes" as rhetorical junctures of choice and political consequence is an important step toward achieving a more just and sustainable world. Without this more engaged sense of critique—including analysis of the myriad of ways we experience alienation and challenges to disalienation in everyday life—the value of studying publics and acting publicly becomes obsolete.

Notes

1. See, for example, Paul Loeb, *Nuclear Culture: Living and Working in the World's Largest Atomic Complex* (Philadelphia: New Society, 1986).

2. Emphasis in original. Gerard A. Hauser, *Vernacular Voices: The Rhetoric of Publics and Public Spheres* (Columbia: University of South Carolina Press, 1999), 49.

3. Like Kim Fortun, we use "disaster" in a way that is "countering tendencies to think of the disaster as isolated in time and space—as an 'incident' (in the words of the chemical industry) that 'can't happen here.'" Naming the polluting impacts of the nuclear weapon production complex a "disaster" is more than an empirical move. "The middle voice," as Fortun argues in her study of anti-nuclear advocates, "is the modality of disaster. It is a way of speaking that builds in awareness that the system that one critiques also operates within the critique." Kim Fortun, *Advocacy after Bhopal: Environmentalism, Disaster, New Global Orders* (Chicago: University of Chicago Press, 2001), 19, 38.

4. According to Michel de Certeau, "three properties characterize the return of the body within the imaginary. It expresses a *transgression*, it connotes *communication*, and it aims at the grasping of a *reality*." Michel de Certeau, *Culture in the Plural*, trans. Tom Conley (Minneapolis: University Minnesota Press, 1997), 22.

5. This chapter includes citations from Fernald Living History interview transcripts, which are available online at http://offo2.epa.state.oh.us/FLHP.htm. The pronoun "we" is used to reflect the collaborative nature of our contributions to this chapter. It is worth noting, however, that one of the authors, Depoe, has lived seven miles from the Fernald site since 1986, has led the initiative for this Oral History Project since 1997, has served on the local Citizens Advisory Board from 2000–2005 (then called the Citizens Task Force), and has published on Fernald elsewhere. Jennifer Duffield and Stephen P. Depoe, "Lessons from Fernald: Reversing NIMBYism Through Democratic Decision-Making," *EPA Risk Policy Report*, February 21, 1997, 31–34; and Stephen P. Depoe, "Public Involvement, Civic Discovery, and the Formation of Environmental Policy: A Comparative Analysis of the Fernald Citizens Task Force and the Fernald Health Effects Subcommittee," in *Communication and Public Participation in Environmental Decision-Making: Advances in Theory and Practice*, ed. Stephen P. Depoe, John D. Delicath, and Marie-France Aepli (Albany: State University of New York Press, 2004), 157–73.

6. Phaedra C. Pezzullo, "Resisting 'National Breast Cancer Awareness Month': The Rhetoric of Counterpublics and Their Cultural Performances," *Quarterly Journal of Speech* 89 (2003): 345–65; Bryan C. Taylor, William J. Kinsella, Stephen P. Depoe, and Maribeth Metzler, eds., *Nuclear Legacies: Communication, Controversy, and the U.S. Nuclear Weapons Complex* (Lahham, MD: Lexington Books, 2007).

7. Ben Highmore, *The Everyday Life Reader* (London: Routledge, 2002), 1–2.

8. In academic writings, "everyday life" generally references two related, but different meanings. Michel de Certeau's understanding broadly addresses our " 'ways of operating' or doing things," and Henri Lefebvre theorizes it to be "what is humble and solid, what is taken for granted and that of which all the parts follow each other in such a regular, unvarying succession that those concerned have no call to question their sequence." Michel de Certeau, *The Practice of Everyday Life,* trans. Stephen Rendall (Berkeley: University of California Press, 1984), xi; Henri Lefebvre, *Everyday Life in the Modern World,* trans. Sacha Rabinovitch (New Brunswick, NJ: Transaction Publishers, 1971), 24. In this sense, their collective interpretation is quite similar to quotidian ones: our everyday life is the practices of our existence that become routine, repetitive, and relatively taken for granted or unquestioned.

9. Henri Lefebvre, *Critique of Everyday Life, Volume 2: Foundations for a Sociology of the Everyday,* trans. John Moore (New York: Verso, 2002).

10. Tarla Rai Peterson, *Sharing the Earth: The Rhetoric of Sustainable Development* (Columbia: University of South Carolina Press, 1997).

11. Kevin DeLuca and Jennifer Peeples, "From Public Sphere to Public Screen: Democracy, Activism, and the 'Violence' of Seattle," *Critical Studies in Media Communication* 19 (2002): 125–51.

12. Pezzullo, "Resisting 'National Breast Cancer Awareness Month.' "

13. Taylor et al., *Nuclear Legacies;* Bryan C. Taylor, William J. Kinsella, Stephen P. Depoe, and Maribeth Metzler, "Nuclear Legacies: Communication, Controversy, and the U.S. Weapons Complex," *Communication Yearbook* 29 (2005), 363–409; Joseph Masco, "Lie Detectors: On Secrets and Hypersecurity in Los Alamos," *Public Culture* 14 (2002): 441–67; Joseph Masco, "The Billboard Campaign: The Los Alamos Study Group and the Nuclear Public Sphere," *Public Culture* 17 (2005): 487–96.

14. On the apocalyptic in nuclear discourse, see Jacques Derrida, "No Apocalypse, Not Now (Full Speed Ahead, Seven Missiles, Seven Missives)," *Diacritics* 14 (1994), 20–31; and David Williams, "Under the Sign of (An)nihilation: Burke in an Age of Nuclear Destruction and Critical Deconstruction," in *The Legacy of Kenneth Burke,* ed. Herbert Simons and Trevor Melia (Madison: University of Wisconsin Press, 1989), 196–223; Karen A. Foss and Stephen W. Littlejohn, " 'The Day After': Rhetorical Vision in an Ironic Frame," *Critical Studies in Mass Communication* 3 (1986): 317–36.

15. The estimated half-life of Uranium-235, which is required to sustain a nuclear fission reaction, is four million years. See Institute for Energy and Environmental Research, "Uranium Fact Sheet," http://www.ieer.org/fctsheet/uranium.html (accessed September 1, 2007).

16. For a more in-depth account, see Peter C. Van Wyck, *Signs of Danger: Waste, Trauma, and Nuclear Threat* (Minneapolis: University of Minnesota Press, 2005).

17. The site includes a Passive Institutional Control plan that is based on a concept called "defense in depth," involving a number of components with redundant messages. U.S. Department of Energy, Carlsbad Field Office, Waste Isolation Pilot Plant, http://www.wipp.energy.gov (accessed August 1, 2006).

18. Taylor et al., "Nuclear Legacies," 378. Alston and Brown report: "According the Center for Defense Information (1991), since 1945 when the United States exploded the first atomic bomb at Alamogordo, New Mexico, six nations—the United States, the Soviet Union, Great Britain, France, China, and India—have detonated a combined total of at least 1,910 nuclear explosives at some 35 sites around the world. That's an average of one explosion every nine days. . . . Since 1974 . . . all U.S. nuclear tests have taken place on Western Shoshone lands at the Nevada Test Site. . . . Since 1962, Great Britain has been testing at the Nevada Test Site, having abandoned its former sites on aboriginal land in Australia and on southern Pacific islands." Dana Alston and Nicole Brown, "Global Threats to People of Color," in *Confronting Environmental Racism: Voices from the Grassroots*, ed. Robert D. Bullard (Boston, MA: South End Press, 1993), 183. For more on the U.S. colonial nuclear legacy, see Joseph Masco, "States of Insecurity: Plutonium and Post–Cold War Anxiety in New Mexico, 1992–96," in *Cultures of Insecurity: States, Communities, and the Production of Danger*, ed. Jutta Weldes, Mark Laffey, Hugh Gusterson, and Raymond Duvall (Minneapolis: University of Minnesota Press, 1999), 203–32.

19. Bryan C. Taylor, "Home Zero: Images of Home and Field in Nuclear-Cultural Studies," *Western Journal of Communication* 61 (1987): 209–34; Eric L. Morgan, "Regional Communication and Sense of Place Surrounding the Waste Isolation Pilot Plant," in *Nuclear Legacies*, ed. Taylor et al., 109–32.

20. Taylor et al., "Nuclear Legacies," 374. These impacts do not compare to the World War II decision by the U.S. government in August of 1945 to bomb the Japanese cities of Hiroshima and Nagasaki, resulting in the deaths of hundreds of thousands of civilians. The United States is the first and, thus far, only nation to use atomic bombs in warfare.

21. De Certeau, *Practice of Everyday*, 117.

22. Masco, "Lie Detectors."

23. "In the domestic realm of U.S. politics," as Masco argues, "the nuclear weapons complex has always maintained two extreme attributes: phenomenal costs and social invisibility. . . . [B]etween 1940 and 1996 the United States spent *at least* $5.8 trillion on nuclear weapons." Masco, "Billboard Campaign," 487. For an understanding of how the U.S. government has used secrecy as a trope in nuclear discourse, see William J. Kinsella, "One Hundred Years of Nuclear Discourse: Four Master Themes and Their Implications for Environmental Communication," in *Environmental Communication Yearbook*, vol. 2, ed. Susan Senecah (Mahwah, NJ: Erlbaum, 2005), 49–

72. This pattern reflects that of toxic disasters more broadly, in which the people most impacted try to socialize their grievances and the people who benefit the most from continuing business-as-usual try to privatize the grievances. See Michael R. Reich, *Toxic Politics: Responding to Chemical Disasters* (Ithaca, NY: Cornell University Press, 1991).

24. In 1985, one year after a series of accidental releases of uranium, fourteen thousand Fernald area residents filed a $300 million class-action lawsuit against the DOE contractor, National Lead of Ohio. In 1989, the suit was settled for $78 million from the DOE (*Crawford v. National Lead of Ohio, 784 F. Supp. 439 [SD Ohio 1989]*). In 1994, another landmark lawsuit was settled when DOE awarded $15 million to Fernald workers, in addition to funding for a lifetime medical monitoring program. *Day v. National Lead of Ohio,* 3 F. 3d 153 (6th Cir., 1993). See also "U.S. Will Pay Settlement in Factory-Radiation Suit," *Wall Street Journal*, July 27, 1994, B6.

25. Fernald's location near Cincinnati, which featured both a large pool of skilled workers and conservative Midwestern values and work ethic, fit perfectly with government goals for the expanding nuclear weapons complex. See Fluor Fernald Corporation, *Fernald at 50: From Weapons to Wetlands* (Fernald, OH: Fluor Fernald, 2001).

26. For additional discussion of the reasons why the government chose the Fernald location, see James R. Wilson, "The Fernald Project of the Atomic Energy Commission: An Agricultural/Industrial Transformation" (MA thesis, Ohio State University, 1956); Michael J. Silverman, "No Immediate Risk: Environmental Safety in Nuclear Weapons Production, 1942–1985" (PhD diss., Carnegie Mellon University, 2000), 263–378.

27. In contrast, Taylor et al. argue that the invisibility of nuclear weapons production and detonation to most people also makes nuclear culture more banal. Taylor et al., " Nuclear Legacies," 364.

28. Peggy O'Farrell, "Final Chapter for Fernald Uranium Plant Goes from A-Bomb Cog to Toxic Site, and Now to Nature Park," *Cincinnati Enquirer*, July 23, 2006, http://news.enquirer.com (accessed October 15, 2006).

29. For a discussion of potential health effects of residential exposure to radiation and other pollutants at Fernald, see Susan M. Pinney et al., "Health Effects in Community Residents Near a Uranium Plant at Fernald, Ohio, USA," *International Journal of Occupational Medicine and Environmental Health* 16 (2003): 139–53.

30. Mr. Young may be referring to Pierre Robin syndrome, a birth defect of unknown origin that presents defects in palate and jaw formation, among other symptoms.

31. For a detailed timeline of events surrounding the transition at Fernald from production to environmental remediation, including the roles played by state and federal regulators, see the Ohio Federal Facilities Oversight Web site, www.offo2.epa.state.oh.us/Fernald.

32. For national media coverage, see Jerome Cramer, B. Russell Leavitt, and

J. Madeleine Nash, "They Lied to Us: Unsafe, Aging U.S. Weapons Plants Are Stirring Fear and Disillusion," *Time*, October 31, 1988, 61–65; Tom Morgenthau, "Nuclear Danger and Deceit," *Newsweek*, October 31, 1988, 28–30.

33. Remediation of the site's polluted production area and surrounding grounds was completed in the fall of 2006. Groundwater remediation will continue for the next several years. In a 2007 ceremony celebrating the cleanup of the area, Lisa Crawford was quoted as saying, "I'm speechless. It's been a long road." Peggy O'Farrell, "Fernald Cleanup Celebrated," *Cincinnati Enquirer*, January 20, 2007, B1, B5.

34. Robert Asen, "A Discourse Theory of Citizenship," *Quarterly Journal of Speech* 90 (2004): 189–211.

35. See, e.g., Barbara L. Allen, *Uneasy Alchemy: Citizens and Experts in Louisiana's Chemical Corridor Disputes* (Cambridge: Massachusetts Institute of Technology Press, 2003).

36. Lefebvre, *Critique of Everyday*, 63.

4
The Ownership Society, or Bourgeois Publicity Revisited

Robert Asen

As a condition of entry into the historical bourgeois public sphere, ownership raised questions about the legitimacy of this realm. Potential problems arose because ownership intimated an apparent contradiction between the universal aspirations of the bourgeois public sphere and the restrictions countenanced by its proponents. Ownership—or any other condition of entry, for that matter—threatened the very legitimacy of the bourgeois public sphere. Only by ensuring the fundamental principle of universal access could this sphere claim to represent the interests of everyone against arbitrary rule. Yet exclusions in practice could be justified in theory so long as everyone had the opportunity to achieve the conditions of entry—that is, so long as everyone had an opportunity to obtain property and education. This was the bourgeois conceit: the bourgeoisie believed that its privileged status had been obtained through the fair competition of the market. If the public sphere sustained exclusion and inequality, it was only because protecting the basic inclusiveness and equality of the economy necessitated a restrictive public sphere. As Jürgen Habermas explains, "only [property owners] had private interests—each his own—which automatically converged into the common interest."[1] In the bourgeois imagination, property ownership, although particular in possession, represented a universal interest insofar as it served the interests of owners and non-owners alike.

Historical practice has laid bare the particular interests of bourgeois property. The recalcitrance and violence directed toward women, laborers, and (in the United States) African Americans who have attempted to redeem the universal promise of bourgeois publicity demonstrate that the bourgeoisie has preferred to represent a universal interest on behalf of others rather than accepting marginalized individuals and groups as active participants in creating a collaborative public life.[2] In light of this history, recognizing that modalities of public engagement are not value-free, contemporary scholars have acknowledged that appeals to universality can function as tools of domination as much as claims for emancipation. Making explicit diverse value commitments, scholars have conceptualized the public sphere as a multiplicity of partially overlapping and intersecting discursive sites against a singular bourgeois public sphere.[3] Scholars also have maintained that the articulation and acceptance of difference can serve public life as well as, if not better than, the search for supposedly universal human interests.[4] Under these circumstances, the intellectual claim that particular conditions of entry can guarantee a general interest has become untenable.

In contrast, among many politicians and policy actors across the globe, ownership has made a comeback. Its political popularity is part of a larger turn over the past three decades to the market as a solution to pressing social problems and, more fundamentally, as a model of human relationships.[5] Buoyed by the resurgence of classical liberal economic thought and propelled by the institutional infrastructure of think tanks and foundations, advocates have championed the market as an ameliorative and revitalizing social force. Advocates have discerned in the market a powerful set of incentives and rewards promising to reduce the costs and increase the returns of ostensibly public goods and services. For some, the market has appeared as a more democratic modality than putatively democratic institutions. As Thomas Frank notes, advocates have insisted that the market has "no place for snobs, for hierarchies, for elitism, for pretense, and it would fight these things by its very nature." Moreover, market modalities constitute an ethically superior realm of society because they enable more authentic expressions of human activity. Frank notes that advocates have embedded markets in human nature: "Markets are where we are most fully human; markets are where we show that we have a soul. To protest *against* markets is to surrender one's very personhood."[6] Market modalities reveal a universal human subjectivity.

In the United States, as many policymakers have embraced the market, ownership has arisen as a primary virtue. Signaling achievement, ownership evidences a citizen's good standing in public. As a societal value, ownership serves as a potentially powerful common bond by magnanimously enabling non-owners to obtain property. Promising to redeem the universal claims of bourgeois publicity, ownership envisages a future that overcomes differences of class, race, and sex and places all citizens on equal ground. Motivated by this vision, advocates of market-based approaches to public issues have called for the realization of an ownership society. David Boaz, executive vice president of the Cato Institute, argues that "individuals take better care of things they own." He maintains that "ownership . . . creates responsible citizens. People who are owners feel more dignity, more pride, and more confidence."[7] Grover Norquist, president of Americans for Tax Reform and a director of the American Conservative Union, contends that "ownership can be revolutionary." Expanding ownership across society would "change the national psyche: increasing the political constituency for lower taxes, stronger property rights, and greater personal responsibility and self-reliance."[8] An ownership society would redress the material and psychological harms that politicians have inflicted on the nation since the "collectivist" New Deal.

During his tenure as president of the United States, George W. Bush was the most prominent proponent of an ownership society. With increasing frequency over the course of his first term, he committed his administration to creating an ownership society for all Americans.[9] Accepting his party's nomination for president in 2004, President Bush held that a "priority for a new term is to build an ownership society, because ownership brings security and dignity and independence."[10] Bush's vision of an "ownership society" served as an invitation for audiences to enact an ownership modality that equated democratic practice and public policy with market norms. This modality of ownership encouraged particular understandings and evaluations of public policy. It also suggested to citizens a perspective for understanding their connections and obligations to each other, as well as the purposes and significance of public engagement. In these ways, ownership promoted ways of being and valuing public. An ownership society constituted public subjectivities, disclosing a substantive process of creating public personae that reified ethical choices as "natural," thereby eliding the values implicated in any modality. An ownership modality invoked a corollary public agenda, delimiting the political realm in ways that benefit specific interests.

The policy centerpiece of the administration's ownership modality entailed an effort to privatize Social Security by creating individual investment accounts in partial or full replacement of traditional, insurance-based retirement benefits. In a press conference two days after his election to a second term, President Bush asserted: "I earned capital in the campaign, political capital, and now I intend to spend it." He promised to begin work on Social Security privatization immediately: "We'll start on Social Security now. We'll start bringing together those in Congress who agree with my assessment that we need to work together. . . . Reforming Social Security will be a priority of my administration."[11] The nearly universal coverage of Social Security made it an appealing case for expanding the benefits of ownership: if the administration could succeed, an ownership society would be close at hand.

This chapter analyzes the qualities of an ownership society as a public modality as well as Bush's advocacy of Social Security privatization as a central policy component of this vision. In Bush's discourse, ownership signaled stakeholding and engendered interest, caring, hope, and compassion. Insisting that ownership empowered individuals, Bush maintained that privatizing Social Security would free citizens from dependence on the federal government for their retirement. However, I argue that his vision of an ownership society promoted a passive mode of publicity that prevented people from engaging as democratic agents. Further, Bush's championing of a widespread investor class ignored important societal inequalities that afforded different opportunities to citizens. As a mode of engagement, ownership publicity keeps important issues off public agendas, treating individual interests as transparent and unchanging. In this way, an ownership modality devalues democratic deliberation.

The Ownership Society as a Public Modality

A primary virtue of the ownership society arose from its intrinsic connection to stakeholding. In his administration, Bush explained, "We understand that when a person owns something, he or she has a vital stake in the future of America."[12] Bush repeated this claim dozens of times during his reelection campaign in 2004, presenting it as the summary justification for his fervently expressed desire to achieve an ownership society. Above all, an ownership society comprised a society of stakeholders. Yet ownership did not appear as one of many ways to obtain a stake in public affairs—it appeared as the only way. The president's discourse subordinated stakeholding to ownership. Bush focused on the creative power of ownership—of homes, businesses, medical accounts, retirement funds, etc. Bush held that "the more ownership there is in America, the more vitality there is in America, and the more people have a vital stake in the future of this country."[13] Ownership appeared as the status that the president wished to grant his constituents, while stakeholding appeared as their reward. As such, stakeholding signified a kind of legal standing for owners. It qualified citizens to participate in the affairs of the nation: only ownership afforded citizens a proper perspective on public issues. Owners had something to gain or lose in the conduct of public policy because they possessed a material interest whereas others appeared as spectators.

Nevertheless, President Bush did not envision an ownership society as an exclusive society. He promised inclusion through the expansion of ownership, insisting, "When I'm talking about ownership, I'm talking about ownership for all people, not just a certain type of person. We want ownership to be a part of every neighborhood. And it's happening in America. It's really what makes us such a wonderful country, isn't it, when people from all walks of life can say, 'I own something.'"[14] Ownership revealed the strengths and weaknesses of America. The nation's strength lay in the opportunities it provided "people from all walks of life" to achieve ownership. Other nations rewarded privilege and tradition, reserving ownership for only "a certain type of person." The United States revealed its wonder in shedding restrictive hierarchies and enabling individual advancement. However, since ownership had not yet reached every neighborhood, the ownership society remained only a partially realized vision. Fortunately, ownership was expanding, and with it a socially ameliorative power. Ownership promised to transcend divisions of race, religion, and ethnicity by bringing people together in common cause as protectors of property.

Owners obtained standing in Bush's vision of society because ownership engendered certain qualities that bolstered the nation. Ownership created interest. Bush explained that promoting ownership would make "sure people have a[n] interest in the future of our country. If you own something, you want to make sure the government makes the right decision so you can continue to own it."[15] Owners could demand a role in policymaking because public policies impacted their possessions directly. Unlike non-owners, they could not escape the consequences of bad policies, since wrong decisions threatened their very ownership status. For these reasons, owners paid attention to the intricacies of policy debates to make sure that government made the right decision. By holding public officials accountable for their decisions, ownership facilitated a system of direct representation. Placing society's stakeholders above special interests and lobbyists as the politician's constituency, ownership upheld democracy. Ownership thus fostered a heightened civic awareness and engagement among citizens, and it compelled an increased civic responsibility among politicians.

Owners cared not just for their possessions but for the nation. Articulating this caring quality, Bush offered an analogy: "There's an old saying here: No one ever washes a rental car. A lot of wisdom in that statement. When you own something, you care about it. When you own something, you have a vital stake in the future of your country."[16] Renters trashed things. They spilled beverages on the seats and made no efforts to clean up their mess, left papers and food wrappers on the floor, rested their shoes on the dashboard, refilled the tank with cheap gasoline. Renters allowed public schools to fail. They made excuses for America's enemies. They adopted the soft bigotry of low expectations while countenancing a culture of permissiveness. One might object to the two cases in Bush's analogy, holding that care for a car implies a direct self-interest that care for the nation lacks. However, Bush connected the two abstractly through the general qualities of ownership. Owning "something" engendered caring—whether this something constituted a mode of transportation or a stake in one's country.

Ownership gave people hope. Bush maintained that "ownership is part of a hopeful America. When you hear me say 'a more hopeful America,' it means I'm going to encourage ownership in our society."[17] The hope entailed in ownership promised a bright future for the nation by combining desire with expectation. When we hope, we entertain the expectation of something desired. Hope entails confidence that we will obtain our desired result. In this way, hopefulness may be contrasted with wishfulness. To wish is also to desire something, but wishing expresses desire without confidence. Indeed, a wish often expresses the fear that the very opposite of the wished for outcome may result. A hopeful America, then, indicated an America confident about its future, signaling a nation capable of setting goals and achieving them. Ownership inspired hope for the nation's future because ownership signified a realization of hope. Owners already achieved their goals. Practitioners of a powerful technē who refused to leave their fortunes to fate or luck, owners exhibited agency in setting themselves on a future trajectory and working to realize it. Encouraging ownership would instill a measure of confidence in Americans who, suffering from economic distress, believed that they could not control their futures. Ownership promised to overcome pessimism and defeat.

Insisting that ownership empowered individuals, Bush asserted that "when people have solid assets, they gain independence and security and dignity and more control over their future."[18] Ownership freed individuals from dependence on others, relieving the nation of its obligation to alleviate their financial and psychological burdens. By relying on the economic prowess of another, dependents reduced their security and fell victim to a future not of their own making. The uncertain economic condition of dependency forced someone to trade a measure of self-respect for the support of another. Suffering a loss of self, dependents carried a severe social stigma. This has been reinforced in U.S. social welfare policy, which historically has cast recipients of public assistance as dependents shamefully subsisting on public largesse. A society of owners would render obsolete policy hierarchies based on distinctions of work and non-work by situating capital, rather than labor, as the basis of public policy. Such a move would empower everyone, even ostensibly independent workers, for they, too, suffered at the hands of government, even in ostensibly "independent" programs like Social Security. Bush explained that government officials had long held the attitude that they controlled the nation, jealously guarding their authority and resisting attempts to shift control to citizens. Bush characterized this view as the "same old Washington mindset." Turning everyone into dependents, policy elites believed that "they'll give the orders, and you will pay the bills." Even though citizens provided the funds for government operations, they held no decision-making authority. Bush promised a change: "America has gone beyond that way of thinking, and we're not going back."[19] Ownership enabled individuals to retain control. Through taxes, politicians could deprive workers of their wages, but they could not relieve owners of their property.

Offering stability in changing times, ownership bolstered individual fortunes in an increasingly mobile society. As jobs and careers changed, people did not stay in one place their entire lives. Speaking to a group of college students, Bush explained that "it was a different society back a couple of decades ago because a person stayed with the same company, had the health plan from the company, retirement plan from the company. Now people are moving around. It's a different world. And there is some uncertainty in that kind of world." Whereas employment might change, ownership offered the stability of assets that remained in the possession and under the control of the owner. Ownership thus offered reassurance to Americans desperately seeking stability and certainty in unsettling times. Bush held that "one way to bring stability and security into a person's life is to encourage ownership. . . . It provides great security and relief."[20] However, the fluidity of global capitalism, which stresses rapid movement of assets across national borders, intimates an instability that belies ownership's assurance. In this context, uncertainty could easily develop into anxiety and fear, including fear of losing the very assets of ownership. Bush did not address these concerns, focusing instead on what he regarded as the promise of ownership. Although he could not resolve concerns about mobility, Bush construed ownership as a basis for acting in an uncertain world.

Activating both figurative and literal dimensions of ownership, Bush asserted that "it's important for people to buy into the future of America."[21] Wanting Americans to adopt his vision, Bush articulated "buying into" as associating with his understanding of the nation's future. In this sense, the phrase "buy into" has circulated in contemporary vernacular discourse in various group and organizational contexts, as managers have asked employees, athletes, volunteers, civil servants, and others to heed their directives. Buying into connotes a collaborative decision-making structure, granting autonomy to the purchaser, who can choose to accept or reject the product. Buying into places the justificatory burden on the seller, who must persuade one's clientele of the value of the offered goods. In vernacular speech, buying into also attributes a potentially gullible or delusional character to an audience that unquestionably accepts the tenets of a dominant ideology. Given his emphasis on hope, Bush may have regarded such connotations as unfairly cynical.

"Buying into" is not only a term of management consulting or cult philosophy; one can literally buy into an organization or commodity. Seeing ownership possibilities in numerous government operations and programs, Bush stressed the literal character of ownership as much as its figurative character. He regularly abstracted commercial exchanges from their larger cultural milieux. As a prominent example, Bush frequently pointed to a rise in home ownership as evidence of his administration's progress toward an ownership society. Expressing considerable pride in this achievement, he beamed, "I love the fact that more and more people from all walks of life are opening the place where they live—open that door up where they live, saying, 'Welcome to my home. Welcome to my piece of property.'"[22] In this statement and others, Bush exploited the warmth associated with "home" to promote the primary value of ownership. Interpellating homeowners as property investors, Bush voiced a typically cordial greeting—"welcome to my home"—as an introduction to an asset portfolio, calling out to Americans to envision themselves as owners of real wealth.[23] Enabling average Americans to obtain a piece of the ownership society, homeownership permitted people to buy into America's future.

Rather than suggesting a cold and calculating way of life, Bush tied ownership to his vision of a compassionate society. In early 2004, he introduced ownership through the frame of compassion.[24] Indeed, the nation could not prosper without the latter. An anonymous society would not engender a successful society, which required direct human contact. People needed to connect with others in meaningful, spiritual ways. An army of bureaucrats could not achieve a fraction of the gains achieved by compassionate citizens. Intimating that the inspired volunteer held the key to America's future, Bush called on his audiences to "rally the armies of compassion, those who mentor our children, those who care for the homeless, those who offer hope to the addicted." Moved by a sense of charity, individuals could enact real change in their communities and across the nation. But how could the inherent compassion of Americans be directed toward pressing social problems? Noting that public officials had to create opportunities for Americans to express their compassion, Bush maintained that "a compassionate society is a society that promotes opportunity for every citizen, including the independence and dignity that come from ownership."[25] Widespread opportunity both enabled compassionate action and served as evidence of its occurrence. And ownership suggested its material attainment.

At first glance, Bush's characterization of ownership as an expression of compassion might appear ill-conceived. The types of volunteering he celebrated—mentoring children, caring for the homeless, giving hope to the addicted—would appear to entail a willing sacrifice of time and wealth, a selflessness not addressed by ownership.[26] Caring for the homeless, for example, likely would consume some of one's assets: work or leisure time would have to be reduced to accommodate volunteering, and one might be asked to donate goods and money to a shelter. Moreover, selflessness seemingly violated the fundamental rule of a market ethics, which Adam Smith famously expressed in his *Wealth of Nations*. Invoking the metaphor of an invisible hand, Smith argued that self-interested behavior benefited everyone, since individuals are "led by an invisible hand to promote an end which was no part of [their] intention." Self-interest actually represented a superior ethical force, promoting society's interests "more effectually than when [an individual] really intends to promote it."[27] The invisible hand intimated that individuals act most selflessly when they pursue self-interest, whereas conscious efforts to improve the condition of others actually reveal a kind of selfishness and self-importance.

Confronting the possibility of undermining the very basis of a market ethics, Bush associated ownership and compassion with the values of respect and responsibility. Ownership connoted respect by transforming dependents into independents, by giving individuals control over their lives. Ownership promoted responsibility by positioning individuals as stakeholders, thus motivating them to seek out information about public affairs and hold public officials accountable. Bush viewed compassion similarly, holding that "in a compassionate society, people respect one another. They respect their religious beliefs. They respect their opinions. And they take responsibility for the decisions they make in life." Responsibility served as the copula connecting compassion and ownership, thereby revealing the spiritual dimension of ownership. "In a responsible society," Bush explained, "each of us is responsible for loving our neighbor just like we'd like to be loved ourselves."[28] Ownership—and, in particular, encouraging its spread—represented a practice of neighborly love. Far from being a starkly material quality, ownership conveyed an inherent moral worth.

Testifying that ownership also saved souls, Bush declared that "it's good for the soul of the country for people to own something." Expanded ownership and the independence it conferred could engender cultural change, establishing responsibility, self-control, and dignity as guiding social norms. To be sure, the president and his supporters believed that dependency had produced the opposite. A culture of dependency dissolved familial ties, defeated the work ethic, and encouraged sexual promiscuity. The negative effects of this culture particularly impacted those least able to withstand its deceptive allure—poor people. And the government only made matters worse by funding this culture of dependency through its social policies. Individual acts of compassion could redress this situation and, in the process, achieve a larger social good. Volunteering for Habitat for Humanity, for example, not only provided people with shelter, it conveyed the moral lessons of ownership. Reaching out in this way, volunteers/owners could make change. Through their efforts, "America will change one soul at a time."[29]

The Ownership Society and Social Security

Since the mid-1990s, policymakers have engaged in extensive discussions over the creation of private accounts in Social Security. Private accounts garnered widespread interest as a potential solution to projected long-term deficits in the program's finances.[30] A familiar story explained these potential shortfalls: increased life expectancies, earlier retirements, and more baby-boomer retirees meant that policymakers would have to raise taxes or reduce benefits to meet future obligations. For many advocates, private accounts have offered the possibility of avoiding these unhappy choices because private accounts would utilize the "power of compound interest."[31] As President Bush explained, "there's something called the compounding rate of interest. In other words, if you set aside dollars over time, they will grow with interest, and it compounds. It gets bigger and bigger and bigger."[32] In the president's view, only compound interest could reshape the gloomy future of Social Security and create wealth for all owners of private accounts. Holding this position, President Bush joined an already existing policy debate. He did not introduce the idea of private accounts, nor was he the first proponent to connect private accounts to ownership. However, President Bush ascribed a more central role to ownership than his predecessors, and he represented Social Security privatization as a central policy expression of his larger social vision.

In the winter of 2005, President Bush launched a barnstorming tour to promote private accounts for Social Security. Holding town-hall meetings in more than twenty states, Bush moderated panel discussions and question-and-answer sessions involving attendees. The panel discussions typically included an expert on retirement policy and laypeople from various walks of life: children, parents, grandparents, young workers, older workers, retirees, farmers, firefighters, small-business owners, warehouse workers, students, single parents, new parents. Laypeople would often participate in pairs or groups. For example, grandparents frequently appeared with their grandchildren. The panelists uniformly voiced concern for the future of Social Security and support for the president's proposed reforms. Retirees expressed confidence that private accounts would not jeopardize their benefits, and younger workers expressed relief that they and their children could anticipate a more secure retirement. President Bush began each meeting with a short speech, then he discussed issues of work and retirement with the panelists. Less often, Bush solicited questions from audience members. Like the panelists, questioners supported his policies.

During these town-hall meetings, President Bush lauded private accounts because they enabled ownership. Utilizing the near-universality of Social Security, private accounts would permit workers to possess capital. While the accounts themselves would be owned by individuals, the spirit of ownership would pervade society as a whole. Recalling the themes of his reelection campaign, President Bush embraced ownership as a modality encompassing multiple policies. He declared: "I strongly believe in an ownership society. I want more people owning their home, owning their own business, owning and managing their own health care account, and owning and managing their retirement account. I think it makes America a better place."[33] Building an ownership society would accentuate admirable American qualities and improve an already enviable way of life.

The ownership offered by private accounts prompted a rethinking of the status afforded citizens by traditional Social Security benefits. Historically, Social Security benefits have been construed culturally as a measure of independence. Retirees have been represented as persons rightfully receiving money owed to them. Social Security benefits have not carried the stigma attached to public assistance benefits. However, through the frame of ownership, traditional Social Security benefits appeared differently. Bush demanded that "Congress ought to consider personal accounts . . . because [they] empower the individual." From this vantage point, traditional benefits actually disempowered individuals, whereas private accounts promised to transform dependency to independence. Assessing the comments of a worker who had discussed managing her 401(k) accounts, President Bush judged: "You listen to Betty's language. She's talking about her assets. She's not relying upon the government. She says, 'These are my assets, and I own these assets.' And that's important."[34] The independence of ownership brought pride and dignity. The resourcefulness and self-reliance of the investor crafted this moral persona, restoring human agency and evidencing the productive, value-laden qualities of modalities as technē. No longer having to act as supplicants beseeching Congress for retirement benefits, retirees could decide for themselves the specific components of a good life.

The independence and self-control of ownership appeared especially important when contrasted with the uncertainty of promised Social Security benefits. President Bush asserted that private accounts would "give our children and grandchildren a chance to replace a burden of uncertainty with a new opportunity. Instead of leaving their full retirement in the hands of future politicians, younger workers will be able to take part of their retirement into their own hands."[35] Self-control engendered peace of mind, since individuals could count on themselves to make the right decisions for their retirement. After all, concern for their retirement constituted a proper self-interest. Politicians, too, acted self-interestedly. But their self-interest did not necessarily coincide with the interests of their constituents—either individually or collectively. Politicians considered a range of factors in determining their self-interests, and they responded to a range of appeals in making their decisions, many of which lay outside the reach of citizens. Unlike politics, ownership did not trade in promises. Stressing the differences between the present Social Security system and personal accounts, President Bush explained: "Your Social Security benefit is simply a promise. You don't own it; the government will decide. If the government can't pay for it, the government says, 'Well, we're going to reduce your benefits.' When you have your own personal account, it's yours. The government cannot take it away."[36] A secure retirement lay in possession, not promises.

The control entailed in ownership found significant expression in President Bush's promise that account owners would be able to leave accumulated assets to heirs. He maintained that "in a personal account, if you had one of those and your assets were growing and you passed away, you could leave it to whomever you want."[37] Since a private account would represent the property of its owner, its assets could be distributed as the owner desired. For Bush, this possible feature of private accounts compared favorably with the present system, which confiscated workers' money. With the present system, he held, "somebody works hard, doesn't live long enough to get the benefits, dies earlier than the national average, and that money that they put in the system—unless you've got younger kids—just is gone, goes to help somebody else."[38] Traditional benefits constituted a coercive income-transfer system. Money distributed to "somebody else," even if helping to secure someone else's retirement, amounted to money lost for the contributor and his or her family. Bush likened this lack of property rights to a disappearance: "Somebody has worked all their life, contributed to the system, dies early, and the money just disappears." Bush declared that the present system "doesn't seem fair to me."[39] Unfairness arose importantly from the compulsion and force that Bush diagnosed in the present system, which undermined the spirit of an ownership modality as purposeful human activity.

Individuals would control private accounts because they provided the funds for the present Social Security system. President Bush insisted to audiences that "when you pay in payroll taxes, it's your money, it's not the government's money; it's your money—you ought to be allowed to take some of your own money and set it aside in a personal savings account that you can call your own."[40] Politicians traditionally demanded that individuals relinquish their money, but they stripped individuals of the authority of capital. For the president, this represented a basic question of trust: "It's your money. I trust you with your own money. To me that's an attitude that Congress ought to take: We trust you with your own money."[41] Trusting people meant treating them as capable agents able to make competent decisions about their futures; in short, trusting people meant treating them as owners. Congress seemed unwilling to do this because decades of paternalistic social policy had made Congress unwilling to relinquish the power of ownership. In contrast, the president hoped to align retirement policy with a longer American tradition of self-determination. He declared that the "strength of our country is trusting the people."[42] In this way, ownership exemplified political values of freedom and liberty.

In addition to empowering people as individuals, private accounts used the power of ownership to foster political engagement. Private accounts promised to turn disaffected and disinterested persons into concerned citizens. Recalling his previous associations of ownership and stakeholding, President Bush asserted repeatedly: "When a person owns something, they have a vital stake in the future of the country."[43] This statement reiterated the position that ownership constituted a necessary condition for political participation. Moreover, Bush implied that wealthy people participated more in government because wealthy people had invested more in government policies: "the more people watch their assets grow, they're going to be saying, 'I better pay attention to fiscal policy in Washington, D.C.' There's nothing that causes more participation in government than if your wealth is directly associated with the decisions of government."[44] Wealthy people possessed real, substantial assets that could be adversely impacted if policymakers made bad decisions. Implicit, too, in the position that wealth served as the primary motivator for political participation was the related notion that other possible motivations were unimportant or improper. Bush's primary emphasis on wealth suggested that the status of citizen itself—with its legal and social rights and privileges—did not motivate sufficient political participation. Indeed, at times he indicated that ownership would compel otherwise inattentive individuals to assume their roles as citizens: "It's a notion of getting people to understand that they've got to pay attention to the future of the country when you, on a monthly basis, in some cases on a daily basis if you want to get on the Internet and look at your asset base."[45] Where appeals to civic obligations had failed, ownership would succeed in reviving the body politic.

However, threatening the purposefulness of its modality, ownership encouraged a specific form of political participation that emphasized spectatorship. President Bush warned that "politicians will be—their actions will be a lot more scrutinized when somebody is watching whether or not the decisions made in Washington is [*sic*] affecting their work on a daily or quarterly basis."[46] This explanation did not indicate clearly whether the "somebody" (presumably, a citizen-owner) watching politicians would undertake the critical inquiry denoted by scrutiny, or whether the person's charge would end with watching alone. Implying the latter, Bush repeatedly cast political participation as "pay[ing] attention" or exhibiting "more interest" in government policies.[47] These phrases suggested that citizen-owners acted like individual shareholders in a corporation: they observed the proceedings in Washington, and they held authority over these proceedings in the form of the vote, but citizen-owners did not participate in governance themselves. In this way, President

Bush circumscribed the agency of participants, constructing a passive mode of citizenship. This passivity did not arise from Bush's use of visual metaphors, but from his separation of seeing from knowing and doing. Scrutiny held the possibility of depicting citizenship as active vision, but Bush reverted to forms of "watching" alone. "Paying attention" indicated increased awareness, but it did not denote the cognition or standing signified in a visual term like "recognizing." Nor did "paying attention" connote the creative, forward-thinking qualities of a visual term like "envisioning." President Bush asked citizens to pay attention, but he did not invite citizens to recognize or envision vibrant democratic practices. Envisioning, for instance, would have encouraged citizens to imagine democratic possibilities. By contrast, watching placed citizens in a reactive mode, leaving the practice of democracy to others.

Although it suggested circumscribed agency, ownership would revive public life because President Bush hoped to extend ownership to all Americans. Bush insisted that "every citizen—every citizen—has got the capacity to manage his or her own money. And if they don't, we help them understand how to. . . . I believe the so-called investor class ought to be every American, regardless of his or her background."[48] Proclaiming his belief in the abilities of ordinary Americans, Bush demystified investing and alluded to the equality of the market. To suggest that every citizen possessed investment competency—or could be taught competency—implied that successful investing did not require a highly specialized set of skills. Investing did not require years of education and training, nor did it require mastery of an esoteric vocabulary. Instead, successful investing drew on judgment and honest effort. In this way, ownership retained a connection between values and everyday practice as it crafted moral action. Resisting a view of morality as transcendent, ownership expressed virtue through specific actions.

Some opponents of private accounts worried that individuals and groups lacked the knowledge and experience to act in the financial arena. Responding to this concern, President Bush appealed to the pedagogical power of ownership itself. Ownership generated interest in asset accumulation and taught owners how to increase their assets. Bush declared that "there's nothing like solving financial illiteracy when you're watching—when you're making decisions for your own money. You start asking questions; there's advisers, there's people around to help you make a rational decision what to do with your own money. And a good way to learn is when you're watching your own money grow."[49] Connoting more than idle spectatorship, observation constituted part of a powerful and multifaceted process of participation in the realm of private accounts. In this process, observation linked directly to decision making. Observation produced better decisions by providing owners with important information, and private accounts provided specific vehicles for enacting financial decisions. Further, account owners could see the results of their decisions immediately because they did not need the concurrence of voters or policymakers to legitimate decisions about private accounts.

President Bush chided opponents of private accounts for what he regarded as an effort to disqualify certain groups of people as capable investors. He observed that "there's a certain notion in America that the investor class is only a certain type of person. I just don't believe that. I don't subscribe to that. I don't think that's what America is about."[50] Subscribing to the notion of an intrinsic investor class betrayed a hereditary-based understanding of social order more appropriate to European monarchies than American democracy. An intrinsic view of investment savvy attached personal characteristics to class standing, denying the social mobility that informed American self-understandings. Moreover, in American history, class discrimination often implicated race, and Bush discerned this linkage in the position against private accounts. The very phrase "investor class" appeared racially coded to interpellate wealthy white suburbanites: "The investor class—it kind of sounds like to me, you know, a certain race of people living in a certain area. I believe everybody's got the capability of being in the investor class."[51] By opposing private accounts, well-meaning defenders of traditional Social Security benefits actually perpetuated racism by representing black workers as incapable of providing independently for their retirement. Defenders of traditional benefits kept black Americans dependent on Social Security because they lacked confidence in black Americans. By contrast, President Bush expressed confidence in all Americans regardless of race and class. Seemingly available to everyone, ownership represented a more "American" approach to retirement.

Conclusion

Sharing his vision of an ownership society, President Bush invited citizens to enact a public modality that he constructed as interested, caring, and hopeful. President Bush imagined a society of compassionate owners acting generously to extend the independence of ownership to others, thereby overcoming disabling social stigmas. Bush linked ownership and compassion through responsibility, as owners took responsibility for their own well-being and expressed neighborly love by treating others similarly. The entrepreneur appeared as the hero of the ownership society, and this figure could flourish only if politicians repositioned government in partnership with owners rather than as a coercive force. President Bush sought to realize his vision of an ownership society by creating private accounts in Social Security, which served well as a vehicle of ownership because of its nearly universal coverage of the population. Moreover, private accounts would transform individuals. Whereas past policy had usurped individual agency and turned workers and retirees into dependents, private accounts placed owners in control. Private accounts also offered benefits for the polity by fostering engaged citizenship. Since ownership appeared as the primary motive for political participation, increased ownership would produce a revitalized democracy. Further, private accounts represented an appropriate response to changing social conditions.

As a mode of public engagement, ownership seeks to redeem the bourgeois promise of universal access. For the historical bourgeois public sphere, expanded participation engendered trouble because it unsettled the shared norms and backgrounds of participants. In a restricted public sphere, the bourgeoisie could focus on a putative common good because their shared socioeconomic standing led them to ask similar questions about public affairs. A shared life experience engendered shared concerns. New participants—women, laborers—brought new experiences, raised different concerns, and asked alternate questions. New participants did not accept settled agendas or modes of interaction. Like its historically specific progenitor, an ownership society discourages new participants from introducing difference into public discourse, leaving existing agendas, participatory modes, and forums intact. Participants themselves undergo transformation as they move from nonownership to ownership status. Engendering an independence that putatively transforms people's needs and interests, ownership promises to transcend such differences as race, ethnicity, and religion, thereby protecting and strengthening the public sphere.

Ownership creates a paradox of expanding participation, however. If ownership constitutes a necessary condition of political participation, then any attempt by non-owners to enter into political discourse must be considered illegitimate. Non-ownership engagement would appear baldly self-interested when compared to the general interest of ownership. Seeking to overcome these exclusions, President Bush proclaimed that an ownership society should increase its stakeholders. Yet this objective can be achieved only by those who already enjoy political legitimacy. Only owners can expand ownership to others, unleashing their entrepreneurial spirit to increase their numbers. Nonowners thus occupy a paradoxically dependent position. Unable to work purposefully to achieve the independence of ownership, they must sit passively while they wait for others to grant their independence.

Ownership promises to expand participation while rendering potential discussion topics off-limits to critical publicity. Ownership constitutes a condition of participation, but ownership does not avail itself to questions concerning its nature, structure, or distribution. Questions of ownership do not appear as properly political questions. Ownership publicity suggests that most economic questions, insofar as they inquire into the basic structures, institutions, or practices of the economy, fall outside of the province of public discourse. The proper response to ownership is awe, not critical investigation. Indeed, the spiritual qualities President Bush ascribed to ownership intimate an almost supernatural force. Bush expressed wonder at the hopeful quality of ownership, professing his love for its ameliorative power. Bush celebrated ownership as a healing medicine. The nation recovered from the terrorist attacks of September 11, 2001, "because there's an ownership society, a culture of ownership in America."[52] At no point, however, did President Bush ask questions of ownership. Nor did he represent ownership as a concept that may be explored, grasped, or refined. Bush encouraged citizens to evaluate existing approaches to governance, but he did not encourage citizens to evaluate conceptions and practices of ownership. Ownership appears as a magical creative force that improves the circumstances of those willing to cultivate its power. One may be able to harness its energy, but one cannot fully understand its operation. Nor should one raise doubts about its expansion, since ownership appears as an unqualified good. Ownership only improves lives, it does not worsen them.

In particular contexts, ownership offers individuals distinct material benefits. For instance, U.S. policy offers home owners income-tax deductions on their mortgage interest payments. However, when advocated as a model for society itself, ownership fails individuals and society. This is because ownership envisions individual and society as combative terms. In an ownership society, the isolated individual reigns supreme. An ownership society cannot imagine individuals working collaboratively to address shared concerns. Moreover, an ownership society cannot account meaningfully for differences among individuals, because doing so would entail acknowledging the influence of social forces like race, sex, and class. In this way, an ownership society imagines a more idealized universality than the bourgeois public sphere. Whereas the former sought to save universality from acknowledged inequalities, an ownership society acts as if inequality does not exist.

Notes

1. Jürgen Habermas, *The Structural Transformation of the Public Sphere: An Inquiry into a Category of Bourgeois Society*, trans. Thomas Burger (1962; repr., Cambridge: Massachusetts Institute of Technology Press, 1989), 87. As my reference to Habermas suggests, my narrative recounts the historical development of the bourgeois public sphere in Europe.

2. See, e.g., Oskar Negt and Alexander Kluge, *Public Sphere and Experience: Toward an Analysis of the Bourgeois and Proletarian Public Sphere*, trans. Peter Labanyi, Jamie Owen Daniel, and Assenka Oksiloff (1972; repr., Minneapolis: University of Minnesota Press, 1993); Joan B. Landes, *Women and the Public Sphere in the Age of the French Revolution* (Ithaca, NY: Cornell University Press, 1988); Catherine R. Squires, "Rethinking the Black Public Sphere: An Alternative Vocabulary for Multiple Publics," *Communication Theory* 12 (2002): 446–68.

3. See, e.g., Robert Asen and Daniel C. Brouwer, "Introduction: Reconfigurations of the Public Sphere," in *Counterpublics and the State*, ed. Robert Asen and Daniel C. Brouwer (Albany: State University of New York Press, 2001), 6–10; Gerard A. Hauser, *Vernacular Voices: The Rhetoric of Publics and Public Spheres* (Columbia: University of South Carolina Press, 1999). Habermas also has endorsed this move. See Jürgen Habermas, *Between Facts and Norms: Contributions to a Discourse Theory of Law and Democracy*, trans. William Rehg (1992; repr., Cambridge: Massachusetts Institute of Technology Press, 1996).

4. See, e.g., Seyla Benhabib, *The Claims of Culture: Equality and Diversity in the Global Era* (Princeton, NJ: Princeton University Press, 2002); Iris Marion Young, *Inclusion and Democracy* (New York: Oxford University Press, 2000).

5. See James Arnt Aune, *Selling the Free Market: The Rhetoric of Economic Correctness* (New York: Guilford Press, 2001); Pierre Bourdieu, *Acts of Resistance: Against the Tyranny of the Market*, trans. Richard Nice (New York: New Press, 1998). On the global rise of neoliberalism, see Helga Leitner, Jamie Peck, Eric S. Sheppard, eds., *Contesting Neoliberalism: Urban Frontiers* (New York: Guilford, 2006); Alfredo Saad-Filho and Deborah Johnston, eds., *Neoliberalism: A Critical Reader* (London: Pluto Press, 2005).

6. Thomas Frank, *One Market under God: Extreme Capitalism, Market Populism, and the End of Economic Democracy* (New York: Doubleday, 2000), 29, xiii.

7. David Boaz, "Ownership Society," *Cato Institute*, http://www.cato.org/special/ownership-_society/boaz.html (accessed March 3, 2007).

8. Grover Norquist, "Ownership Can Be Revolutionary," *American Enterprise*, March 2005, 50.

9. A keyword search for the phrase "ownership society" in the online edition of

Weekly Compilation of Presidential Documents reveals that Bush mentioned the phrase with greater frequency annually over the course of his first term. The phrase did not appear in Bush's public statements and speeches in 2001. In 2002, the phrase appeared in his public speeches and statements four times. In 2003, this number increased to fifty-six. The number increased again in 2004 to eighty-one.

10. George W. Bush, *Weekly Compilation of Presidential Documents*, vol. 40 (Washington, DC: Government Printing Office, 2004), 1799.

11. Ibid., 40:2789–90.

12. Ibid., 40:42.

13. Ibid., 40:1093.

14. Ibid., 40:1188.

15. Ibid.

16. Ibid., 40:2420.

17. Ibid., 40:1874.

18. Ibid., 40:295.

19. Ibid.

20. Ibid., 40:1506.

21. Ibid., 40:1734.

22. Ibid., 40:1985.

23. Althusser has written famously that "ideology 'acts' or 'functions' in such a way that it 'recruits' subjects . . . by that very precise operation which I have called *interpellation* or hailing, and which can be imagined along the lines of the most commonplace everyday police (or other) hailing: 'Hey, you there!'" Of course, Althusser viewed ideology through a structural lens. He held that "ideology has always-already interpellated individuals as subjects." Louis Althusser, "Ideology and Ideological State Apparatuses (Notes towards an Investigation)," in *Lenin and Philosophy and Other Essays*, trans. Ben Brewster (New York: Monthly Review Press, 1971), 174–75. Bush's recruiting represented a more active hailing of citizens as property owners.

24. In one of his very first public articulations of the phrase "ownership society," which occurred in 2002, Bush portrayed his vision as an expression of a compassionate society. He held that "an *ownership society* is a compassionate *society*." George W. Bush, *Weekly Compilation of Presidential Documents*, vol. 38 (Washington, DC: Government Printing Office, 2002), 1773.

25. Bush, *Weekly Compilation*, 40:42.

26. In a dialogue on whether markets facilitate moral behavior, for example, economist Rebecca Blank argues that markets promote self-interested behavior whereas religiously inspired action (Blank draws on her Christian beliefs) call for people to be "*other-interested* as well as self-interested." Rebecca M. Blank, "Viewing the Market Economy Through the Lens of Faith," *Is the Market Moral? A Dialogue on Religion, Economics, and Justice*, ed. E. J. Dionne Jr., Jean Bethke Elshtain, and Kayla M. Drogosz (Washington, DC: Brookings Institution Press, 2004), 23.

27. Adam Smith, *An Inquiry into the Nature and Causes of the Wealth of Nations*, ed. Edwin Cannan (Chicago: University of Chicago Press, 1976), 4:2.9.

28. Bush, *Weekly Compilation*, 40:43.

29. Ibid., 40:269, 1569.

30. The report of the 1994–96 Advisory Council on Social Security sparked interest in private accounts for many policymakers. Predicting a 25 percent shortfall for Social Security beginning in 2030, members of the Advisory Council offered three plans to bolster the program's finances. One plan proposed solutions that followed the traditional social-insurance structure of Social Security. The other two plans introduced versions of private accounts. See Advisory Council on Social Security, *Report of the 1994–1996 Advisory Council on Social Security*, Washington, DC, 1997.

The long-term financial outlook for Social Security has improved since the mid-1990s. Whereas the 1994–96 Advisory Council projected a deficit beginning in 2030, the Social Security trustees' 2006 report projected that full funding could be sustained through 2040. Even without any changes to the program, three-fourths of benefits could be paid through 2080. The trustees noted that "present tax rates would be sufficient to pay 74 percent of scheduled benefits after trust fund exhaustion in 2040 and 70 percent of scheduled benefits in 2080." Board of Trustees, Federal Old-Age and Survivors Insurance and Disability Insurance Trust Funds, *2006 Annual Report of the Board of Trustees of the Federal Old-Age and Survivors Insurance and Disability Insurance Trust Funds*, Washington, DC, May 2006, 8.

31. However, private accounts themselves would not improve the finances of Social Security and would actually exacerbate financial deficits by diverting payroll taxes. Taxes still would have to be increased and benefits decreased to address the deficits. The proponents of private accounts on the 1994–96 Advisory Council conceded this point. Proponents noted that "there is a cost of transition to the new system." They explained that "in moving toward a system in which each generation pays for its own benefits rather than those of its elders, some workers have to pay for the benefits that come due under the old system to earlier generations as well to prefund their own retirement" (Advisory Council, *Report*, 30).

The 2001 President's Commission to Strengthen Social Security, which was appointed by Bush, also acknowledged that private accounts would require additional funds. The President's Commission urged that these costs be regarded as investments: "Like any sound investment program, investing in personal accounts requires additional resources up front." The President's Commission proposed decreasing traditional Social Security benefits and transferring additional general tax revenues to the program. President's Commission to Strengthen Social Security, *Strengthening Social Security and Creating Personal Wealth for All Americans*, Washington, DC, December 21, 2001, 67, 76.

32. George W. Bush, *Weekly Compilation of Presidential Documents*, vol. 41 (Washington, DC: Government Printing Office, 2005), 373.

33. Ibid., 41:142.
34. Ibid., 41:477, 613.
35. Ibid., 41:626
36. Ibid., 41:149.
37. Ibid., 41:464.
38. Ibid., 41:167.
39. Ibid., 41:834.
40. Ibid., 41:373.
41. Ibid., 41:532.
42. Ibid., 41:929.
43. Ibid., 41:430.
44. Ibid., 41:412.
45. Ibid., 41:874.
46. Ibid., 41:612.
47. See, e.g., Bush, *Weekly Compilation*, 41:430, 495.
48. Bush, *Weekly Compilation*, 41:242.
49. Ibid., 41:839.
50. Ibid., 41:363.
51. Ibid., 41:401.
52. Ibid., 40:334.

5
(In)Hospitable Publics
Theorizing Modalities of Access to U.S. Publics

Sara McKinnon

Immigration has always been recognized as a modality of access to U.S. publics. Codified through federal law and legal precedent, the U.S. immigration system entails a complex of rules, regulations, policies, and procedures that must be navigated by people seeking entry.[1] The process stratifies people into different categories (e.g., asylum seekers, undocumented migrants, resident aliens) and uses those divisions to determine the protocol and procedure of their potential access. These procedures include technologies of discipline and bio-power that instill in subjects the proper values and practices of the U.S. citizenry, while overwhelming potential subjects' sense of self with the sense of surveillance.[2] The methods of these technologies involve dense applications, court hearings, medical examinations, and interviews, all shrouded in technical and legal language that can be the difference between access and deportation. Thus, prospective subjects of the state must become experts of the technical and legal discourses that constrain and enable their possibilities for access to U.S. publics.

The possibility of mastering and maneuvering these discourses became immensely more difficult during the 1990s as neoliberal policies designed to renationalize politics in response to the denationalizing of economics began to be implemented.[3] In 1995, President Clinton decided that asylum seekers must wait 180 days before they could begin to work in the United States. Clinton also signed the 1996 Illegal Immigration Reform and Immigrant Responsibility Act, which required asylum seekers to make their claims within one year of entering the U.S. while expanding the grounds for denying asylum claims. The act also provided justifications for holding asylum claimants in detention centers and introduced "expedited removal," giving "immigration officers the authority to remove 'improperly documented aliens' arriving in the US 'without further hearing or review.'"[4] More recently, the 2001 Patriot Act and the 2005 Real ID Act continue the trajectory of such exclusionary legislation.

The shift in immigration policies and, more specifically, the shift in asylum law directly relate to questions of the modality of access, or hospitality, in U.S. publics. Refugees and asylum seekers, by their very positions as subjects, are bound to the nation-state. Contrary to the popular belief that refugees are "problems" caused by the failure of nation-states, Emma Haddad posits that displaced persons are central to the system of nation-building: "as long as there are political borders constructing separate states and creating clear definitions of insiders and outsiders, there will be refugees."[5] Though the nation-state is no longer the primary mode through which citizenship is constituted or performed,[6] for those seeking asylum the state continues to be the primary conductor in determining their access to publics. In this context, when an asylum seeker stands at the front door of the state and asks for asylum—hospitality within the home(land) and its publics—the state is the only possible conduit to that access, thus constituting a modality to the public.[7]

The symbolic connection between homes and nation-states is prevalent and proverbial. For instance, individuals frequently hail a home or homeland, or they invoke a motherland or fatherland in naming their ancestral or national belonging. Inquiries about one's language of birth often call individuals to name their mother tongue. Furthermore, state offices and departments often use the symbol of home in institutional rhetoric to emphasize the necessity of their particular goals, such as protection and security. As a condition of its emergence, the U.S. Department of Homeland Security (DHS) announced its primary purpose in relation to the home as "preserving our freedoms, protecting America. . . . [W]e secure our homeland."[8] The use of the term *homeland* deliberately implies intimacy and familiarity among those members of the home. Hailing the figure of the home and close relations within the home provides a strong rationale for the DHS to protect and secure. In this deployment of home, the state becomes the host of the home-nation—determining who has access, monitoring how they enter, deciding who can stay—all because it has positioned itself, or has been positioned, as the arbiter of hospitality.

As should be clear, an ontological assumption of this chapter is that subjects are not afforded equal access to the public and publicness; not all subjects can access the public, though the possibility of access is perpetually present. I read the possibility to access the public through the concepts of home and hospitality because this framework not only envisions a public that has permeable limits,[9] but imagines a process of invitation or request between subjects of the public and those whose subjectivity is defined by their positions outside of the home.

In this chapter I consider how the possibility of participation in publics is constituted by the state and question how modalities of access to publics are conditioned through particular values, discourses, and logics that, in the current moment, reflect market regimes. I mobilize the tension between political and ethical hospitality to examine the actualities of access to publics and to further consider the potential for publics to be hospitable. I first develop a conceptual framework of hospitable publics to explore how access is often constituted through states in neoliberal globalization. Next, attending to the claims of asylum seekers, in particular those asking asylum for reasons of gender and sexual orientation persecution, I use the framework of hospitable publics to demonstrate what happens around, through, and beyond publics. I argue that the current logics of late capitalism place conditions on available modalities of access through the following lines: First, guests are made coherent in their relation to global capital along lines of productivity and the threat of reproductivity. Second, guests are recognized through the logic of exchange in their positions as gifts either to the host or to the home. Finally, guests are organized via the logic of publicness that evaluates the political and state connections possessed by refugees. These logics work in tandem to frame the ways asylum seekers and other guests maneuver this modality of access to U.S. publics.

Hospitable Publics

Hospitality provides a fortuitous way to complicate constitutions of publics as it forecloses upon a question of how publics might be similar to homes. These homes are spatially and temporally bound modalities of invitation, but also of invention and action. Furthermore, publics as home connotes invitation and reception as *guests* are also proper subjects of the home. While hosts are recognized as primarily belonging *in* or even *to* the home, the host does not exist as host without the guest. And the *home* cannot be hospitable unless there is a guest to receive. Publics as home thus calls forth questions of hospitality, or the ways that subjects are invited to belong and participate within the home-public.

In theorizing hospitality Jacques Derrida uses the polysemic meaning of the word *hôte* to work through and consider the significance of the aporia between political hospitality and ethical hospitality. In this analysis, political hospitality is best understood as "a question of law, an obligation, a duty, and a right; it refers to the welcoming of an alien/stranger other as a non-enemy."[10] It provides spatial boundaries, limits, and conditions to the forms such welcoming can take. The hospitable home, "whether public or private, is dependent on and controlled by the law and the state police."[11] State laws and actors regulate what should happen in the home, manifest in city codes restricting the presence of "unsightly" broken cars, loud noise extending beyond the home, and underage drinking. State officials also monitor and restrict who can enter and exit homes. This is evident in the ways that home security systems are directly linked to police stations and how certain subjects are placed under "house" arrest with electronic devices surveying their movement.

In contrast, the ethically hospitable home is open to the radically other guest. The host allows, even invites, the guest to be at home despite risking the security of self, space, and family in that invitation. Through this exchange, however, the host is invited home by the radically other guest her/himself. Ethical hospitality requires that the host open up her/his home without invitation or common language,[12] knowing nothing of the guest, and without the expectation of reciprocity. This relationship is truly hospitable because both host and guest are *host* to one another by endowing each other with the gift of surviving life without necessitating reciprocity of exchange.[13] Ethical hospitality disrupts notions of ownership and property, for the home is no longer owned in a singular sense.[14] Moreover, the space of home must first invite the host to enter and reside. Derrida writes, "The *hôte* who receives (the host), the one who welcomes the invited or received *hôte* (the guest), the welcoming *hôte* who considers himself the owner of the place, is in truth a *hôte* received in his own home. He receives hospitality that he offers *in* his own home; he receives it *from* his own home—which, in the end, does not belong to him. The *hôte* as host is a guest."[15] To be ethically hospitable, the host must first recognize the ways she/he is a stranger in/to the home.

The tension between political and ethical hospitality fundamentally concerns who can be a subject and the process of gaining access to spaces constituted as homes. This matter of access is certainly not new to scholars of publics as some of the first critiques of public sphere theory engaged questions of who could be present and participate in publics.[16] Importantly, many of the most trenchant critiques concerned the (in)accessibility of publics for women.[17] Feminist theorists challenged the Habermasian articulation of access and bracketing of the social differential, rightly noting that the proposed modes of deliberation and formalities of address were structures of patriarchal, racial, and socioeconomic exclusion as only certain subjects had the means and maneuverability to publicly participate in those ways, or to even be present in those publics.

Importantly, counterpublics offer a modality for marginalized groups to gain access and garner publicity for their particular needs and concerns.[18] Yet even the ability to forge these counter arenas speaks to the ways subjects already belong, in some way, in the home. This is not to say that counterpublics are not valuable to political and social change as there are abundant examples of counterpublics that galvanize instrumental politics to effect social change.[19] Rather, I figure access to examine not how those already within home find or constitute political space, but the conditions of access to the public and the ability to be public. For as theories of hospitality suggest, and the following analysis of asylum claims demonstrate, even those who are denied access to the public are unswervingly constituted by the publics (and states) that exclude them.

I argue that access to publics has been constituted in large part through the renationalizing policies of neoliberal globalization in the contemporary United States.[20] Renationalizing policies are responsive to the lack of sovereign control in globalization because of the seemingly unrestricted movement of information, people, and resources in and out of the home nation-state.[21] In feeling this sense of "losing control,"[22] the host increasingly relies on "Janus-faced state strategies" to maintain control over the home. These strategies, as Adam Tickell and Jamie Peck note, are "absorbed in the task of making, extending, and managing markets in the broad field of economic policy, while at the same time meeting its expanding social and penal policy objectives in an increasingly activist and authoritarian manner."[23] The strategies are employed for the sake of instituting the "free-market" as the primary system of exchange. Neoliberal globalization thus produces "growing economic and financial linkages that integrate territorial formations more extensively over time."[24] The presence of these global linkages and transactions might be taken as a fact of the contemporary moment, yet it is vital to denaturalize the "free-market" and recognize it as instituted not only in global finance capital, but through the political and social institutions that constitute everyday life.[25]

The integration of neoliberalism in everyday social and political processes means that market logics now function as normative cultural logics in mainstream discourse. These logics presently work "across much of the developed and developing capitalist world, while shaping the architectures of the multilateral institutions and regional state structures (such as the European Union and the North American Free Trade Agreement)."[26] While on the surface it may appear that the state relinquishes sovereignty for the sake of the free market in neoliberalism, the state nevertheless remains a central actor in the institution of neoliberal market logics as sociocultural logics. This is evident most in the wave of neoliberal legislation of the 1990s, including the Defense of Marriage Act, the Personal Responsibility and Work Opportunity Reconciliation Act, and the Illegal Immigration Reform and Immigrant Responsibility Act.[27] Policymakers incorporated market logics in this legislation through provisions privileging and upholding ideas such as "personal responsibility," "individualism," and traditional "family values."[28]

As a result of such policies, the possibilities for political hospitality are now contingent upon and function first through the market logic of late capitalism where flexibility is emphasized, production and labor are increasingly privatized, and belief in the self-regulating market is upheld above all. Indeed, late capitalism necessitates a push to "minimizing cost and maximizing flexibility."[29] The emphasis on flexibility and the spatial mobility of capital and production are strongly related to circulation-based capitalism, where the inadvertent goal is to "subordinate and eventually efface historically discrete cultures and capitalisms and to create a unified cosmopolitan culture of unimpeded circulation."[30] The logic of exchange emerges from this emphasis on flexibility as actors seek to know what they will get for what they put in. For asylum seekers, the logic of exchange turns on a question of what they bring as figurative gifts for/to the host.[31] While many immigrant subjects have much to offer the U.S. state in exchange for access to publics, the logic of exchange largely disempowers immigrant subjects by rendering their skills, stories, and forms of labor intelligible as deficits to the state.

This logic of exchange is founded on the ideal that things of value circulate not in private realms but in the public where they can be observed and witnessed by many. Publicness thus becomes another organizing principle of late capitalism intervening in the recognition of asylum seekers. In this vein, publicness intercedes in the recognition of certain actions or processes as public matter. For example, while business endeavors, such as corporate mergers, outsourcing, and trade speculation, are certainly recognized as productive exchanges of the public, the relationship between a man who abuses a woman and the woman he targets remains off many public agendas. The logic of publicness also works in the perception of certain actors as public, who are always already situated as masculine, leading Cindy Griffin to note that the public functions as a space of "second birth" for men, where their productivity is lauded.[32]

The distribution of publicness is infused in the final logic of late capitalism functioning in asylum cases—the emphasis on productivity and the connected threat of reproductivity. Aihwa Ong explains that guests and hosts in the United States materialize through these logics in which "citizenship is defined as the civic duty of the individual to reduce his or her burden on society, and instead to build up his or her own human capital—in other words, to 'be an entrepreneur of her/himself.'"[33] She contends that certain groups, particularly those associated as "parasites" or "dependents" of the state, are recognized through "racializing schemes that serve to blacken and stigmatize" their bodies.[34] Important here are the implications concerning the process of subjectification that happens in claiming asylum; even before guests pass into modalities of access, their bodies are classified, regulated, and constituted through values of democracy, human capital, and race that materialize bodies when they appear on the doorsteps of a home. When not seen as productive to the public home, the asylum seeking subject is read as a private subject and consequently understood as the reproductive threat to the public.

Asylum in the Hospitable Public

That women around the world believe they can come to the United States, ask for asylum on the basis of gender, and possibly gain residence speaks strongly of the global publicity of the United States as a hospitable nation-state to women.[35] Within the U.S. home it is true that many women have gained access to publics, achieving recognition as public, productive, and value-added subjects to the home's external image as a defender of women's rights. While many women have gained asylum in the United States on the basis of gender,[36] barriers remain because gender is not formally named as a social group and certain forms of gender persecution are deemed private matters. To be sure, these omissions result from patriarchal laws, but the ways appointed immigration judges interpret these laws to determine access increasingly involve the logics of publicness, productivity and the threat of reproductivity, and exchange.

Publicness and the Reproductive Threat

Olimpia Lazo-Majano's claim for asylum on the basis of gender is one of the first recognized times gender was enumerated as a social group and form of persecution in asylum law.[37] In 1981, Lazo-Majano's husband fled El Salvador because he was a member of a rightist parliamentary group and no longer wanted to participate. Lazo-Majano stayed in El Salvador to work as a domestic, and through this work she began washing the clothes of childhood acquaintance Rene Zuniga, a sergeant in the armed forces of the Salvadoran military. After news circulated that Lazo-Majano's husband had fled El Salvador, Zuniga began to threaten her as well as physically and sexually violate her. Zuniga told Lazo-Majano that if her husband returned to El Salvador, he would "cut both of them into pieces" for being subversives.[38]

In 1982, Lazo-Majano entered the United States and later applied for political asylum on the grounds of the enduring sexual assault, torture, and threats she experienced in El Salvador. The first immigration judge denied her case, as did the Board of Immigration Appeals (BIA), which noted that "the evidence attests to mistreatment of an individual, not persecution."[39] Lazo-Majano revised her argument in appealing to the federal court to claim that she had endured persecution on the basis of her political opinion, which Zuniga regarded as "subversive." In reviewing the case the judges granted Lazo-Majano asylum, deciding that while the claimant's political opinion was in "camouflage," "when Zuniga manipulatively chooses to regard Olimpia as a subversive, he attributes to her the political opinion of a subversive, and she is being persecuted on account of political opinion."[40] Notably, however, the asylum grant was not on the grounds of gender persecution. In his dissenting opinion Circuit Judge Cecil Poole illuminates the complexities of gender that Lazo-Majano negotiated in her arguments: "She may indeed have suffered emotional and physical abuse in the course of her personal relationship with Sergeant Zuniga, but such mistreatment is clearly personal in nature and does not constitute political persecution with the meaning of the immigration laws."[41]

The logics underlying the different court receptions of Lazo-Majano's plea starkly attest to the conditions placed on access to the public. The immigration judge, the BIA, and those dissenting appellate judges conflated the sexual assault and physical abuse she experienced with the "personal" and nonpolitical. The framing of the persecution she experienced as "personal" accomplishes two things. First, it positions her ultimately as a private subject. Lazo-Majano is figured as an actor in private realms and private exchanges when Judge Poole intimates that the violations she names result from her "personal relationship" with Zuniga. This analysis implies that Lazo-Majano is partially culpable for the abuse she experienced because she elected to have a "personal relationship" with Zuniga. These insinuations, made directly by Judge Poole but resonant with the lower court decisions, mark Lazo-Majano as a private subject with personal issues because of a personal relationship. In this framing, she is no longer a guest who is intelligible as a proper public subject at the front door of the U.S. home. This case illuminates that the modality of access evident in U.S. immigration is highly monitored and reinforced by the values through which judges read the cases presented in their courtrooms.

Despite the final grant of asylum, Lazo-Majano's claim must also be read through the logic of productivity and the threat of reproductivity, for it is only when Lazo-Majano is named as a political "subversive" that she is seen as a guest with a claim necessitating access to the home. In the first claim of gender persecution, Lazo-Majano's case was intelligible to the courts through a reinforcement of the public-private split that positioned her as unproductive to the public and thus less worthy of access. Because Lazo-Majano worked as a domestic in El Salvador, she seemingly did not contribute to public realms of finance, nor did she obtain a high profile as a political activist, nor did she evidently strengthen access to global capital for the U.S. state. Her visibility as female, read historically as a "private subject" and the most "socially dependent" (due to reproductivity and kin connections), constructs her as the least able to be productive publicly in terms of human capital for the state-host.[42] Her (in)access to global capital, recognized through her inability to gain access in any way other than asylum for gendered reasons (private reasons), illustrates that women seeking gender-based asylum are recognized, according to Ong's classificatory system, as the most racialized and the least productive.[43] Her access to U.S. publics thus can only happen when Lazo-Majano is named by another *as* a public subject—a subject with political power enough to be "subversive" and to pose a threat to Zuniga. This case demonstrates the ways that entrance into the home hinges upon one's recognized subjectivity.

The logics of publicness also frame the denial of Rodi Alvarado's claim for asylum on the basis of gender persecution.[44] Native Guatemalan Rodi Adali Alvarado Peña[45] fled to the United States in 1995 after ten years of unremitting physical, emotional, and psychological violation by her husband, Francisco Osorio. Despite Alvarado's repeated attempts to involve the police in Guatemala, they refused to intervene in the assaults. Alavardo also tried to divorce Osorio but was prohibited from doing so without her husband's consent. Upon entry in the United States, Alvarado applied for asylum. In 1996, the judge hearing her case favorably decided that international human rights statutes and U.S. political asylum definitions protected Alvarado. The judge not only ruled that her experiences constituted persecution, but that the Guatemalan government demonstrated its "unwillingness" to protect her. After the Immigration and Naturalization Services (INS) appealed the ruling, the BIA denied the case in 1999 on two grounds. First, the board rejected Alvarado's articulation of her social group membership, deciding "that a social group defined on the basis of gender and male relationship must fail because it is simply a reiteration of the social group of 'battered women.' "[46] Additionally, the BIA determined that Alvarado lacked evidence that the persecution was on account of her membership as a Guatemalan woman with certain views about male dominance.

Similar reasoning appears in many of the cases where gender stands as the social group and motivation for persecution. Salvadoran refugee Sofia Campos-Guardado claimed that guerrilla forces raped her because of family connections to the agriculture industry. Basing her asylum claim on her political opinion and social group membership, she held that "she was persecuted in El Salvador for political opinions attributed to her by her assailants, on account of her family membership, and because of the concomitant association of the family with the agrarian land reform movement."[47] In response, the BIA "concluded that Ms. Campos 'had not shown that the attackers harmed her in order to overcome any of *her own* political opinions.' "[48]

Additionally, the denial of gender as a social group can be seen in the case of Carmen Gomez, a Salvadoran woman who suffered gendered violence by guerrilla forces. She fled to the United States, where she lived illegally for ten years before being arrested. Gomez claimed that she was the member of a social group of "women who have been previously battered and raped by Salvadoran guerrillas."[49] In refusing this framing of social group, the court wrote: "Gomez failed to produce evidence that women who have previously been abused by the guerillas possess common characteristics—other than gender and youth—such that would-be persecutors could identify them as members of that purported group. Indeed, there is no indication that Gomez will be singled out for further brutalization on this basis."[50] In another case, Rosalba Aguirre-Cervantes sought asylum from Mexico because of physical abuse by her father. Aguirre-Cervantes argued that her family constituted a social group, since her father abused each family member. She also claimed that rampant gendered violence in Mexico placed her in a gendered social group. While the first immigration judge affirmed her case, the INS appealed the case to the BIA, which contested her social group positioning. Eventually, she was granted withholding of removal, yet the BIA left the asylum decision up to the attorney general.[51]

In these cases, because gender is not formally iterated as an immutable characteristic of one's identity (such as race, religion, or nationality), claimants must first define their social group membership. Since gender is not enough—as in Gomez's case, when the court reasoned that gender is not a common enough characteristic (or perhaps too common)—women making these claims rhetorically have to craft their membership so that there is a clear linkage between the social group and the persecution. Furthermore, the political nature of the social group membership and the persecution must be present in readily understood terms. In almost all of these cases, being a woman who has experienced gendered violence does not quite count, for both gender and gendered violence are rarely intelligible as political.

Rather, the relations of hospitality in asylum configure the host as a public (male) subject and the guest as public (male) actor so that hospitality is no hospitality at all for women claiming gender persecution. Indeed, it took Zuniga naming Lazo-Majano as a political "subversive" for her to be figured through the logics of publicness as a guest worthy in the modality of access. Alvarado, Gomez, Campos-Guardado, and Aguirre-Cervantes never obtained this status, even as the states they fled were unable and/or unwilling to secure their safety. The forms of persecution they experienced were not intelligible as political to the U.S. state, nor were their positionalities as feminine subjects.[52] Mireille Rosello notes that "women are often a barometer of hospitality, because groups do not let them act as agents capable of granting or denying hospitality. In other words, they sometimes constitute part of the exchange of favors that the guest and the host negotiate as gifts, signs, and symbols."[53] This point is vital to understanding the late-capitalist logics at work in the conditions placed on access to publics, for contemporary political hospitality hinges upon the question of what the subject *brings* to the home.

Because of their feminine bodies, nationality, productivity, and the details of their gendered persecution, Lazo-Majano, Alvarado, Campos-Guardado, Gomez, and Aguirre-Cervantes were not even intelligible within the guest-host relation as gifts to the host. I posit that guests who gain access to U.S. publics most notably gain access as gifts. Sometimes this gift is in the form of the laboring body, for while the late-capitalist economy tries to rid itself of labor, remnants of the need—though compartmentalized and privatized—remain. Circulation-based capital, though it tries to diminish the demand for the human, still needs the gift of production-based labor to function.[54] In this exchange, the host recognizes the guest's labor but not the guest. Because of this, the guest is seen first as an object that gives something to the host rather than as a capable subject.

Productivity and Exchange

Sometimes guests bring gifts with them that improve the host's home. These gifts serve to reassure the host of the home's value and to project an image of the home to other sovereigns. Several instances of gender-based asylum have been accepted along these logics, most notably cases on the basis of female genital circumcision.[55] As Jacqueline Bhabha illustrates, these cases function positively within the logic of exchange for they allow the host-state to be seen as a maintainer of human rights.[56] The gifts that the host receives are not the gifts of surviving life as Derrida posits.[57] Rather, these are gifts of surviving in globalization through projects of modernity. It is this element that complicates Derrida's theorizing about hospitality and the ideal gift that functions in ethical hospitality. Survival does not mean surviving past life for the state; it means survival in the competition for access to global flows of capital. In this way, many women claiming gender persecution as a reason for asylum are unintelligible in hospitality, since they ostensibly bring nothing—not even the gift of productivity—for the host's survival. In contrast, as we will see, gay men seeking asylum provide a gift to the home in their claims for asylum, all the while not posing the threat of reproductivity that women claiming gender persecution do.

Since 1994, gay male asylum seekers have been relatively successful in gaining access to asylum in the United States because of persecution based on (perceived) sexual orientation.[58] In this instance, however, the dynamics of modernity play to the advantage of those seeking access. First of all, it is once again men who are gaining asylum as the cases of women asylum seekers on the basis of sexual orientation are miniscule in comparison to both the gay male applicants and gay men who are granted asylum.[59] In part, this gender disparity demonstrates the androcentrism implied in constructions of the citizen and refugee, for the model refugee or asylum seeker has also historically been "'someone heroically trying to assert his (typically male) individuality against an oppressive state.'"[60] Thus, the subject (whether host or guest) invited to the public home is always already coded as a male subject.

Furthermore, within the host-guest relation, accepting gay asylum seekers acts as a gift to the home for it allows the United States to paint itself (and the state the asylee leaves) in particular imaginations of modernity. Rosello explains:

> The definition of the refugee recognizes that the principle of hospitality has already been violated, and that asylum is an exceptional remedy, a moment of excess in the system: an excess of hospitality here responds to a lack of hospitality elsewhere. The body that grants asylum both condemns that lack of hospitality elsewhere while recognizing that, within that space, inhospitality has become the norm, or at least the reality of a law, of a given power. Helping asylum seekers is also an admission of powerlessness, the sign that inhospitality, somewhere, prevails unchallenged.[61]

In this, the modernity of the nation left behind is one that is failing by not protecting the rights and lives of its citizens—the modernity of an inhospitable future. This is evident in the case of Nasser Mustapha Karouni from the Tyre region of Lebanon, where being gay is "punishable by death."[62] Similarly, Kwasi Amanfi testified that his life would be in danger if he returned to his native Ghana, where he had witnessed "prior public torture of homosexuals."[63] This logic of exchange is also present in the case of Giovanni Hernandez-Montiel. Born in Mexico, Hernandez-Montiel knew he was gay from age eight, when he realized his attraction to other men.[64] At age twelve, Hernandez-Montiel began dressing as a woman, propelling her expulsion from school, threats by parents of other children warning her not to "pervert" their sons, and arrest and rape by police officers because "it was illegal for homosexuals to walk down the street and for men to dress like women."[65] The first immigration judge denied Hernandez-Montiel's case, claiming that she failed to demonstrate that the persecution was on account of membership in a social group. Overturning this decision, an appellate court came to understand that "sexual orientation and sexual identity are immutable; they are so fundamental to one's identity that a person should not be required to abandon them. . . . Sexual identity goes beyond sexual conduct and manifests itself outwardly, often through dress and appearance."[66] For Hernandez-Montiel, this recognition shifted the grounds for her membership. Instead of the named social group being "Mexican gay men," her persecution appeared intelligible when she was named as "a member of the 'particular social group' of gay men in Mexico with female sexual identities."[67] Importantly, this case set a precedent for distinguishing between sexual orientation and sexual identity as immutable "social group categories."

Following Hernandez-Montiel, Salvadoran Luis Reyes-Reyes was granted withholding of removal under the Convention Against Torture (CAT), which states "an applicant qualifies for withholding of removal if 'it is more likely than not that he or she would be tortured if removed to the proposed country of removal.'"[68] Reyes-Reyes's "sexual identity" figured importantly in her successful grant of withholding. Court documents describe her as "a homosexual male with a female sexual identity. He dresses and looks like a woman, wearing makeup and a woman's hairstyle. Although Reyes has not undergone sex reassignment surgery, he has had a characteristically female appearance, mannerisms, and gestures for the past sixteen years. He has a 'deep female identity' and has gone by female names such as Josephine, Linda and Cukita."[69] Although the court did not grant Reyes-Reyes asylum because she did not file within one year of entering the United States, the court did not deport her because it recognized that the Salvadoran state was inhospitable to gay men with "female sexual identities." Accepting persecuted guests in this instance allows the United States to justify the recognition of other modernities as inhospitable while recognizing itself as a safe, welcoming nation. As Gabriel Giorgi writes, "gay visibility stands out as a symbol, a token of social tolerance and achieved freedom."[70] While it might seem on the surface that this is merely a gift of the political or social elements of modernity in relation to other nations, the ties to global capital are strong and significant.

Hospitable access to gay asylum seekers projects something to gays and lesbians in the nation and throughout the world, namely, that the United States is a safe home for gay men to enter. This gift is one that adorns the exterior of the home while also reflecting something back to those existing within the home. Saying that your home is safe is a gift with enormous economic implications in regards to tourism, real estate, small businesses, entertainment, and the arts. As Arnaldo Cruz-Malavé and Martin Manalansan write: "Queerness is now global. Whether in advertising, film, performance art, the Internet, or the political discourse of human rights in emerging democracies, images of queer sexualities and cultures now circulate around the globe."[71] It is as though the U.S. state that grants access understands clearly what this will do for the image of the home.

In discussing queer citizenship, David Bell and Jon Binnie note that queers in the United States are recognizable as consumer-citizens, hailed "as pioneers—by doing-up run-down areas of town, by spending their way out of recession and by being at the forefront of the new creative economy."[72] Dereka Rushbrook contends that queers are not only a conditionally accepted class within cities, but have become the "ethnic group" one should have in order to be considered cosmopolitan.[73] It would seem, then, that greater recognition and access granted to gay male asylum seekers also signal something about the state's cosmopolitanism. While certainly not the case thirty years ago, the values maintained in this modality of access have shifted so that hospitality to gay asylum seekers becomes a gift of a cosmopolitan image. The state-host relies on the gay asylum seeker to prove that U.S. publics are safe, modern places to enter for queers with access to global capital. And this matters at a time when gays and lesbians are increasingly mobile.[74] Accepting gay asylum seekers almost allows the public to ignore oppressive national laws because the state, in relation to other sovereigns, is recognized as hospitable, non-violent, and progressive. Even if the state morally opposes homosexuality, it does not oppose queer capital or the figure of the cosmopolitan gay who can aid in local economies. This welcoming of queer capital is even embodied in one of the capitalist bastions of conservative hetero-patriarchy, the Disney Company, which has recently decided to sell wedding packages to gays at their resorts despite homophobic protests.

Gay asylum seekers are recognized as guests worthy of access because they do not enter the home with the threat of reproduction posed by women claiming gender persecution and, perhaps, female guests in general. Since gay men are not popularly known for their ability to reproduce, they are not read as potentially dependent on social welfare in the same ways as women. They also do not arrive with the threat of future kin that intercedes in the recognition of women claiming gendered persecution. Instead, the intelligibility of the cosmopolitan queer subject partially enables recognition of gay male asylum seekers through the logic of productivity. Since queers in the United States are rendered visible as economically mobile, the threat of social dependency does not enter in the making of this guest's subjectivity.

As we see with women claiming gender-based persecution and gay men claiming persecution on the basis of sexual identity or orientation, one condition of access is that guests bring something valuable with them to contribute to the home. A home is not just an invitational space but is politicized, surveyed, critiqued. Because of this, political hospitality always forecloses upon a question of what the guest will bring to the host and home. The economic logic at work in asylum cases demands that something be gained in the exchange of hospitality for refuge. For asylum seekers, access to U.S. publics comes at a cost.

The (In)Hospitable Public

Throughout this chapter I have explored the hospitable limits of access to U.S. publics. Following Nancy Fraser and others, I demonstrate that states largely shape their publics.[75] Not only do states influence modes of participation within their publics, they are central actors in determining the conditions of access to participation in publics. They do this through processes that evaluate guests according to values of publicness desired in subjects in the state. Increasingly, guests are intelligible through these values even before they set foot on the doorstep of the home as guests because they already exist within the imagination of what it means to be a proper citizen-subject. Three primary logics of late capitalism constitute this imagination: first, guests are intelligible through the logic of publicness; second, guests are recognized as worthy of access in relation to their productivity or the threat of reproduction; third, guests are rendered visible through a logic of exchange in what they bring to the home.

In pushing the recognition of subjects in publics, Derrida posits that ethical hospitality must always rest on the foreseeable horizon of political hospitality. However, I argue that neoliberal globalization and the logics of late capitalism diminish the possibility of ethical hospitality informing modalities of access. Guests are increasingly required to do the work of both the host and guest in the hospitable relation, while the host—and the home for that matter—receive survival in late capitalism through the guest's productivity, publicness, and gifts. These manifestations of the guest foreclose upon the possibilities of ethical hospitality because the guest is increasingly less intelligible as human. Rather, the guest is recognizable for what she/he *brings* to the host. For this reason, I contend that modalities of access to U.S. publics, particularly those related to immigration, are largely inhospitable. In order for processes of immigration to push into the ethical realm, guests would need first to be recognized *as* guests, as full subjects worthy of hospitality, rather than as objects bringing benefits to the host and home. States would also have to understand, admit, and act upon their participation in the (in)hospitality of other homes. This would mean a comprehension of the ways that hosts and guests function in each other's survival and livable life.[76] This also entails formulating modalities of access through an ethic of vulnerability, calling subjects to question the ways they partake in home together as speaking subjects.

As its exclusion as a social group category under the definition of refugee vividly illustrates, gender has effectively been expunged from access to U.S. publics. One of the reasons why gay men have not experienced this exclusion is because the male body is coded as neutral rather than gendered. And in this neutrality, men are always figured as appropriate subjects for belonging in the U.S. nation-state. Male subjects, in claiming a right to refuge, do not challenge state sovereignty because they are always already figured as belonging. So when biologically male applicants (who have not had surgery) claim asylum for reasons involving what could be described as their gender identity, their claims are read through sexuality and sex. Gender thus remains associated with a woman's identity, separating gender (and women) even further from the possibility of gaining access to publics and publicness through U.S. immigration processes.

The complexities of the relationship between gender and sexuality are perhaps best evidenced in Hernandez-Montiel's arguments for asylum. Although the court accepted her claims of persecution, it rejected the gendered basis of these claims, advancing instead a distinction between sexual orientation and sexual identity, where "sexual identity goes beyond sexual conduct and manifests itself outwardly, often through dress and appearance."[77] In this instance, Hernandez-Montiel's biology meant that she could only ever be figured as a male. This is clear in the very wording of the court in hailing her as a member of the "'particular social group' of gay men in Mexico with female sexual identities." Sexuality was the only logical description of Hernandez-Montiel's identity for the members of the court, because the biological male subject is not coded as a gendered subject—regardless of outward appearance.

If men were also coded as gendered subjects in political hospitality, a legal fissure might appear for gender and the gendered claims that women make in asylum cases to be seen as public, and hence political. Further, this discursive shift might create a way of understanding the complexities of gender that play out in male asylum cases. At the same time, this shift would risk catapulting gender into the public at the expense of femininity. If men are recognized as gendered, then all manifestations of femininity potentially would be recognized as private, forcing those who do femininity on their bodies to withdraw from publics. Figuring men as gendered could render femininity as the marker of public and private, which also would threaten the asylum cases of transgender people. Nevertheless, even if femininity becomes the ultimate other—

thereby expunging femininity from public—the biological male subject would remain exempt from being read through the threat of reproductivity. Even if gender would enter political hospitality, biology and the binary of sex would remain the primary discourse intervening in the recognition of gendered guests who seek access to hospitable spaces.

Notes

1. I should note that individuals do not have to engage in state processes of immigration in order to enter a state. The millions of undocumented migrants, students, tourists who overstay visas, and many others in diverse situations demonstrate that someone may gain access to a nation-state in non-sanctioned ways. Yet, the state appears as a primary relationship partner for undocumented people living in the United States. This relationship might manifest in the complex strategies a person deploys for avoiding Immigration and Customs Enforcement officers. It is also present in the fastidious records a migrant keeps to demonstrate her/his contributions to the state. In addition, a primary modality of a migrant's subjectivity in the United States is secrecy, or privateness, the experience of living to "not be found out." I contend that non-citizen-subjects must move through the state-mandated processes of immigration to access publicness in the U.S.

2. Aihwa Ong, *Buddha Is Hiding: Refugees, Citizenship, the New America* (Berkeley: University of California Press, 2003); Katarzyna Marciniak, *Alienhood: Citizenship, Exile, and the Logic of Difference* (Minneapolis: University of Minnesota Press, 2006).

3. Saskia Sassen, *Losing Control? Sovereignty in an Age of Globalization* (New York: Columbia University Press, 1996).

4. Matthew J. Gibney, *The Ethics and Politics of Asylum: Liberal Democracy and the Response to Refugees* (Cambridge: Cambridge University Press, 2004), 164.

5. Emma Haddad, "The Refugee: The Individual between Sovereigns," *Global Society: Journal of Interdisciplinary International Relations* 17 (2003): 297.

6. Aihwa Ong, "Cultural Citizenship as Subject-Making: Immigrants Negotiate Racial and Cultural Boundaries in the United States," *Current Anthropology* 37 (1996): 737–62.

7. Transnational and Third World feminists have long explicated that for women the primary modality to publicness is the state. The state politicizes women's bodies while simultaneously de-politicizing their subjectivities as private. Furthermore, state governance practices, meaning "not only the effects of governance on women or 'what happens to women' under state rule but also the way the entire apparatus of government treats women," starkly limit (and enable) the possibilities for women to be seen as public subjects with political identities. M. Jacqui Alexander and Chandra Talpade Mohanty, "Introduction: Genealogies, Legacies, Movements," in *Feminist Genealogies,*

Colonial Legacies, Democratic Futures, ed. M. Jacqui Alexander and Chandra Talpade Mohanty (New York: Routledge, 1997), xxviii; Radha S. Hegde, "A View from Elsewhere: Locating Difference and the Politics of Representation from a Transnational Feminist Perspective," *Communication Theory* 8 (1998): 271–97; Raka Shome, "Transnational Feminism and Communication Studies," *Communication Review* 9 (2006): 255–67.

8. U.S. Department of Homeland Security, *Strategic Plan—Securing Our Homeland*, http://www.dhs.gov/xabout/strategicplan/index.shtm (accessed September 1, 2007).

9. Jacques Derrida and Anne Dufourmantelle, *Of Hospitality*, trans. Rachel Bowlby (Stanford, CA: Stanford University Press, 2000).

10. Meyda Yegenoglu, "Liberal Multiculturalism and the Ethics of Hospitality in the Age of Globalization," *Postmodern Culture* 13 (2003): 15.

11. Jacques Derrida, *On Cosmopolitanism and Forgiveness*, trans. Mark Dooley and Michael Hughes (London: Routledge, 2001), 22.

12. Derrida makes clear that hospitality in the traditional sense means that "if I were foreign, you would accept with more tolerance that I don't speak as you do, that I have my own idiom, my way of speaking that is so far from being technical, so far from juridical, a way that is at once more popular and more philosophical." This explanation implicates that any necessity for the foreigner to speak the language of the state forecloses the possibility of true hospitality. Conversely, political hospitality relies on the question of language to demarcate who can have access to the home. Derrida and Dufourmantelle, *Of Hospitality*, 21.

13. Jacques Derrida, *Given Time: I. Counterfeit Money*, trans. Peggy Kamuf (Chicago: University of Chicago, 1992).

14. Yegenoglu, "Liberal Multiculturalism," 33.

15. Jacques Derrida, *Adieu to Emmanuel Levinas*, trans. Pascale-Anne Brault and Michael Naas (Stanford, CA: Stanford University Press, 1999).

16. Rita Felski, "Politics, Aesthetics, and the Feminist Public Sphere," in *Beyond Feminist Aesthetics: Feminist Literature and Social Change* (Cambridge, MA: Harvard University Press, 1989), 164–74; Nancy Fraser, "Rethinking the Public Sphere: A Contribution to the Critique of Actually Existing Democracy," in *Habermas and the Public Sphere*, ed. Craig Calhoun (Cambridge: Massachusetts Institute of Technology Press, 1992), 109–42; Oskar Negt and Alexander Kluge, *Public Sphere and Experience: Toward an Analysis of the Bourgeois and Proletarian Public Sphere*, trans. Peter Labanyi, Jamie Owen Daniel, and Assenka Oksiloff (Minneapolis: University of Minnesota Press, 1993); Lauren Berlant and Michael Warner, "Sex in Public," *Critical Inquiry* 24 (1998): 547–66; Catherine R. Squires, "Rethinking the Black Public Sphere: An Alternative Vocabulary for Multiple Public Spheres," *Communication Theory* 12 (2002): 446–69; Cindy L. Griffin, "The Essentialist Roots of the Public Sphere: A Feminist Critique," *Western Journal of Communication* 60 (1996): 21–39; Jane Mansbridge,

"Using Power/Fighting Power: The Polity," in *Democracy and Difference: Contesting the Boundaries of the Political*, ed. Seyla Benhabib (Princeton, NJ: Princeton University Press: 1996), 46–66.

17. Derrida also contributes to this critique in his lectures on hospitality, especially his discussion of Lot's daughter. Derrida reads this biblical story of Lot as a moment where the law of hospitality is privileged above every other principle or relationship. Lot invites foreigners to the city of Sodom to take repose in his house. They first refuse but with persistence Lot urges them to enter his home. Later that night, the people of Sodom siege Lot's home, demanding that he send the foreigners out so that they can "penetrate" them. In response, Lot urges the people to leave the foreigners alone and take his virgin daughters instead. As Derrida writes, "the same law of hospitality gives rise to an analogous bargaining, a sort of hierarchy of the guests and the hostages." The underlying relationality of hospitality, then, is homosociality with women as the figure of exchange. Quite literally, women who have access to the home, or public, are not figured as the foreigners who should be endowed with hospitality, but the "hostages" of exchange between men. Derrida and Dufourmantelle, *Of Hospitality*, 151–52.

18. Felski, "Politics, Aesthetics, and the Feminist Public Sphere"; Fraser, "Rethinking the Public Sphere."

19. Robert Asen and Daniel C. Brouwer, "Introduction: Reconfigurations of the Public Sphere," in *Counterpublics and the State*, ed. Robert Asen and Daniel C. Brouwer (Albany: State University of New York Press, 2001), 1–32; Nilüfur Göle, "Islam in Public: New Visibilities and New Imaginaries," *Public Culture* 14 (2002): 173–90; Katherine Jane Hauser, "George Tooker, Surveillance, and Cold War Sexual Politics," *GLQ: A Journal of Lesbian & Gay Studies* 11 (2005): 391–425; Haideh Moghissi, "September 11 and Middle Eastern Women: Shrinking Space for Critical Thinking and Oppositional Politics," *Signs: Journal of Women in Culture & Society* 29 (2004): 594–97; Thomas Olesen, "In the Court of Public Opinion: Transnational Problem Construction in the HIV/AIDS Medicine Access Campaign, 1998–2001," *International Sociology* 21 (2006): 5–30; Michael Warner, *Publics and Counterpublics* (New York: Zone Books, 2002); Melissa W. Wright, "The Paradoxes of Protests: The Mujeres De Negro of Northern Mexico," *Gender, Place & Culture: A Journal of Feminist Geography* 12 (2005): 277–92.

20. Sassen, *Losing Control?*

21. Derrida and Dufourmantelle, *Of Hospitality*.

22. Sassen, *Losing Control?*

23. Moghissi, "September 11." Adam Tickell and Jamie Peck, "Making Global Rules: Globalization or Neoliberalism," *Globalization and World Cities Study Group and Network Research Bulletin* 102 (2003): 9.

24. William Tabb, *Economic Governance in the Age of Globalization* (New York: Columbia University Press, 2004), 41.

25. Karl Polanyi, "The Economy as Instituted Process," in *Trade and Market in Early Empires*, ed. Karl Polanyi (Glencoe, IL: Free Press, 1957).

26. Tickell and Peck, "Making Global Rules," 7–8.

27. Eithne Luibhéid, "Heteronormativity, Responsibility and Neo-Liberal Governance in U.S. Immigration Control," in *Passing Lines: Sexuality and Immigration*, ed. Brad Epps, Keja Valens, and Bill Johnson González (Cambridge, MA: Harvard University Press, 2005).

28. Ibid.

29. Evelyn Hu-DeHart, "Globalization and Its Discontents," *Frontiers: A Journal of Women Studies* 24 (2003): 248.

30. Benjamin Lee and Edward LiPuma, "Cultures of Circulation: The Imagination of Modernity," *Public Culture* 14 (2002): 210.

31. Derrida did not factor reciprocity into the gifting scenario. Much like ethical hospitality, the gift is given without an expectation for a return, and fundamentally without the receiver's knowledge of the gift. I deploy this notion of the gift with mindfulness of Derrida's intention, but use it to draw out the tensions of hospitality in neoliberalism. I figure hospitality, or potential access to the public, as the gift; because of the predominant logics of the hospitable relationship, however, an exchange is expected of the receiver of hospitality. This is not a gift that is given in response, but one that precedes and creates the possibility for the actual moment of hospitality.

32. Griffin, "Essentialist Roots."

33. Ong, *Buddha Is Hiding,* 12.

34. Ibid., 13.

35. For excellent discussions of the contradictions that asylum-seekers claiming gender-based persecution experience between the ways the United States positions itself as a defender of women's rights and the complexities of state sovereignty, see Inderpal Grewal, *Transnational America: Feminisms, Diasporas, Neoliberalisms* (Durham: Duke University Press, 2005); Jacqueline Bhabha, "Embodied Rights: Gender Persecution, State Sovereignty, and Refugees," *Public Culture* 9 (1996): 3–32.

36. See, for example, *Abankwah v. INS*, 185 F.3d 18 (1999); *Abay v. Ashcroft*, 368 F.3d 634, 38 (2004); *Abebe v. Gonzales*, 432 F.3d 1037 (2005); *Gao v. Gonzales*, 440 F.3d 62 (2006); *Re Kasinga*, 21 I. & N. Dec. 357 (1996); *Lopez-Galarza v. INS*, 99 F.3d 954 (1996); *Nwaokolo v. INS*, 314 F.3d 303, 08 (2002); *Zheng v. INS*, 44 F. 3d 379 (1995).

37. *Lazo-Majano v. INS*, 813 F.2d 1432 (1987).

38. Ibid., 1434.

39. Ibid., 1435.

40. Ibid., 1436–37.

41. Ibid., 1437.

42. Deirdre M. Moloney, "Women, Sexual Morality, and Economic Dependency in Early U.S. Deportation Policy," *Journal of Women's History* 18 (2006): 95–122; Ann Marie Nicolosi, "'We Do Not Want Our Girls to Marry Foreigners': Gender, Race, and American Citizenship," *NWSA Journal* 13, no. 3 (2001): 1–21.

43. Ong, *Buddha Is Hiding.*

44. *Re R-A-*, 22 I. & N. Dec. 906 (2001).

45. Rodi Adali Alvarado Peña self-identifies as Rodi Alvarado in her position on the advisory board for the Center of Gender and Refugee Studies, and so I take cue from her in using the name Rodi Alvarado when talking about her case.

46. Karen Musalo et al., "Brief of Amici Curiae," Refugee Law Center and International Human Rights/Migration Project, 1997, 34.

47. *Campos-Guardado v. INS*, 809 F.2d 285, 289 (1987).

48. Ibid., 289.

49. *Gomez v. INS*, 947 F.2d 660, 664 (1991).

50. Ibid., 665.

51. *Aguirre-Cervantes v. INS*, 242 F.3d 1169 (2001).

52. While Attorney General Janet Reno ordered the BIA to reconsider Alvarado's case in one of her last acts in office, Attorney General John Ashcroft immediately rescinded this order and withheld a decision during his tenure. With the shift from the INS to the Department of Homeland Security, Alvarado's case changed hands again and was left unevaluated or not decided. Finally, on September 30, 2008, Attorney General Michael Mukasey called the BIA to re-hear the case. This decision, unavailable as of this writing, could either set precedent for intimate violence to be seen as political persecution, or severely limit the human rights of women making gender-related claims.

53. Mireille Rosello, *Postcolonial Hospitality: The Immigrant as Guest* (Stanford, CA: Stanford University Press, 2001), 57.

54. Lee and LiPuma, "Cultures of Circulation."

55. *Abankwah v. INS; Abay v. Ashcroft; Abebe v. Gonzales; Azanor v. Ashcroft*, 364 F.3d 1013 (2004); *Hassan v. Gonzales*, 484 F.3d 513 (2007); *Re Kasinga; Nwaokolo v. INS; Uanreroro v. Gonzales*, 443 F.3d 1197 (2006).

56. Bhabha, "Embodied Rights."

57. Derrida, *Given Time*.

58. I say *perceived* here because there are several cases when men were persecuted because they were thought to be homosexual, though in testimony they rejected this characterization.

59. Eithne Luibhéid, *Entry Denied: Controlling Sexuality at the Border* (Minneapolis: University of Minnesota Press, 2002).

60. Jacqueline Bhabha quoted in Luibhéid, *Entry Denied*, 148.

61. Rosello, *Postcolonial Hospitality*, 153.

62. *Karouni v. Gonzales*, 399 F.3d 1163 (2005).

63. *Amanfi v. Ashcroft*, 328 F.3d 719, 724 (2003).

64. In writing about Hernandez-Montiel and others I use pronouns appropriate to their ascribed gender identities. I also maintain the pronouns used by court officials within quotations in order to highlight the complexities and complications of sex, gender, and sexuality present in the cases.

65. *Hernandez-Montiel v. INS*, 225 F. 3d 1084, 1089 (2000).

66. Ibid., 1094.

67. Ibid., 1096.

68. *Reyes-Reyes v. Ashcroft*, 384 F.3d 782, 788 (2004).

69. Ibid., 786.

70. Gabriel Giorgi, "Madrid En Transito: Travelers, Visibility and Gay Identity," *GLQ: A Journal of Lesbian & Gay Studies* 8 (2002): 161–62.

71. Arnaldo Cruz-Malavé and Martin F. Manalansan IV, "Introduction: Dissident Sexualities/Alternative Globalisms," in *Queer Globalizations: Citizenship and the Afterlife of Colonialism*, ed. Arnaldo Cruz-Malavé and Martin F. Manalansan IV (New York: New York University Press, 2002), 1.

72. David Bell and Jon Binnie, "Authenticating Queer Space: Citizenship, Urbanism and Governance," *Urban Studies* 41 (2004): 1817.

73. Dereka Rushbrook, "Cities, Queer Space, and the Cosmopolitan Tourist," *GLQ: A Journal of Lesbian & Gay Studies* 8 (2002): 183–206.

74. Lionel Cantú Jr., "De Ambiente: Queer Tourism and the Shifting Boundaries of Mexican Male Sexualities," *GLQ: A Journal of Lesbian & Gay Studies* 8 (2002): 139–66; Cruz-Malavé and Manalansan, *Queer Globalizations*; Giorgi, "Madrid"; Lawrence La Fountain-Stokes, "De Un Pajaro Las Dos Alas: Travel Notes of a Queer Puerto Rican in Havana," *GLQ: A Journal of Lesbian & Gay Studies* 8 (2002): 7–33; Michael Luongo, "Rome's World Pride: Making the Eternal City an International Gay Tourism Destination," *GLQ: A Journal of Lesbian & Gay Studies* 8 (2002): 167–81; Jasbir Kaur Puar, "Circuits of Queer Mobility: Tourism, Travel and Globalization," *GLQ: A Journal of Lesbian & Gay Studies* 8 (2002): 101–37.

75. Asen and Brouwer, "Introduction"; Fraser, "Rethinking the Public Sphere"; Göle, "Islam."

76. Judith Butler, "On Never Having Learned How to Live," *Differences: A Journal of Feminist Cultural Studies* 16 (2005): 27–34.

77. *Hernandez-Montiel v. INS*, 1094.

6

Eyeing New Publics

Veiling and the Performance of Civic Visibility

Radha S. Hegde

> Muslim women who wear the veil are not aliens.
>
> —Aisha Azmi, a British Muslim teaching assistant

> Our tolerance is part of what makes Britain, Britain. So conform to it; or don't come here.
>
> —Tony Blair, former prime minister of Britain

Colonial legacies and the demands of the global economy have led to vast demographic movements of people in new directions and pathways. These new patterns of migration have stirred debates on border controls, and the implications are being felt in the rhythms of everyday life in various corners of the world. In these connections and collisions of people, issues of nationalism, identity, and belonging are brought into visibility in complex ways while at the same time creating new forms of invisibility. Inflected by local politics, the subject of immigration is inevitably entangled with issues concerning religious, racial, and gendered identities. Sensationalized by the media, the scripting of immigration by different constituencies serves as a point of departure to address how cultural and social issues are drafted into public debate in the complex, transnational environment that we are in today.

The growing presence of transnational Muslim communities in the West has sparked explosive discussions about the politics of citizenship and the integration of immigrants. New migrants articulate modes of civic participation and assert claims on nationhood that run counter to normative frames of public life. The patterns of Muslim migration in both Europe and the United States have to be situated within the current geopolitical context of war, terrorism, and the currents of neoliberal capitalism. The desire and effort to define the national body is accompanied by aggressive identification of the non-assimilative Other. How do issues of Islam, especially with respect to gender, surface in the public realm of Western modernity? How does Islam test the limits of the secular, liberal state? How does the West perceive Islamic identity as a viable modality of public presence and engagement? How does this impact the enactment of citizenship and its performative possibilities available to Muslims in the West?

The encounter between Islam and the West is routinely described in polarities that reinforce existing stereotypes of Muslims as antithetical to the rational subject of the West. Ahistorical explanations of the friction that ensues from these points of contact only serve to quarantine Muslims in a culturalist discourse which legitimizes their exclusion and exaggerates their Otherness. A politics of cultural avoidance, according to Nilüfer Göle, is no longer possible, yet there is a growing anxiety about "a perceived breakdown of boundaries, a loss of identity that accompanies the dynamics of this encounter and is leading to the reinforcement of national and religious identities."[1]

Over the years, Muslim women have been used strategically as a rationale for the exertion of benevolent power. A predictable, civilizational logic inevitably accompanies dominant Western discourse describing Islam's stance toward women. In particular, the dress codes of Muslim women have come to signify their subordinate status and lack of agency. The veil has been endowed with a formidable range of political and symbolic meaning, and the practice of veiling almost instantaneously marks the Muslim woman as a premodern subject by embedding her within a religious system that is portrayed as inherently illiberal and oppressive.[2] The rhetoric about veiling, which has surfaced in various registers throughout European colonial history, is currently being reshaped and deployed within the context of global migration and the security state. This chapter will discuss the politics of the veil from the point of view of the limits that are enforced on the processes through which immigrants can engage modalities of public participation.

These patterns of representation about Islamic communities and their presence in the Western liberal state force a reexamination of the presence of alterity in public life. In a time of transnational mobility and complex forms of national affiliation, the transparency of the public sphere cannot be assumed. By foregrounding the processes of public engagement, it is possible to understand how social worlds are reproduced and regulated. The manner in which questions are being raised about citizenship, integration, and community has serious consequences for democratic public engagement. The tensions between national master narratives and transnational cultural processes heighten the contested nature of public life in contemporary European society.[3] When the topic of Muslim women appears in the media, cultural differences are cast in terms of a civilizational clash, and the gendered body of the Other surfaces only in terms of rescue. The narrative is typically of the enlightened West exerting its pastoral power to save the gendered body from a putative premodern and oppressive religious structure. A stand on the veil becomes an ideological "litmus test," according to Joan Scott, who writes that "having an opinion about it serves to establish one's credentials on the heady topics of individualism, secularism, and the emancipation of women."[4]

Global diasporic movements have set a very complex transnational circuitry in motion through which various discourses about nation, belonging, citizenship, and community travel. This chapter specifically examines comments made by two British politicians about Islam and the veiling practices of Muslim women. The comments serve as a point of departure to elaborate on how questions of difference and religio-political issues are publicized in a global context, especially with respect to Muslim women. In late 2006, Jack Straw, a senior British politician, wrote a newspaper column that sparked intense discussion around the world. Straw confessed that he felt "uneasy talking to someone face-to-face who I could not see."[5] This was immediately followed by a speech highly critical of multiculturalism by the then–prime minister Tony Blair, who admonished immigrants to adhere to the nation's "essential values."[6] The column by Straw presents the actual demand to conform to performative conventions, and Blair's remarks about integration set the abstractions about the imagined community of the nation. Together they advance a discussion about the nature and form of publicness and its largely unquestioned universality. Michael Warner argues that there are "ambiguities, even contradictions" in the idea of the public and notes that as it extends "to new contexts and new media, new polities and new rhetorics, its meaning can be seen to change in ways that we have scarcely begun to appreciate."[7] Responding to this challenge, this chapter discusses these questions: What do forms of publicity and public belonging mean in the transnational context when global Islamic communities are scripting new forms of public comportment and presence? What are the modalities of public engagement that are set into motion when actors with distinct cultural and political trajectories interact? Particularly, how are questions of modernity and tradition inserted into the discussion and managed both in terms of symbolic and material meaning?

Uncovering the Alien Within

Since September 11, 2001, Muslim women's head cover, long a trope for the oppression and subordination of women, has surfaced as a prominent subject of attention. The conflation of the veil with women's passivity and Islam's primitivism both essentializes and flattens the Muslim experience in highly problematic ways. In October 2006, Jack Straw, a British Labor Party politician and former foreign secretary, stirred one more round of publicity for the gendered Islamic dress code and its appropriateness in British public life.

In his weekly column in the *Lancashire Telegraph,* Straw described a meeting where he had requested a Muslim woman, who had come to his constituency's advice bureau, to remove her veil. The woman, whom he does not name, was wearing a *niqab,* or a full veil, where her face except for her eyes was fully covered. To Straw, this was a "visible statement of separation and of difference."[8] The article sparked national debate in Britain about identity, inclusion, and the very possibility of a multicultural society. As expected in the media-saturated environment, the comments caused international ripples, escalated debate, and drew heated reactions from around the world.

Straw notes that he defends the right of the woman to wear a headscarf and wearing a full veil breaks no laws. However, he thinks:

> The conversation would be of greater value if the lady took the covering from her face. Indeed, the value of a meeting, as opposed to a letter or phone call, is so that you can—almost literally—see what the other person means, and not just hear what they say. I thought it may be hard going when I made my request for face-to-face interviews in these circumstances. However, I can't recall a single occasion when a lady has refused to lift her veil; most seem relieved I have asked. Last Friday was a case in point. The veil came off almost as soon as I opened my mouth. I dealt with the problems the lady had brought to me. We then had a really interesting debate about veil wearing. This itself contained some surprises. It became absolutely clear to me that the husband had played no part in her decision. She had read books and thought about the issue. She felt more comfortable wearing the veil when out. People bothered her less.[9]

One must pay attention to the tenor of Straw's comments and to the juxtaposition of facts that he presents: "the husband had played no part in her decision." Straw also adds earlier in the column, "Her husband, a professional man whom I vaguely knew, was with her. She did most of the talking. I got down the detail of the problem, told the lady and her husband that I thought I could sort it out, and we parted amicably."[10] To Straw, the fact that the husband was silent in this interaction is a very important indicator of her autonomy and agency. He goes on to say that she had read books and thought about the issue. The very articulation of this statement reinforces the stereotypical construction of the Muslim woman who through her own veiling marks herself as unthinking and premodern.

Why is Straw so ill at ease? After all, they got the work done, as he claims in the column. In his own words, the lady in question was perfectly articulate, and they transacted the business for which she came; in addition, she seems to have graciously lifted her veil at his request. Straw continued to defend himself by saying the veil was "a visible statement of separation and difference." He believed it stood in the way of community relations and reinforced the creation of parallel communities. Straw's admission about his discomfort comes from the belief in the revelatory aspect of the face and its primacy in the Western modes of sociality. Several questions emerge: Should he have made the request? Why is the veil relevant to the conduct of his duties? Why the need to see her face unveiled? What are the assumptions about the face with respect to comportment in public? How does Straw's role as a public official authorize and/or legitimize his request? As Patricia Williams writes in the *Nation*, "when Straw insists that Muslim women who come to his office remove their veils for his comfort, who is the host, who is the guest? Is his role properly the accommodating public servant or more the gatekeeper of Anglican mores?" Muslim women's avowals of choice and assertions of comfort with the veil are most often dismissed, argues Williams, as false consciousness.[11]

Lecturing to an interfaith gathering after the heated reaction to his column, Straw continued on the theme of assimilation: "Simply breathing the same air as other members of society isn't integration."[12] Many might consider these comments to be harmless statements or requests from a senior politician with an impeccable record of service. However, the drift of the statements and the position of privilege which authorizes them warrant further consideration. After the speech, the BBC reported that a veiled woman in the audience said to Jack Straw: "I recognise that you feel uncomfortable. I sympathise in a way but I don't understand that these women who visited your surgery [office] are less integrated. I don't feel any less British or feel any less common value with

British society."[13] It is this space of hybrid cosmopolitanism that unsettles the normative narrative of citizenship.

Modes of Publicizing Difference

At the heart of this debate lies the subject of Britishness and the ideological constructs embedded within what are considered core British values. The Muslim women's *niqab,* or full cover, gains center stage as an impediment to assimilation, or as "a mark of separation," as Tony Blair termed it. The discourse first focuses on what is essentially a woman's choice of clothing; it then moves in linear sequence to larger questions of the nation and the imagined community. In the analysis of this debate, what is striking and becomes increasingly predictable is the easy slippage of issues by which questions of veiling, oppression, and terrorism fold into one another.

"We have to deal with the debate," Tony Blair said at a press conference, commenting both on Straw's remark and the suspension of a British Muslim teaching assistant, Aisha Azmi, by a local council for refusing to remove her veil in school.[14] "People want to know that the Muslim community in particular, but actually all minority communities, have got the balance right between integration and multi-culturalism."[15] This characterization and framing of the debate provides a telling comment on the state of multiculturalism in Britain. Blair and Straw assert that the debate is not about choice but about effective communication. To the Muslim community in Britain, the debate is about yet another form of stigmatization that further separates them from the larger polity. Blair's comments reveal the limits of the national imaginary with respect to immigrants and the performative modalities deemed permissible for participation in public life.

Islam is considered the fastest growing religion in Europe, and one of the reasons is the rising number of Muslim immigrants. The Islamic presence becomes a flash point to trigger discussions about religion, cultural integration, and citizenship. The dominant discourse inevitably reverts to one of loss and anxiety about the passing of a homogenous public together with an aggressive blaming of immigrants for their resistance and inability to assimilate. In the process of subtracting Muslim presence from the public whole, a long and complex history of transnational connections between Islam and the West is forgotten and erased. In addition, the political conversation about immigration and diversity is substituted for a cultural and civilizational discourse, which ultimately oversimplifies and aggravates the situation. As Nilüfer Göle writes, "Europeanness appears as an identity defined by shared history and common cultural values rather than as a project for rethinking the political bond."[16]

It is the evocation of intangible abstractions that serves as the fault line for separating the truly integrated from the resistant immigrants. In the 2006 speech on multiculturalism, Tony Blair provided a series of declarations stating that immigrants should subscribe to the essential values that give citizens the right to be called British. Blair's comments set the tone for the larger political climate in which Straw's comments have to be situated. "Integration . . . is not about culture or lifestyle. It is about values. It is about integrating at the point of shared, common, unifying British values. It isn't about what defines us as people, but as citizens, the rights and duties that go with being a member of our society."[17] By appealing through abstractions to a lost homogeneity, the discussion on the politics of multiculturalism is deferred and, instead, the rhetoric refocuses on the implosion from within: "But how do we react when that 'difference' leads to separation and alienation from the values that define what we hold in common?"[18]

This warning about liberal multiculturalism arises from an underlying antipathy for immigrants that is fortified by the argument regarding cultural incompatibility. There is also an aggressive stance that confounds the very logic of tolerance and acceptance that Blair propounds: "Our tolerance is what makes Britain, Britain. So conform to it; or don't come here."[19] Blair's insistence that immigrants have a "duty" to integrate was termed by the media as Blair's declaration that "Britain's multiculturalist experiment was over."[20] Both Blair's remarks and media reports reflect British society's attitude toward difference and the gaze of surveillance directed toward Muslim citizens. The broader controversy is also a comment about the impossibility of operating with a template or fixed notion of a pure and pristine public sphere. What we see happening here is the resurrection of a national community which resists the very idea of difference as a basis for a global community.

The presence of deterritorialized cultures and transnational communities destabilizes the definition of publics hinged on dominant assumptions about national boundaries and allegiance. Blair unequivocally upholds the transcendence of a national community that supersedes and envelopes all other counterpublics: "But when it comes to our essential values—belief in democracy, the rule of law, tolerance, equal treatment for all, respect for this country and its shared heritage—then that is where we come together, it is what we hold in common; it is what gives us the right to call ourselves British. At that point, no distinctive culture or religion supersedes our duty to be part of an integrated United Kingdom."[21]

Muslim immigrants are being told to separate the public and private in ways that deny the complexities of material life and cultural politics. Globalization has given rise to transnational communities with webs of affiliations that exceed national borders. They produce new forms of translocal cultures that both threaten and produce a crisis in the Western imaginary.[22] Globalization constitutes a complex disjunctive order that is clearly not captured by the smooth metaphor of flows but is rather full of jagged contours which can no longer be understood by simple binaries that characterize center-periphery models. Categories such as the here and there, West and East, can no longer be seen in isolation but are, and actually have been, deeply implicated in one another. The debate about who's in and who's out is rehearsed everywhere, from schools to hospitals and airport security. And, of course, in scholarship, such as Samuel Huntington's warning that Hispanic immigration threatens to disrupt the core Anglo Protestant culture of the United States.[23] The presence of Muslim immigrants today has led to a growing Orientalist and violent discourse of the dangerous, inscrutable Islamic other.

As people cross borders, cultures are reinvented and mix on the street, but the language of assimilation and obligation to the mythos of national community ironically gains momentum. In the context of globalization and increased security, it is revealing to see, as Daniel Brouwer and Robert Asen write in the introduction to this book, how publics are actualized. The public sphere, in its ideal Habermasian form, is an arena where the rational discourse and deliberation of citizens can influence public policy and the generation of public opinion. But what we see happening here is both an active steering of the nature of public debate about immigration and a specification of the terms under which a national public is constituted. Various regimes of cultural normativity are cited to structure the ways in which private citizens should be inducted into fields of publicity as rightful citizens. Blair's comments cited here demonstrate how the constructs of public and public good are shaped and mobilized within fields of power. The debate is significant as it involves the demarcation of national boundaries and the valorization of a singularly defined national public.

In spite of cultures becoming increasingly deterritorialized and transnationalized in everyday practices, the conception of the public and the public sphere also remains deeply entrenched within nationalist presuppositions.[24] Immigration provides a revealing example of the fact that the state and the public sphere are not as distinct or separate as in the original Habermasian formulation.[25] The state is closely involved in the constitution and surveillance of the public through the demarcation of boundaries to identify both national spaces and rightful citizens. Ironically, as Saskia Sassen points out, in most developed countries, economic policies are striving to create border-free spaces for the free circulation of capital and commodities, while immigration policies remain rooted within older conceptions of the bounded nation-state and national borders.[26]

The Islamic immigrant wearing visible symbols of religion becomes the ultimate marker of difference in a national space that considers itself cosmopolitan, anti-racist, and tolerant. In a self-congratulatory note, Blair extols: "Our public culture is also completely different. We now have more ethnic minority MPs, peers, and Ministers though not enough. We have had the first black Cabinet minister. The media are generally more sensitive, and include ethnic minority reporters and columnists. Racism has, for the most part, been kicked out of sport. Offensive remarks and stupid stereotypes have been driven out of public conversation. The basic courtesies, in other words, have been extended to all people."[27] Blair's view of a culture of tolerance uniting the country presents a view of the social landscape that is totally disconnected both from the complexities of the imperial past and from the contested terrain of contemporary life. Deep-seated antagonisms cannot be unsettled and much less *kicked out* at will. Selectively recognizing public culture in terms of a superficial multiculturalism, Blair claims a national victory over racism. For both Blair and Straw, the idea of the public is deeply entrenched within the ideological framework of a dominant Euro-American discourse of citizenship. Reading the racial and gendered modalities of Othering enables an interrogation of the assumptions that drive the machinery of the national imaginary. "Stupid stereotypes" he claims have been "driven out" and "basic courtesies" have been "extended to all people." Through such rhetorical fiats, racism is presented as an individual and behavioral lack. In the process, the systemic politics of racism is discounted in keeping with the growing ethos of neoliberal privatization.

Nationalism and a fervent call for rehomogenization become the primary response to the belief that the arrival of immigrants has caused the demise of cohesion and social harmony. The reality of colonialism and the contested relationship between transnational and putative national cultures are erased from the discussion in a drive to sanitize the public sphere. As Paul Gilroy writes, "The fascination with immigrants should be made part of Europe's history rather than its contemporary geography."[28] By assigning the immigrant "problem" to the immediate present, the politics and histories of difference are elided, and solutions are posed as strategies for assimilation. Instead, it recuperates a nationalist narrative premised on the hegemony of Western modernity, whose exclusivity is enacted through the stipulation of a series of exclusions. The next section will return to Jack Straw's comments to examine the conditions of possibility that are presented to the gendered transnational subject in the context of this beleaguered multiculturalism.

Staging of the Modern Citizen

Driving the abstractions of citizenry are very real performative regulations that are evoked by Straw and others. The long colonial history behind the Western gaze directed at Islam has received a new Orientalist twist, conflating Islam, irrationality, fundamentalism, violence, gendered oppression, and terrorism.[29] The veiled woman becomes the focus of attention where fears and prejudices about the Muslim world are channeled through a discourse of benevolence and righteousness. The justification of the war on terror as one to liberate women, Laura Bush's cry of outrage about the oppression of her Afghan sisters,[30] and the remarks by Straw and Blair all follow suit in their easy assignment of victim status to Muslim women. As several feminist scholars ask, Why has the veil become "the almost exclusive sign of radical cultural difference" between Islam and the West?[31] The refrain around the veil has been consistent—Muslim women are denied agency and need to be liberated by Western enlightenment. The veil sets off a series of doubts and questions about not only gender oppression in the Islamic community and the ability of Muslim women to act independently but also the very possibility of Muslim women partaking of modernity. The veil radically unsettles the private/public distinctions of the secular liberal paradigm by changing the conditions of intelligibility and public culture.[32]

The perception of Muslim women as a threat to secular democracy provides a striking illustration of the rigidity and the privileged religio-political referents worked into the constitution of the public sphere. Straw's request to abandon the veil to facilitate conversation is fraught with assumptions that lay out the terrain against which difference is measured and regulated. With no swerving from the register of polite benevolence, the expectations and regulations are mobilized to secure the national space.

Let us return to a few of Straw's assertions where he notes inconsistencies between the attire of the woman who was in his office and her performative stance. Straw notes that the woman spoke in "a broad Lancashire accent" and that she was with her husband, "a professional man whom I vaguely know," but that "she did all the talking." After acknowledging that the particular encounter was polite and respectful on both sides, Straw writes that it got him thinking: "In part, this was because of the apparent incongruity between the signals which indicate common bonds—the entirely English accent, the couples' education (wholly in the UK)—and the fact of the veil."[33] Her visual presentation and material presence wearing a niqab call into question the authenticity of her Britishness and her performance of citizenship. This exchange cannot be dismissed as a request from a seasoned politician about the inability of making contact with the full face of a member of his constituency. It speaks to the contested politics of multiculturalism and the conflict between the realities of global migration and the assumptions that underwrite the national community.

Straw's comment emanates from the liberal premise of the speaking subject and a particular type of visual representation. To Straw, the woman (who is never named or identified), her persona, and her public performance are misaligned with the contemporary. Her embodied presence, characterized by Straw as "a visual statement of difference,"[34] defies a certain type of transparency that prohibits her admittance into the community of citizens. The niqab does not allow the woman, in Straw's interpretation, to participate in modernity as she lacks the appropriate look, and hence she and other Muslim women are actively setting themselves apart in "voluntary apartheid" as another British politician termed it.[35]

Straw pays no attention to the complex colonial and racist overtones of his own so-called request. Saving women, as mentioned earlier in the chapter, has been a central trope in the legitimizing of colonial projects and continues to be in the current geopolitical context. Straw repeats the same formulaic Western response to veiled Muslim woman by reducing the veil to a visible sign of disempowerment and collapsing the diversity of the Muslim experience to a singular and reductive explanation centered on the veil.[36] Using the rhetoric of neoliberalism, Straw also couches the issue as one of personal choice by arguing that someone with a Western education should know better. Straw is basically arguing how someone with a British education and upbringing could be so regressive as to accept a veil as a form of attire. Not only does Straw simplify the cultural practice of veiling, but he links it to the question of his comfort in communication: "Above all, I felt uncomfortable about talking to someone 'face-to-face' who I could not see. It was such a visible statement of separation and of difference."[37]

Ultimately, it is Straw's discomfiture that triggered off the demand to remove the veil, the global media attention about the ability of Muslim women to integrate, and the expected anti-Muslim reaction. As a white male politician, Straw could wield attention to his interpersonal discomfort and bypass the power differential embedded in the encounter. He bypasses the fact that he is able to make this request from his position of privilege as a white male MP (member of Parliament). Madeline Bunting in her column in the *Guardian* writes, "Comfort is a disastrous new measure for interactions in a diverse society."[38] In his concern for Britishness, Straw's comments led to more intense anti-Islam reactions and, in fact, reproduced the presence and politics of parallel communities. The veil becomes the target to isolate Muslim women and cast them as stigmatized figures not belonging to the modern.

The narrative of modernity has been constructed with Europe at the center both in terms of its geographical location and temporal flow. The linear path of progress against which other cultures are measured and regulated is normed on the West. With the universalism of the project established, modernity reproduces itself through "assigning a different and lesser significance to things deemed purely local, non-Western and lacking a universal expression."[39] What is incompatible with the so-called modern is rendered marginal or deficient, only to be measured as a lack or an aberration. In the essentialized discourse about culture that is widely circulated today, cultures are distinguished in simplistic terms or described as innate and static qualities that inhere to groups of people. The "culture talk" we hear today splits the world, according to Mahmood Mamdani, into the modern and the premodern who either are lagging behind on the road to modernity or else are resistant and decidedly antimodern.[40]

Dipesh Chakrabarty advances a compelling argument that modernity is always depicted as a transition narrative for the non-West and a narrative about a lack. The West stands in as the end point, the destination for the rest of the world, which is forever delegated to the "waiting rooms of history," lacking coevalness and contemporaneity with the West.[41] The veiled woman, by extension, exists in an ahistorical framework; her status is reified as out of pace with modernity and its rational expectations. In a re-narration of a colonial gesture, Straw's remarks stand in for the imperial center offering its benevolence to help the Muslim woman step across the threshold. The operative assumption being that rescuing the gendered subject from her cultural confines will deliver her into the present and a communicable modernity. Straw, in fact, wants to assist in the birth of the modern Muslim subject.

Postcolonial scholars theorize that modernity and its institutions should be linked to the colonial modes of knowledge production and structures of power rather than be viewed as merely a European invention or a time period through which all societies must pass. The space of colonial difference has always been a precondition for the staging of the modern with the subaltern subject defined as the constitutive Other of modernity. In order to perform its authority, modernity must distinguish itself aggressively from what it conceives of as the non-modern. To do so, it defines its rationality and enlightenment in opposition to traditionalism and the irrationality of Others. This tension is framed as the divide that stipulates how and which forms and modalities of Otherness can be accommodated within the space of West.

Conclusion

There is an obsessive focus on Muslim women, and politicians like Jack Straw and Tony Blair never tire of the subject of immigrant women. Blair in his speech even apologizes for this attention but returns right back to the topic by saying, "I know it is not sensible to conduct this debate as if the only issue is the very hot and sensitive one of the veil." Yet stressing the need to find the right balance between integration and diversity, he remarks, "It is really a matter of plain common sense that when it is an essential part of someone's work to communicate directly with people, being able to see their face is important."[42] By evoking common sense, Muslim women are further marginalized from the very process of rational action. The constructedness of this modality of publicity is further naturalized by rendering it as familiar and commonsensical. The woman in Blackburn who came to Straw's office for assistance is singled out as the body that is out of place and spectacularly misfit for modern forms of social interaction. Her body is publicized as the one that refuses integration with the national community by not complying with obvious, commonsensical expectations of social interaction.

The patriarchal gaze devalues the Muslim woman's social presence and compromises her political agency by fixing her in terms of Otherness. Veiling disqualifies her from being a liberal, autonomous subject; and, in fact, she is reprimanded for her dress, deemed a deviation from what the state considers to be a commonsensical prerequisite of performing citizenship. The responsibility to integrate to privileged norms is placed squarely on the individual immigrant, and the role of the state's responsibility to immigrant groups is bypassed. These two examples both demonstrate the extent of the state's failure in responding to the transnational transformations in the national scene. Instead of living up to a professed multicultural vision, these speeches and injunctions to Muslim women only serve to exacerbate the tensions between communities and reproduce the rhetoric of civilizational differences.

The insistence on homogeneity is untenable and even anachronistic in the current global context. With the increased flow of migrants from postcolonial worlds into the old imperial centers, the public sphere is changing radically in terms of its composition, its form, and even its function. There is a disconnect between the state's call for assimilation to a set of core national values and the materiality of quotidian practices in transnational communities. It is impossible to think of community in today's context in terms of purity or to define nationalism outside of the global processes of mobility and migration. In fact, community and cohesion are misrecognized in normative abstractions in order to maintain the hegemonic "face" of the public. In the eyes of Muslim groups, this is another instance of Islamophobia through the invocation of strong nationalist ideologies.

From their position of power, status, and white privilege, Jack Straw and Tony Blair stage this unveiling as an elaborate liberation or coming-out ritual for Muslim women. In fact, the insistence on face-to-face communication ironically shrouds the real discussion about the politics of integration to one of gender and the control and regulation of Muslim women. Gender becomes a focal point in these minoritizing maneuvers that are actively directed toward the Muslim community in Europe. Issues related to women, such as the headscarf or arranged marriages, are inevitably linked to discussions about the assimilability of Muslims and Islam in Western societies. The veiled woman is brought into public view only through the benevolence of the patriarchal gaze. As Joan Scott writes, "This creates a hierarchy that promotes and reinforces a sense not just of Western superiority, but of Western women's superiority—the old colonial relationship emerges intact, an operation of domination in the guise of a mission of salvation."[43]

Enmeshed in the circuitry of nationalism and citizenship are various systems of regulation that operate at multiple levels and at the same time are deeply classed, raced, and gendered. What we see happening here is the production of the civic body through particular systems of exclusion. Minoo Moallem makes the point that it is through the production of the civic body that the parallel process of embodiment and disembodiment takes place: "Embodied particulars compose a unity, creating a transcendental subjectivity that seeks to comprehend all entities within itself, thereby perpetuating a 'logic of identity'—an identity that seeks to eliminate all uncertainty by eliminating otherness."[44] The veil attaches the Muslim woman to her Otherness and disallows her from entering the privileged frames of publicity.

The statements about the veil resurrect "fictitious unities" about cultural differences by mapping coherent systems of meaning to cultural groups.[45] The consequences of this in a global environment are critical as they reproduce the exclusionary logics on which the civic body is constructed. The unnamed woman in Straw's surgery claimed her right to be a British citizen and at the same time exercise her freedom to express her religious affiliation and belief through the choice of her mode of dress. Here she was being an active citizen, exercising her civic identity, and taking her problems to her elected representative. The only problem seems to be her choice of attire, which makes for the professed discomfort. It touches a space of contradiction that poses a radical challenge to the conventional boundaries of private and public. Interestingly enough, Straw's and Blair's comments and active protest of the Islamic clothing come at the same time as the popularity of *hijabs* (head scarfs) with younger Muslim women has been increasing. Media reports state that for the first time there are now more than a million hijabs distributed in Britain.[46] The point is not whether this surge is a response to Straw's comments, as the media would like us to believe. The significant fact is that women are choosing to veil, refuting the easy formulaic equation of veiling with oppression and acquiescence to patriarchal oppression. The use of the head cover is part of the performative expression of Muslim identity and in this context can be read as an active choice of an alternate modality of public presentation. As Myra McDonald writes, "Expressions of surprise, even in the twenty-first century, that veiled Muslim women can appear as Olympic athletes, 'suicide bombers,' feminist politicians, musicians or even comedians, underline the tenacity of beliefs that Islamic veiling is intrinsically incompatible with women's agency in the construction of their identities."[47]

Veiling inserts an aspect of private identity into the public sphere and problematizes the neutrality of the secular public sphere. When Muslim women in the West decide to follow an Islamic dress code, they are performing forms of embodied citizenship that test the limits of liberal discourses of freedom.[48] It calls into question the conditions under which the gendered transnational immigrant's body will be accepted as a legitimate actor in the public sphere. Other forms of head cover or even types of religious attire used by men have not drawn the same level of scrutiny as the Muslim women's head cover.[49] The Muslim woman in Straw's office is making a claim to exercise her rights as a citizen and is dismissed on the grounds of open communication. In this case, the woman's veil defies the scopic penetration of the eye of the state as symbolized by Straw and reverses the norms of visual symmetry where the gaze of the powerful male has full access to the body of the subaltern. By achieving her interactional objective through repositioning the role of the auditory, the veiled woman unsettles the sensory balance of Western modernity and its public privileging of the ocular.

Straw ends his column in the *Lancashire Telegraph* with a question: "I thought a lot before raising this matter a year ago, and still more before writing this. But if not me, who?"[50] Actually, Straw is hardly the only one who is raising questions about the veil today. Instead of working from naturalized notions of differences in a bounded public sphere, the case discussed in this chapter reveals the need to account for new modalities of public participation that constitute the transnational dynamic of contemporary life. Straw, however, mentioned in a follow-up interview that "communities are bound together partly by informal chance relations between strangers—people being able to acknowledge each other in the street or being able to pass the time of day. That's made more difficult if people are wearing a veil. That's just a fact of life."[51] Communities are held together by history, politics, and shared experiences and not by chance relationships. Communication is neither transparent nor direct in the complex modalities through which publics come to be.

Notes

1. Nilüfer Göle, "Islam in Public: New Visibilities and New Imaginaries," *Public Culture* 14 (2002): 12.

2. Media representations of the current debates about the veil in the West have been receiving a great deal of research attention from feminist scholars. See, e.g., Kevin J. Ayotte and Mary E. Husain, "Securing Afghan Women: Neocolonialiam, Epistemic Violence, and the Rhetoric of the Veil," *NWSA Journal* 17 (2005): 112–33; Judith Ezekiel, "French Dressing: Race, Gender and the Hijab Story," *Feminist Studies* 32 (2006): 256–78; Vron Ware, "Info-War and the Politics of Feminist Curi-

osity: Exploring New Frameworks for Feminist Intercultural Studies," *Cultural Studies* 20 (2006): 526–51.

3. See Arjun Appadurai and Carol A. Breckenridge, "Public Modernity in India," in *Consuming Modernity: Public Culture in Contemporary India*, ed. Carol A. Breckenridge (Minneapolis: University of Minnesota Press, 1995).

4. Joan Scott, *Politics of the Veil* (Princeton, NJ: Princeton University Press, 2007), 17.

5. Jack Straw, "I Want to Unveil My Views on an Important Issue," *Daily Telegraph*, October 10, 2006, http://www.telegraph.co.uk/news/main.jhtml?xml=/news/2006/10/06/nveils106.xml (accessed August 3, 2007).

6. Tony Blair, "Full Text of Blair's Multiculturalism Speech," *Daily Telegraph*, September 12, 2006, http://www.telegraph.co.uk/news/main.jhtml?xml=/news/2006/12/08/ublair208.xml (accessed December 13, 2006).

7. Michael Warner, *Publics and Counterpublics* (New York: Zone Books, 2002), 8.

8. Straw, "I Want to Unveil."

9. Ibid.

10. Ibid.

11. Patricia J. Williams, "Keeping Up Appearances," *Nation*, November 27, 2006, 9.

12. "Muslims Must Feel British," November 2, 2006, http://news.bbc.co.uk/2/hi/uk_news/politics/6110798.stm (accessed November 10, 2008).

13. Ibid.

14. Aisha Azmi made international news after being suspended by a school board in Yorkshire on account of wearing the full veil. For a full account, see Alan Cowell, "For Multiculturalist Britain, Uncomfortable New Clothes," *New York Times*, October 22, 2006, http://select.nytimes.com/ (accessed August 2, 2007).

15. Allen Cowell, "Blair Criticizes Full Islamic Veils as 'Mark of Separation,'" *New York Times*, October 18, 2006, http://www.nytimes.com/2006/10/18/world/europe/18britain.html (accessed February 8, 2007).

16. Nilüfer Göle, "Islam Resettling the European Agenda?" *Public Culture* 18 (2006): 14.

17. Blair, "Full Text."

18. Ibid.

19. Ibid.

20. Phillip Johnston, "Blair: Paying Religious Groups Is a Mistake," *Daily Telegraph*, September 12, 2006, http://www.telegraph.co.uk/core/content/displayPrintable.jhmtl?xml (accessed December 13, 2006).

21. Blair, "Full Text."

22. For a discussion of the rise of new normativities with reference to the global visibility of emergent transnational Asian publics, see Aihwa Ong, *Flexible Citizenship: The Cultural Logics of Transnationality* (Durham: Duke University Press, 1999).

23. Samuel P. Huntington, *Who Are We: The Challenges to America's National Identity* (New York: Simon & Schuster, 2004).

24. Nancy Fraser, "Transnationalizing the Public Sphere," Republicart.net, March 2005, http://www.republicart.net/disc/publicum/fraser01_en.htm (accessed December 5, 2005).

25. Robert Asen and Daniel C. Brouwer, eds., *Counterpublics and the State* (Albany: State University of New York Press, 2001).

26. Saskia Sassen, *Guests and Aliens* (New York: New Press, 1999).

27. Blair, "Full Text."

28. Paul Gilroy, *Postcolonial Melancholia* (New York: Columbia University Press, 2004), 148.

29. Leila Ahmed, *Women and Gender in Islam: Historical Roots of a Modern Debate* (New Haven: Yale University Press, 1993).

30. After the U.S. invasion of Afghanistan, Laura Bush, in a radio address, stated that "the fight against terrorism is also a fight for the rights and dignity of women" and that "the brutal oppression of women is the central goal of all terrorists." Laura Bush, "Radio Address to the Nation," WhiteHouse.gov, November 17, 2001, http://www.whitehouse.gov/news/releases/2001/11/20011117.html (accessed June 15, 2005).

31. Afsaneh Najmabadi, "Gender and Secularism of Modernity: How Can a Muslim Woman Be French?" *Feminist Studies* 32 (2006): 244.

32. I draw here from Lauren Berlant and Michael Warner, who in their important 1998 essay argue that queer social practices demonstrate the changed possibilities of "identity, intelligibility, culture and sex that appear when the heterosexual couple is no longer the referent or privileged example of sexual culture." Lauren Berlant and Michael Warner, "Sex in Public," *Critical Inquiry* 24 (1998): 187.

33. Straw, "I Want to Unveil."

34. Ibid.

35. The term "voluntary apartheid" was used by David Davis, a conservative member of Parliament. See "Davis in 'UK Apartheid' Warning," BBC, October 15, 2006, http://news.bbc.co.uk/1/hi/uk/6052232.stm (accessed August 3, 2007).

36. Lila Abu-Lughod, "Do Muslim Women Really Need Saving? Anthropological Reflections on Cultural Relativism and Its Others," *American Anthropologist* 104 (2002): 783–90.

37. Straw, "I Want to Unveil."

38. Madeline Bunting, "Jack Straw Has Unleashed a Storm of Prejudice and Intensified Division," *Guardian*, October 9, 2006, http://www.guardian.co.uk/comment/story/0,,1890698,00.html (accessed August 2, 2007).

39. Timothy Mitchell, "Introduction," in *Questions of Modernity*, ed. Timothy Mitchell (Minneapolis: University of Minnesota Press, 2000), xi.

40. Mahmood Mamdani, *Good Muslim, Bad Muslim: America, the Cold War and the Roots of Terror* (New York: Doubleday, 2005).

41. Dipesh Chakrabarty, *Provincializing Europe: Postcolonial Thought and Historical Difference* (Princeton, NJ: Princeton University Press, 2000).

42. Blair, "Full Text."

43. Joan Scott, "Feminist Reverberations," *Differences* 13 (2002): 9.

44. Minoo Moallem, *Between Warrior Brother and Veiled Sister: Islamic Fundamentalism and the Politics of Patriarchy in Iran* (Berkeley: University of California Press, 2005), 62.

45. I draw the term "fictitious unities," coined by Dennis Riley, from Scott, "Feminist Reverberations," 9.

46. Lewis Hanman and Samantha Haque, "Veil Sales Surge Post Straw's Comment," http://www.channe14.com/news/articles/society/religion/veil+sales+surge+post+straw+comments/570367 (accessed September 7, 2007).

47. Myra McDonald, "Muslim Women and the Veil: Problems of Image and Voice in Media Representations," *Feminist Media Studies* 16 (2006): 19.

48. See Seyla Benhabib's discussion of the challenge to the French idea of *läicité* and secularism. Seyla Benhabib, *The Claims of Culture: Equality and Diversity in the Global Era* (Princeton, NJ: Princeton University Press, 2002).

49. Karen Armstrong, "My Years in a Habit Taught Me the Paradox of Veiling," *Guardian*, October 26, 2006, http://www.guardian.co.uk/commentisfree/2006/oct/26/comment.politics1 (accessed August 29, 2007).

50. Straw, "I Want to Unveil."

51. "Remove Full Veils Urges Straw," October 6, 2006, http://news.bbc.co.uk/2/hi/uk_news/politics/5411954.stm (accessed November 13, 2008).

7
Mediating Modalities
Practicing Popular Politics

Helene A. Shugart

The tradition of "public sphere" scholarship, as Jim McGuigan has noted, has generally given short shrift to popular cultural forms and venues, implicitly if not explicitly dismissing them as superfluous or irrelevant to political engagement and debate.[1] But this attitude, as McGuigan and others have argued, is extremely shortsighted if not naïve, for popular culture, especially as mediated, constitutes a powerful, pervasive, and virtually endless source of—and resource for—information and attitudes regarding the very matters that occupy the ostensibly "legitimate" public sphere. Accordingly, McGuigan favors the more inclusive theoretical designation of the "cultural public sphere," which he defines as "the articulation of politics, public and personal, as a contested terrain through affective (aesthetic and emotional) modes of communication."[2]

Historically, most cultural studies scholarship across disciplines reflects this assumption, positioning popular culture, more broadly, and media fare, specifically, as significant sites of political contestation—as powerful, if not more so, than more conventional designated, "official" spaces. Yet if the implicit acknowledgment of an expanded notion of "the public sphere" has driven the work of cultural studies in decidedly positive ways, it has also constrained scholarship through the sometimes static, reductive, discrete, or exclusive shape that the sphere has assumed.[3] Cultural studies scholarship has tended to implicitly characterize "the media" collectively as a prominent, powerful, and increasingly pervasive public sphere in which cultural politics are variously reflected, manufactured, contested, and reinforced. In this vein, the bulk of that work has attended to those very entities and agents who control the media industry and thus define this public sphere.[4] Although Douglas Kellner sounds an optimistic note regarding popular culture, he acknowledges the classic cultural studies perspective that "the system of [media] production shapes what sorts of cultural texts will be produced, what structural limits there will be as to what can and cannot be said, and what sorts of ideological codes and effects these texts will generate."[5] Simply put, the contemporary mainstream mediascape, these critics aver, comprises a venue of domination and oppression that functions primarily, if covertly, to "reproduce a repressive social system."[6]

Uncomfortable with the fairly static and homogenous rendering of audiences as passive "cultural dupes" afforded by such a characterization, and reflective of similar concerns on the part of public sphere scholars who chide the exclusion of marginalized voices in such a conception, several contemporary cultural critics have examined audiences more closely as they "read" and respond to cultural texts. Such contributions have ranged from identifying various possible readings that audiences might perform in relation to dominant cultural fare to how audiences make sense of such texts in the context of their own experiences and perceptions and how those texts might be employed resistively by audiences.[7] However, these perspectives do not necessarily dismantle the problems inherent to a conception of "the media," as a collective public sphere, as an exclusive space designed, managed, and occupied by designated official agents. While powerful, dominant institutions and the constraints they impose are very real and significant and must be acknowledged, such a conceptualization apprehends media as a distinct realm or container for dominant or resistive ideas. If audiences are afforded agency, even to the extent that they engage the text, they are not afforded voice or participation within that sphere; at best, they are rendered inhabitants of disenfranchised "counterpublic" spheres that, even if they are embedded in a constellation of other publics, reinforce the boundaries and presumption of "the" public sphere,[8] contributing to a bifurcation of text and audience.

In keeping with critical public sphere scholarship that seeks to complicate how we understand public engagement and the constitution of "public(s)," I want to suggest another approach to the question of the negotiation of power in conventional mediated contexts of constraint: one that considers contemporary mediated forms in terms of *modalities* by which discourses are circulated and contested. Although many contemporary cultural critics have examined the strategies, patterns, and practices of popular cultural media fare and of audience readings (although decidedly emphasizing the former and with relatively few exceptions),[9] these approaches, with their loci in either text or audience, do not attend to the modes through which text and audience intersect in the negotiation of meaning and power or, accordingly, the dynamic, fluid, volatile, and infinitely contested nature of that intersection. Critical examination in this vein is particularly warranted in light of the fact that contemporary media technologies are characterized by distinctive forms, sensibilities, and practices that are increasingly sophisticated in their apprehension of audiences. The distinctive aesthetic character of many contemporary media texts, I suggest, might productively be engaged as a process through which contexts and conditions of constraint are negotiated, thereby further illuminating the relationship between texts and audiences. Such an endeavor further reveals the resonance between aesthetic modalities and everyday experience to the extent that identification is implicated by a modalities approach, albeit as a highly fluid concept: that is, particular practices and processes invite audiences to engage with and variously accept, reject, and/or modify the norms and values promoted in a given text. Accordingly, aesthetic media modalities serve as conductors for creative engagement between text and audience, resulting in particular kinds of knowledge that enable productive ends.

To this end, I draw on "landmark" contemporary popular mediated texts that engage sexual "alterity" (as measured against the conventional discourse of heteronormativity). Namely, I examine the mainstream television programs *Ellen*, *Will and Grace*, and *Queer Eye for the Straight Guy*—all programs that, although no longer in active production, have been cited as key cultural events in the "mainstreaming" (however problematically, as many have noted) of queerness.[10] Specifically, I argue that these texts all featured pastiche and parody, contemporary aesthetic practices that are productively apprehended as modalities to the extent that they can illuminate the ways in which meaning and power are negotiated at the intersection of text and audience.

Modus Operandi

My argument in this chapter is that certain aesthetic patterns and practices characteristic of contemporary media fare might be understood as "public modalities" through which power and meaning are contested between text and audience, even as those patterns and practices are produced within and for "dominant" discourses. I do not suggest that this is the norm; in fact, I am convinced that most mainstream mediated texts are fairly straightforwardly reflective of conventional discourses of constraint, and this is especially true of apparently resistive messages that are, upon closer inspection, altered in important ways that undermine them and ultimately reify those very discourses of convention. In raising the specter of exceptions, I also do not subscribe to the argument that contemporary media texts, in particular, are infinitely available for resistive readings on the part of audiences who may impose or infer meaning at will—or, for that matter, that resistance is exclusively located in audiences or particular "publics." Rather than apprehending the text and the audience as discrete, static, and oppositional entities, I locate my argument within particular practices that are characterized by instability and malleability and, as such, invite if not require engagement between text and audience. If that engagement is not necessarily critical, it at least contains the potential thereof. My broader interest is in examining how public engagement and the notion of "public" are constituted via these resultant processes, or modalities, especially in such a way that acknowledges the political significance, implications, and possibilities of popular cultural forms.

One of the overarching aesthetic features of contemporary media fare that has been identified by numerous cultural critics is pastiche.[11] Pastiche as available in mediated texts is "a hodgepodge of random images that are not organized so as to say anything or take a position. There is no narrative logic inherent in the presentation of images; they are just randomly recognised as mechanical permutations."[12] Todd Gitlin characterizes pastiche as "cultural recombination" that permits "anything [to be] juxtaposed to anything else."[13] This is manifest, for instance, in the barrage of incoherent images and sound bites that comprises most contemporary media: for instance, graphic images of violence followed by touching "Hallmark" family moments, followed by satirical political commentary, followed by sexually provocative images in quick succession, each of which may or may not belong to particular genres such as news, advertising, or programming. Although Jean-François Lyotard, like John Fiske and others, has argued that the disruption and rejection of a grand master narrative in this fashion can be empowering,[14] other cultural critics disagree, arguing that pastiche "overwhelms [the audience's] ability to interpret meaning rationally," rendering an apathetic audience, at best, or an entirely passive one, at worst.[15] Some scholars have cited this very defiance of rationality as a virtue, however, noting that it lends itself to "bricolage," wherein audience members might cobble together—in entirely idiosyncratic and ungovernable ways, in keeping with pastiche—resistive messages from the random collage of images with which they are presented.[16]

Parody is another aesthetic practice that is characteristic of contemporary media fare. If not unique to that milieu, it is deployed there in novel ways. Parody, at base, is defined as mimicry to the end of "send[ing] up . . . convention" in the form of, for example, a cultural or political icon (such as a celebrity or president) or, more broadly, a concept (like femininity).[17] Its pervasiveness in contemporary popular, especially mediated, culture is indisputable. In that context, it is typically characterized by other aesthetic practices, like self-reflexivity, referencing historical cultural moments or symbols,[18] or recombination, wherein more than one historical reference is invoked or historical and contemporary references are presented in ironic combination. Pointing to the complementarity if not confluence of pastiche and parody, Frederic Jameson characterizes pastiche as "blank parody," in that the fleeting, random, and incoherent qualities of pastiche ensure that representations occurring in that context are rendered devoid of substance and, thus, rather nonsensical.[19] Like Jameson, many critics who have examined parody in the context of popular culture have assessed it as a device or vehicle in the service of dominant discourses.[20] Others, however, have lauded parody for its critical potential irrespective of context, citing its inherent moorings in critique as a mine from which audiences might draw to the end of resistive readings.[21]

As relevant to cultural studies approaches more broadly, and as apparent in scholarship attending to pastiche and parody specifically, the debate regarding the critical implications of pastiche and parody tends to be located in either the text, as devices employed to convey conventional content, or the audience, insofar as they function as resources for resistance. If engagement between text and audience is acknowledged and addressed, an assessment of the negotiation of meaning and power is limited by these respective conceptualizations. These approaches and their attendant contributions are not wrongheaded; to the contrary, they illuminate and make salient the conditions, contexts, and constraints that characterize both pastiche and parody as contemporary media practices. Certainly, they are invoked and organized in strategic ways in particular texts, designed to at least convey if not reproduce conventional discourses. By the same token, their inherently inchoate (in the case of pastiche) and ironic (in the case of parody) qualities render them at least somewhat accessible and ambiguous and thus arguably more available for resistive readings. A modalities approach does not negate these features, but instead seeks to examine them as processes, that is, where and how they intersect, acknowledging more fully and explicitly that both things can be true. Assessing pastiche and parody—especially as they occur in tandem with each other—as modalities can illuminate further how publics are configured and constituted and how meaning and power are negotiated in ways that likewise more fully acknowledge their fluidity, dynamism, and volatility.

One of the key advantages of a modalities approach in this regard is that it defies ownership of meaning by, respectively, "dominant interests" or audiences. Rather, the very notion of "modality" affords primacy to the processes of *engagement*, an orientation that is endowed with very different assumptions, consequences, and implications than either a devices or vehicles (for dominant discourses) or resources (for resistive audiences) orientation—approaches that, while they do not belie processes of engagement, deemphasize if not implicitly dismiss them. Accordingly, a modalities approach further resists an apprehension of those patterns and practices as infinitely malleable. If rules do not necessarily govern the engagement, it does occur in a context of constraint, as defined by venue and by the cultural conditions of consumption. Thus, if pastiche and parody arguably provide access for apparently resistive representations, incorporate or invite critique, and are predicated on ambiguity, they nonetheless are organized by or in relation to established cultural conventions that manage both the production of said representations and readings thereof—as modalities, they are neither inherently oppressive or resistive but instead implicate certain values via particular engagements and configurations. Apprehending pastiche and parody as modalities, then, foregrounds the intersection of and tensions between text and audience rather than privileging one or the other, as vehicle or resource approaches tend to do.

Indeed, pastiche and parody are especially promising practices to apprehend as modalities given their ambiguous and ironic qualities. They are reflective of contemporary cultural sensibilities, for instance, of detachment, randomness, irony, and cynicism—sensibilities that are both reflected and produced by contemporary media fare. Even if, as some critics contend, those sensibilities—more specifically, practices that reflect them—are configured in hegemonic ways in that fare, the fact remains that they are, by their very natures, ambiguous and unstable: in other words, if they are (re)historicized and (re)contextualized, they are nonetheless inherently characterized by fluidity. This is certainly true of pastiche and parody, as well as other practices stemming from these contemporary sensibilities, including, for instance, juxtaposition, reflexivity, spectacle, and camp—none of which are novel, to be sure, but each of which is rendered especially agile and fluid in light of contemporary conventions and sensibilities.[22] As relevant to pastiche and parody, in the former case, a host of "alternative" and apparently resistive representations are afforded entrée under the guise of randomness and discordance. Similarly, parody is predicated on critique and reflection to the end of consulting and discerning multiple meanings in order to "get it." While both occur within defined parameters established by and within the text, their instability is inherent. This is true of each practice on its own terms; however, I am especially interested in how they function in tandem. This is so because while modalities may be generally characterized by dynamic engagement, certain modalities are arguably richer and more complex than others. In the texts that I examine in the foregoing analysis, I argue that parody and pastiche can also be understood as a collective modality through which discourses of convention and resistance are negotiated in ways that further illuminate the relationship between text and audience. Specifically, a modalities approach reveals the extent to which political discourses are in constant flux, continually reconfiguring and recalibrating themselves in relation to each other at any given moment. Particular modalities provide the framework for that contestation, but it is a framework that is simultaneously governed by that very contestation.

In particular, I assess three highly culturally significant, landmark television programs dealing with sexual "alterity," in these cases asexuality and homosexuality, that have had a significant impact on cultural discourses of sexuality: *Ellen*, *Will and Grace*, and *Queer Eye for the Straight Guy*. Notably, each of these programs prominently featured pastiche and parody, respectively and in tandem. I argue that these aesthetic practices constituted modalities to the extent that they established the scaffolding for the political negotiation of cultural discourses of sexuality in ways that did, indeed, significantly alter U.S. popular cultural understandings of sexuality. Rather than characterize or evaluate a particular outcome as a result of these shows as critical or oppressive, I want to foreground the actual mobilizations and contestations of those discourses, via pastiche and parody, as available in the texts. Such an approach—a modalities approach—holds considerable promise for furthering our understanding of the complex ways in which power is actively negotiated—not by and within a text or by and within its audience, or even at the margins that separate them, but among them.

The "Homosexual Wink"

Both pastiche and parody are highly available in each of the texts at hand, which may be more broadly significant in terms of the utility of those tandem modalities in navigating resistive political discourses in contexts of constraint.[23] The "groundbreaking" situation comedy *Ellen* (originally titled *These Friends of Mine*) was originally broadcast on ABC network television between 1994 and 1998,[24] and it continues to be broadcast in syndication. The show featured a single woman, Ellen Morgan, who was portrayed as heterosexual for the first three years but who eventually came out as a lesbian. Parody, specifically of femininity, was especially apparent prior to her coming out in two primary ways: the highly stereotypical renderings of the female characters surrounding her as well as her own parodic performances of femininity. In the former case, the women against whom Ellen's character was drawn essentially represented the three primary stereotypes of women: her friend Paige, the *femme fatale* replete with revealing clothes, high heels, lots of makeup, and big hair; Audrey, the (adult) little girl who consistently wore pink, baby doll dresses and "Mary Jane" shoes, her hair in pigtails, and spoke in a childish voice; and Donna, Ellen's mother, who was "ditzy" and quintessentially maternal—vague, not too bright, but kindhearted and nurturing. In the latter case, on some occasions, Ellen, a highly androgynous character as compared to her female foils and to most prime-time female leads, was forced to "perform" femininity under duress and with no other option available—for example, as a stripper, as a seductive personal trainer, and as a woman making a dating video—in highly excessive and parodic ways. In both cases, while these parodic performances certainly play on and arguably reify conventional discourses of gender, Ellen's comparatively "normal"—and consequently normalized—androgynous, decidedly "unfeminine" persona rendered them suspect and thus available for critical reflection. Indeed, they also provided effective camouflage for arguably the more subversive representation of Ellen's asexuality: her abject failure at heterosexual romance and, more tellingly, her strong aversion to it (as evinced especially by her enormous relief when she escaped every romantic scenario) seemed perfectly reasonable given the bizarre heterosexual endeavors and practices of her friends and family members, which included such things as alarming sex role plays, promiscuity, and disturbing fetishes—all notably connected to the gender parodies of femininity noted above, especially the *femme fatale* and the little girl. Although homosexuality was never explicitly invoked in the early years of the series, during which parody and pastiche thoroughly characterized the show, the representation of an androgynous and decidedly, explicitly asexual female lead character constituted a signal departure from conventional representations and discourses of femininity and heteronormative female sexuality.

Importantly, these parodies all occurred in a pastiche-laden context, in large part as relevant to the configuration of quirky characters that may be the stuff of situation comedy; but, I argue, these parodies assumed especially dissonant and incoherent dimensions in the show. Characters like Joe, Ellen's obese playboy bookstore manager; Adam, her effeminate heterosexual roommate; and Spence, her macho and extremely insecure cousin, provided a backdrop into which the parodies of femininity noted above blended. While those parodies accordingly could be dismissed as simply more of this playful, inchoate absurd pastiche—which is, according to some critics, the very purpose of ensconcing alterity in pastiche—pastiche could also be understood as the vehicle and camouflage for those parodies. After all, the male characters, while they may indeed have tweaked gender and sexual conventions, were not caricaturish or parodic in the ways that the female characters were. Moreover, the extreme caricatures of femininity featured were anchored in and drawn against Ellen's androgyny, which was accordingly normalized. Pastiche and parody were thus configured in *Ellen* in such a way as to circulate resistive discourses regarding the cultural politics of gender and sexuality immediately alongside highly conventional discourses and generic forms. The organization of those discourses in relation to each other, or more precisely in contestation with each other, offers key insights into the ways in which audience and text can be fully implicated and engaged via the modalities of pastiche and parody: multiple reference points may well have been arrayed and sequenced in considered ways within the text, but whatever meaning inhered was entirely contingent upon the reference points to which the audience attended.

On the heels of the demise of *Ellen*, which was cancelled one year following DeGeneres's/Morgan's coming out, ostensibly because the situation comedy had become "too gay" for mainstream tastes, NBC launched the highly successful and popular situation comedy *Will and Grace*, featuring a gay man and straight woman best-friend duo as its "hook." In active production from 1998 through 2006, like *Ellen*, it too continues to be broadcast in syndication. More important, also like *Ellen*, it was praised as a landmark cultural event in terms of the "mainstreaming" of homosexuality.[25] Many critics noted the problematic ways in which the pairing and, especially, Will (the gay male lead) were rendered; that is, other than being nominally gay, Will was highly consistent with the conventions of the romantic heterosexual male lead, and his relationship with Grace, his best friend, bore all the hallmarks of an intimate romantic relationship or even marriage, save for actual sexual relations.[26] Furthermore, Will and Grace's gay male friend Jack was highly stereotypically rendered as a "flaming" homosexual, characterized by very feminine behaviors and actions. Grace's secretary and friend, Karen, rounded out the ensemble, and her relationship with Jack mirrored that between Will and Grace insofar as she, like Grace, was heterosexual and Karen and Jack were kindred spirits.

Pastiche was available in the show primarily in terms of genre: that is, it cobbled together conventions of various genres in random and absurd ways. As suggested above, the romantic comedy was one such genre, featuring as it did the intimate relationship between a fairly childlike woman and a relatively paternalistic man characterized by witty banter and madcap escapades. Elements of the soap opera characterized the show as well, albeit often in parodic ways, thus suggesting further ways in which pastiche and parody may function together. Examples of this include Will and Grace's endeavors to have a child together; Grace's tumultuous marriage; and the saga of Karen's marriage, her husband's prison sentence, his subsequent apparent death, her relationship with his mistress, her affair with the mistress's father, and her husband's resurfacing. The show also, perhaps not surprisingly, featured aspects of political satire, especially as relevant to sexuality but to race and ethnicity as well, as when the controversy of two men kissing on television was the subject of a few episodes, or when Will and Grace disagreed over the merits of political candidates, one of whom was gay and one of whom was a woman. The characters of Karen and Jack, who were highly caricaturish in their renderings, contributed greatly to the pastiche that characterized the show. Karen, an extremely wealthy socialite, nonetheless worked as Grace's secretary, although she was useless in that capacity, devoting her time to boozing, drugging, and imperiously criticizing Grace. Jack, of course, was the epitome of the stereotypical gay man: effeminate, promiscuous, emotional, and flighty. Profoundly selfish, immature, and dedicated to amusing themselves at the expense of others, Jack and Karen engaged in all manner of bizarre and wacky antics—for instance, working as a magic team together, making a politically incorrect sexual harassment training video, and catching pickpockets red handed in gay bars.

Parody, perhaps obviously, was also a staple feature of the show in ways that fully complemented its pastiche. For instance, the soap opera dynamic noted above was extremely "camp"—outrageous, over the top, and satirical, thus constituting a parody of the genre itself—and in much the same way, Karen's character was a parody of the "rich bitch" socialite familiar in characters ranging from Joan Crawford to Joan Collins.[27] But parody was particularly salient in the show as relevant to sexuality, for that cultural discourse was the nexus of the show, after all, and, more broadly, the focal point of contestation in the mediated context of constraint. Certainly, Jack's character was a parody of queerness that, as many critics have argued, reified heteronormative sensibilities and heterosexist assumptions. But rejecting the parody out of hand risks dismissing its critical and subversive qualities. Indeed, Jack was the avenue for a considerable amount of subversive humor; for instance, he often made disparaging comments about "breeders" and their unfathomable lifestyles, and he made much of being physically repulsed by the specter of heterosexuality, as when he undergoes a terrible identity crisis upon becoming aroused by a female lap dancer—until he discovers, to his enormous relief, that she is transgendered (a preoperative transsexual, more precisely and significantly). All of these are obvious spoofs of homophobic attitudes and practices, and accordingly, they promote inclusiveness and diversity by dint of ridiculing intolerance and exclusivity—indeed, parody is the modal vehicle for those values. I would argue that it is precisely *because* his character was hegemonically rendered and drawn so sharply against Will that Jack was afforded subversive license, via pastiche and parody. Perhaps it is in this vein that A. J. Jacobs asserts that "by having Will, we earned the right to have Jack."[28]

But I would suggest further that the character of Will—the apparent "straight man," so to speak, to Jack's buffoon—ought likewise to be read against an apprehension of Jack in light of those subversive sensibilities—that is, as opposed to the superficial read afforded by Jack's buffoonery. As noted, several critics have identified the ways in which Will was "heterosexualized" by virtue of his near-perfect conformity to mainstream conventions of ideal heterosexual masculinity: he was traditionally masculine, wealthy, white, attractive, and intimately involved with a woman. Accordingly, and in tandem with the fact that he was rarely depicted in a romantic context with a man or even in a broader gay community,[29] Will was a very problematic character, homogenized and heterosexualized as a very paean to heteronormativity, with virtually all traces of queerness either eradicated or diffused to the point of irrelevance. But for these same reasons and specifically in light of the subversive moments afforded by pastiche and parody in the show, Will's character *also* is viable as a parody of heterosexuality. After all, his nominal homosexuality was the key premise of the series, and his virtually unqualified rendering of ideal male heterosexuality and heteronormativity exposed the arbitrariness of those conventions. As perhaps definitive evidence for this parody, gay male sexuality was sold, in the character of Will, as "doing" male heterosexuality one better in that, as a gay man, Will was demonstrated as having much greater (especially sexual) access to, license with, and control of women than a straight man could have precisely because he was gay. For instance, he could do and say things to women, like touching their bodies and seeing them in various states of undress, that were considered harmless in the context of his sexual orientation but that would be considered highly inappropriate if performed by a straight man who was not a lover.[30] Accordingly, in the character of Will, heterosexual male privilege was arguably parodied and mocked as wanting on its very own terms, even as it was reified.

In *Will and Grace*, then, pastiche functioned as the backdrop and context for the engagement of cultural discourses of sexuality. The amalgam of apparently inchoate and "piecemeal" genres and characters that comprised the show arguably served to camouflage contestations revolving about those discourses, even as they might also have appropriated them. That is, even as resistive messages might have been usurped, deflated, or trivialized by dint of a perhaps strategically rendered hodgepodge, particular cues could also be attended to and configured from that hodgepodge that could support subversive messages. The parody that characterized the show in various respects worked in tandem with pastiche, both in terms of honing and organizing that (apparently random) aesthetic and in terms of how particular, seemingly dissonant parodies were drawn against each other. I refer, especially, to the parody of queerness that is Jack and the parody of heterosexuality that is Will. These two gay men could not have been more different or, for that matter, more caricaturish in their respective parodic performances. Their juxtaposition against each other itself constituted a form of pastiche, one that was further founded upon the substratum of pastiche comprised by the genre blending that marked the show. My point is not that transgressive messages trumped hegemonic ones in *Will and Grace*; indeed, the reverse could just as likely be true. Rather, I suggest that the modalities of pastiche and parody, respectively and collectively, by which these representations were configured actually constituted the grounds for the public engagement and contestation of cultural discourses of sexuality—engagement that furthermore directly entailed the interaction of text and audience in negotiating its terms, conditions, and significance.

The Bravo cable network and (for two seasons) NBC prime-time program *Queer Eye for the Straight Guy*, in active production from 2003 through 2007, constituted a brief but significant moment in the contemporary popular cultural consciousness, hailed as yet another landmark popular cultural event relevant to the cultural politics of sexuality, this time by forging an alliance between gay and straight men.[31] The show featured five gay men, each of whom boasted an area of expertise, who were collectively assigned each week to "make over" a straight man and his home for, typically, a special occasion with a wife or girlfriend. Ushering the concept of "metrosexuality" into the U.S. popular vernacular, the show was organized around the premise that gay (male) sensibilities could be usefully employed by straight men to make them more attractive to and successful with straight women. The problematic nature of the program, then, is clear at the outset, irrespective of the fact that the five men were "positively" portrayed: that positive portrayal was entirely contingent upon their reification of heteronormativity. Queerness was trivialized as a handmaiden—or manservant—to heterosexuality; and homosexuality was rendered entirely devoid of substance, in general, and sexuality (in terms of practice and references thereto), in particular, articulated instead as interchangeable with excellent taste. Indeed, several critics have made this case, further noting the function of *Queer Eye,* specifically, and metrosexuality, more broadly, as vehicles for the cultivation of consumptive practices and the restabilization of broader political discourses.[32] I concur with these assessments, and I suggest that the show might also be usefully apprehended through the critical framework of public modalities in order to examine more precisely how the cultural politics of sexuality were engaged and contested in the program. A consideration of the particular modalities that characterized that engagement, respectively and in relation to each other, may lend further insight into the patterns and practices by which resistance is negotiated in contexts of constraint.

Certainly, parody was *Queer Eye*'s hallmark, and it was evident at the very outset, via the opening montage that heralded each episode as well as the "superhero" motif that set the tone for the show. In that montage, each of the so-called Fab Five received a call to service, then was frozen in a dramatic still shot as he prepared to embark on his mission. Once convened, they raced to the site of that newest challenge (and they raced everywhere, underscoring the urgency of their mission), running down the facts of the straight man in question. They then proceeded to rush into the man's house and promptly take over, whirling through his house and his life and leaving in their wake a new and much-improved version of both. At the conclusion of each episode, the Fab Five observed the culmination of their enterprise—typically, a momentous event such as a marriage proposal, a special birthday dinner, or the first meeting of the parents of the heterosexual couple—on video monitor from afar, ensconced in a sort of urban contemporary "bat cave" and furnished with appropriately retro martinis, where they interjected their comments on the straight man's absorption and/or performance of all they had taught and bestowed upon him. The superhero is clearly invoked via all the aesthetic markers of the characterization of the Fab Five: their dramatic interventions, special powers in the service of others, and ultimate restoration to a separate plane of existence. The parodic dimensions of that invocation were secured through irony, which aesthetically dramatized and caricatured the image of the superhero.

Placing gay men in this role further ironized the trope by challenging (in the case of male superheroes) its conventional, heteronormative, masculine basis.

Parody was also vividly available in the form of stereotypes. In the case of the Fab Five, their respective areas of specialization were fashion, interior design, hair and grooming, food and wine, and "culture"—in terms of happening or desirable trends. Of course, these are the primary heterosexist tropes of gay men, and the "experts" certainly played to those tropes, for instance, via their emotional obsession with their areas of expertise: when Carson, the fashion expert, clutches his heart at the sight of his slovenly charge, for example, or when Ted, the food and wine expert, pretends to swoon upon opening the subject's pantry. The straight men also were stereotypical to a parodic extreme, typically representing "worst-case scenarios" of men who were well meaning but entirely clueless about how to present themselves effectively, especially in a romantic context. For instance, they may have worn a hideous, alarmingly obvious toupee, kept their hair unshaven or uncut for years, treated their partners only to fast-food dinners, or never spent more than two dollars at a flea market on gifts for their partners.

Pastiche was inherent in the program primarily insofar as these parodic performances were situated in relation to each other—that is, as both juxtaposed against and allied with each other. Male heterosexuality and homosexuality were established as fairly absolute extremes in terms of, especially, gender and authenticity, and yet they were allied with each other for the common purpose of salvaging heteronormativity—as explicitly noted in the title, after all, *Queer Eye for the Straight Guy*. Parodically rendering gay men effeminate—by virtue of their "feminine" areas of expertise if not by their personas—made straight men more successfully heteronormatively masculine. Pastiche inhered in the juxtaposition and alliance between authenticity and artifice; that is, the straight men were portrayed as "authentically," substantively masculine, including as drawn against the superficiality of the gay men and their interest in appearances, décor, and details. Yet the straight men's masculine prowess was ultimately fully realized by assuming or partaking of that very superficiality. In the case of *Queer Eye*, then, pastiche appeared in the configuration of the parodies and their implications in relation to each other and more specifically in the invocation and juxtaposition of discordant elements.

As noted, the show undeniably reproduced heteronormative conventions and discourses, the ostensibly progressive portrayal of the gay men as knowledgeable, helpful, and even endowed with superpowers notwithstanding. Furthermore, the modalities of parody and pastiche cultivated this articulation, underscoring the point that modalities are not inherently either liberating or oppressive. However, I suggest even when those modalities bolstered conventional discourses of sexuality and gender, they were not simply static, passive devices deployed in the service of those discourses. Rather, they were dynamic and fluid, even volatile, and afforded transgressive possibilities. Under the guise of parody and pastiche, the show included some very sharp critiques of heterosexuality. This was frequently evident in elitist critiques of taste predicated on the sharp juxtapositions between straight and queer masculinity, wherein the gay men would snidely comment on the straight men's choices of plastic dinnerware and utensils, their pathetic taste in clothes, and their inability to absorb instruction. Furthermore, the straight men were almost always cast, even after the makeover, as inferior to the gay men in terms of physical attractiveness, charm, sophistication, and wit. While this could be attributed to the necessity that straight men fail in some regard in order to preserve the "authenticity" of heteronormative masculinity, critiques were also, both more subtly and significantly, directed to broader social conventions, such as family, work, and gender. Often, the Fab Five would make comments, as they watched from their bat cave, about the straight men, comments that were ostensibly laudatory but also condescending or, at least, sarcastic: for example, during a family hug as one makeover is restored to his family, one of the men comments, "What a cute, cute family. Really, they're cute as buttons!" In another case, as a middle-aged man is reconciled to his baldness and has burned his toupee, one of the Fab Five says, "Now he looks just like your average successful lawyer!" In yet another episode, a newly made-over man, painfully awkward as he attempts but fails to prepare a meal for his girlfriend, ultimately requires her help to salvage the situation. As the event closes on the couple sharing an awkward kiss, one of the "queer eyes" comments, "Well, our work here is done; he's all man now!" These comments were not inherently or even remarkably subversive in the context of the show. To the contrary, in fact, they explicitly endorsed heteronormativity (not to mention, implicitly, normative discourses of class and race).[33] Furthermore, they occurred within the parameters of parody and pastiche that, after all, were the modalities that ultimately reified heteronormative masculinity. But those modalities, as I have argued, are notoriously unstable, and thus are always simultaneously available as resistance to the very things that they represent.

In this vein, a number of scenes also included a strong homoerotic component that could be configured as transgressive. For instance, the "culture"—or romance—advice was often dispensed by the gay male expert to the straight man in a softly lit environment while the two were alone, frequently as they reclined on the straight man's bed, with music playing in the background. "Touch her like this," Jai (the cultural guru) instructs in one such episode, lightly tracing the subject's face. Ostensibly, this was a natural sequence of events insofar as the culture expert was helping his charge set the right atmosphere in the bedroom. However, the scenes were semiotically charged with homoerotic signifiers. More to the point, parody and pastiche are the modalities by which that critique is made available: the ostensibly gay man assumes the role of straight man, while the straight man assumes that of a woman in this overarching parody of heteronormativity. The reconfiguration or layering of parodies, of course, constitutes pastiche. Similarly, Carson, the fashion expert, frequently would dress or undress the straight man in the dressing room, undoing his belt buckle, unzipping his pants, or kneeling down in front of him to examine the trouser break, all to the end of getting him into the right clothes. In one episode, as well, Kyan, the hair and grooming expert, accompanied the straight man into a spray-on tanning booth where the men, both in skimpy swimsuits, stood closely together. Even as the straight man expressed his discomfort at being nearly naked and confined with a gay man, the stylist did not relent, and the straight man acquiesced to the conditions of instruction. Here, too, parody and pastiche are the vehicles by which this implicit critique of heteronormativity—as unstable and insecure—is made available: the ostensibly effeminate gay man is rendered dominant, even aggressive, while the ostensibly authentically masculine straight man is accordingly rendered submissive, intimidated, and passive. Although the gender binary informing this interaction is significant and undeniably problematic, parody and pastiche afforded critique through a recombination of representations and an inversion of power.

Pastiche and parody, even as they constituted the warrants for appropriation for alterity, thus simultaneously functioned in *Queer Eye* as camouflage for subversive messages that, in this case, were rendered in such a way as to expose the tenuousness and vulnerability of the heteronormative conventions of masculinity. This underscores the point that political engagement and contestation in a context of constraint—in this case, mainstream media fare—might be productively examined in terms of the modalities that characterize them. Such a lens affords a more extensive understanding of how cultural politics are contested and negotiated in light of the contemporary aesthetic practices and sensibilities that drive public cultural forms. A public modalities framework can illuminate the complexity of political engagement and thus lend further insight into the ways in which publics are invoked and constituted as well as how political discourses are circulated and contested.

This dynamic is illustrated further by an important distinction between the texts I have assessed here. Both *Will and Grace* and *Queer Eye for the Straight Guy* unambiguously featured homosexuality and, more to the point, openly gay men as their premises. Accordingly, as I have described, parodies of those very characters and, at times, others, as well as (and in tandem with) the context of pastiche images, plots, and references, are the axes on which both appropriation and subversion turn. This dynamic appears to have characterized *Ellen* only prior to the character's coming out; her androgyny and asexuality as established in the pre–coming out episodes—which was enabled by the caricatures of femininity displayed by the other female characters—contested the tropes of femininity and heteronormative female sexuality. However, upon Ellen's coming out, parodies of femininity no longer figured prominently for Ellen or other female characters in the show. Accordingly, the pastiche qualities of the show receded as well as Ellen was depicted navigating her life as a lesbian. Although humor certainly was retained in the program, the over-the-top, satirical, random, and incoherent aesthetics that characterized the show prior to Ellen's coming out virtually disappeared as the issues surrounding Ellen's lesbianism emerged as the central theme. The consequent cancellation of the show could be explained by the fact that its primary focus on Ellen's lesbian identity and relationships may have been too much for mainstream audiences to accept at the time—the "too gay" argument.[34] But perhaps the eradication of the modalities that permitted entrée of transgressive representations—pastiche and parody—was at least as significant a factor in the show's demise. That is, had queerness in *Ellen* been appropriated, parodied, and qualified in ways palatable to conventional heteronormative tastes, as they unquestionably were in *Will and Grace* and *Queer Eye for the Straight Guy*, perhaps it would have remained popular—*and* managed to be transgressive under cover of its own appropriation.

Popular Politics

The notion that popular culture is a political space drives cultural studies scholarship, an acknowledgment that does much to advance an appreciation of the circulation of political discourses.[35] However, imposing a public sphere framework on popular cultural forms and venues also is limiting—ironically, explicitly designating it as such clarifies how powerfully that assumption also undergirds cultural studies scholarship. That is, it reinforces the idea of "the popular" as a sanctioned, discrete space to which particular agents have access and from which other agents (or "publics"), in the form of spectators or consumers, are excluded. This is especially apparent as relevant to a construction of "the media" as a powerful purveyor of the popular. Typically conceptualized as ideologically driven, collective vehicles for dominant discourses, media texts are understood as specific, concrete sites of contestation, or, more precisely, of the conditional invocation and subsequent management of resistance. Audiences, when they are acknowledged, accordingly assume the role of other publics or manifestations thereof, ranging from entirely passive spectators who grant presumption to the dominant discourses that are advanced and reinforced to resistive readers who might creatively mine those texts to craft transgressive messages. While this conceptualization may acknowledge the existence of agency and multiple publics, it nonetheless maintains a highly continent boundary between the relatively official public sphere and alternative, inherently marginalized (counter)publics.

A public modalities framework, conversely, offers considerable promise in complicating and extending our understanding of the relationship and engagement *between* text and audience. Such an approach directs greater attention to the actual contestation of political discourses in a context of constraint and to how publics and publicities might be imagined, invoked, and constituted in multiple and fluid ways. Furthermore, a public modalities approach reframes patterns and practices of engagement as exactly that, rather than as, for instance, devices either deployed by dominant agents or resistively read by audiences. By way of illustration, I have examined three media texts that have been identified as highly significant cultural moments—*Ellen*, *Will and Grace*, and *Queer Eye for the Straight Guy*—each of which turned on the representation of sexual alterity as drawn against heteronormative conventions. Although they all have been lauded as key to the mainstreaming of queerness and progressive cultural politics, various cultural critics have qualified those enthusiastic sentiments, chronicling the problematic and ultimately hegemonic nature of the renderings of queerness in each of them. I do not dispute these conclusions, but I suggest that a closer look at the *modalities* by which cultural discourses of sexuality were engaged in these texts is productive in terms of lending insight into the processes of public engagement and contestation, especially as they occur in the intersections between text and audience.

In particular, I have suggested here that at least two aesthetic patterns and practices that characterize much contemporary media fare—pastiche and parody—might be apprehended not simply as tools defined and deployed by particular agents in sanctioned venues or resources that might be mined for resistive readings, but as modalities that constitute political contestation as well as invoke publics in that contestation. In these cases, I have argued that pastiche and parody, even as they are familiar motifs of contemporary media fare that may promote conventional discourses, also may invoke and afford transgression of greater or lesser degrees. Pastiche and parody not only secure entry for representations of gender and sexual "alterity" in each of these instances. As inherently unstable practices, they also afford subversive messages regarding heteronormativity *even as* they promote heteronormative discourses. Both messages are simultaneously available, wholly integral while tightly intertwined, signaling the complex ways in which political contestation is engaged in popular cultural texts. The contestation between these articulations necessarily entails the active intersection of text and audience—not via static texts or strategies of deployment or appropriation, but by engaging cues conveyed by those modalities to craft meaning.

Contemporary popular cultural forms and venues are volatile sites of political engagement, and a public modalities framework is instructive precisely to the extent that it trains our eyes upon the processes of that engagement. The location of engagement, defined as it is by convention and constraint, is certainly salient; and affording primacy to modes of engagement does not dismiss this focus so much as reposition it, more appropriately as context than as centerpiece, and, in so doing, illuminate the complexities of discursive contestation. A modalities approach to cultural studies, especially of mediated popular cultural forms, further invites a reconsideration of the relationship between text and audience. While modalities may certainly be tailored and shaped by histories, contexts, and agents, they are inherently unstable and therefore implicate other political discourses, thereby inviting, even requiring, a symbiosis between text and audience. How modalities are configured within particular texts certainly varies with respect to their critical significance and implications. But the benefit of a modalities framework is that it privileges contestation and thus directs critical attention precisely to the ways in which particular practices of political engagement can be (re)configured and the vital function of audience *in* the text, and vice versa. Thus, a modalities orientation to public engagement promotes a more sophisticated understanding of the practices and politics of that engagement. Especially as relevant to contemporary cultural forms, modalities are perhaps more appropriately understood not simply as the means but as the very loci of political contestation.

Notes

1. Jim McGuigan, "Cultural Policy Studies," in *Culture and the Public Sphere* (London: Routledge, 1996).

2. Jim McGuigan, "The Cultural Public Sphere," *European Journal of Cultural Studies* 8 (2005): 435.

3. Robert Hariman and John Louis Lucaites, *No Caption Needed: Iconic Photographs, Public Culture, and Liberal Democracy* (Chicago: University of Chicago Press, 2007); G. Thomas Goodnight, "The Personal, Technical, and Public Spheres of Argument: A Speculative Inquiry into the Art of Public Deliberation," *Journal of the American Forensic Association* 18 (1982): 202–23; Michael Schudson, "The 'Public Sphere' and Its Problems: Bringing the State (Back) In," *Notre Dame Journal of Law, Ethics & Public Policy* 8 (1994): 519–44; Lisa McLaughlin, "Feminism, the Public Sphere, Media and Democracy," *Media, Culture & Society* 15 (1993): 598–620.

4. E.g., Todd Gitlin, "Looking Through the Screen," in *Watching Television*, ed. Todd Gitlin (New York: Pantheon 1986), 3–8; Stuart Hall, "Encoding/Decoding," in *Culture, Media, Language: Working Papers in Cultural Studies, 1972–79*, ed. Stuart Hall (London: Hutchinson, 1980) 128–38; Douglas Kellner, "Toward a Multiperspectival Cultural Studies," *Centennial Review* 26 (1992): 5–41; Mark Poster, *The Mode of Information: Poststructuralism and Social Context* (Chicago: University of Chicago Press, 1990).

5. Kellner, "Toward," 19.

6. John B. Harms and David R. Dickens, "Postmodern Media Studies: Analysis or Symptom?" *Critical Studies in Mass Communication* 13 (1996): 219–21.

7. Hall, "Encoding/Decoding"; Celeste M. Condit, "The Rhetorical Limits of Polysemy," *Critical Studies in Mass Communication* 6 (1989): 103–22; Celeste M. Condit, "Hegemony in a Mass-Mediated Society: Concordance about Reproductive Technologies," *Critical Studies in Mass Communication* 9 (1994): 311–24; John Fiske, "Television: Polysemy and Popularity," *Critical Studies in Mass Communication* 3 (1986): 391–408; John Fiske, *Television Culture* (New York: Methuen, 1987); John Fiske, *Understanding Popular Culture* (New York: Routledge, 1989).

8. E.g., Nancy Fraser, "Rethinking the Public Sphere: A Contribution to the Critique of Actually Existing Democracy," in *Habermas and the Public Sphere*, ed. Craig Calhoun (Cambridge: Massachusetts Institute of Technology Press, 1991), 109–42.

9. Harms and Dickens, "Postmodern," 222; David Tetzlaff, "Divide and Conquer: Popular Culture and Social Control in Late Capitalism," *Media, Culture & Society* 13 (1991): 9–33; Helene A. Shugart, Catherine Egley Waggoner, and D. Lynn O'Brien Hallstein, "Mediating Third-Wave Feminism: Appropriation as Postmodern Media Practice," *Critical Studies in Media Communication* 18 (2001): 196. For exceptions, see, e.g., Brian L. Ott, "(Re)Locating Pleasure in Media Studies: Toward an Erotics of Reading," *Communication and Critical/Cultural Studies* 1 (2004): 194–212; Helene A.

Shugart and Catherine Egley Waggoner, *Making Camp: Rhetorics of Transgressions in U.S. Popular Culture* (Tuscaloosa: University of Alabama Press, 2008).

10. Kathleen Battles and Wendy Hilton-Morrow, "Gay Characters in Conventional Spaces: *Will and Grace* and the Situation Comedy Genre," *Critical Studies in Media Communication* 19 (2002): 87–105; Bonnie J. Dow, "Ellen, Television, and the Politics of Gay and Lesbian Visibility," *Critical Studies in Media Communication* 18 (2001): 123–40; Dana Heller, "Taking the Nation 'from Drab to Fab': *Queer Eye for the Straight Guy*," *Feminist Media Studies* 4 (2004): 347–50; Katherine Sender, "Queens for a Day: *Queer Eye for the Straight Guy* and the Neoliberal Project," *Critical Studies in Media Communication* 23 (2006): 131–51; Helene A. Shugart, "Reinventing Privilege: The (New) Gay Man in Contemporary Popular Media," *Critical Studies in Media Communication* 20 (2003): 67–91

11. See, e.g., David L. Altheide and Robert P. Snow, *Media Worlds in the Postjournalism Era* (New York: Aldine De Gruyter, 1991); Frederic Jameson, *Postmodernism, or, the Cultural Logic of Late Capitalism* (Durham, NC: Duke University Press, 1991); Elizabeth Ann Kaplan, *Rocking Around the Clock: Music Television, Postmodernism and Consumer Culture* (New York: Methuen, 1987).

12. Harms and Dickens, "Postmodern," 216.

13. Todd Gitlin, "Postmodernism: Roots and Politics," in *Cultural Politics in Contemporary America*, ed. Ian Angus and Sut Jhally (London: Routledge, 1989), 350.

14. Jean-François Lyotard, *The Postmodern Condition*, trans. Brian Massumi (Minneapolis: University of Minnesota Press, 1984).

15. Harms and Dickens, "Postmodern," 216; see also Hall, "Encoding/Decoding"; Gitlin, "Postmodernism"; Jameson, *Postmodernism*.

16. Angela McRobbie, *Postmodernism and Popular Culture* (London: Routledge, 1994). See also Jim Collins, *Uncommon Cultures: Popular Culture and Postmodernism* (New York: Routledge, 1989).

17. Caryl Flinn, "The Deaths of Camp," in *Camp: Queer Aesthetics and the Performing Subject*, ed. Fabio Cleto (Ann Arbor: University of Michigan Press, 1999), 440.

18. Harms and Dickens, "Postmodern."

19. Frederic Jameson, "Postmodernism and Consumer Society," in *The Anti-Aesthetic: Essays on Postmodern Culture*, ed. Hal Foster (Seattle: Bay, 1983), 113.

20. Judith Butler, *Gender Trouble: Feminism and the Subversion of Identity* (New York: Routledge, 1990); Judith Halberstam, *In a Queer Time and Place: Transgender Bodies, Subcultural Lives* (New York: New York University Press, 2005); Linda Hutcheon, *Splitting Images: Contemporary Canadian Ironies* (Toronto: Oxford University Press, 1991).

21. Butler, *Gender;* Nicola Evans, "Games of Hide and Seek: Race, Gender and Drag in *The Crying Game* and *The Birdcage*," *Text and Performance Quarterly* 18 (1998): 199–216; Pamela Robertson, *Guilty Pleasures: Feminist Camp from Mae West to Madonna* (Durham, NC: Duke University Press, 1996); Helene A. Shugart,

"Parody as Subversive Performance: Denaturalising Gender in *Ellen*," *Text and Performance Quarterly* 21 (2001): 95–113.

22. Shugart and Waggoner, *Making Camp*.

23. The phrase "homosexual wink" is drawn from the work of James Creech, *Closet Writing/Gay Reading: The Case of Nelville's Pierre* (Chicago: University of Chicago Press, 1993), 93–100.

24. See, e.g., Dow, "Ellen."

25. Michael Schneider, "Emmys Go 'West'—Into Peacock's Nest," *Variety*, September 18, 2000, 21–28.

26. See Battles and Hilton-Morrow, "Gay Characters"; Shugart, "Reinventing."

27. Shugart and Waggoner, *Making Camp*.

28. A. J. Jacobs, "When Gay Men Happen to Straight Women," *Entertainment Weekly*, October 23, 1998, 23.

29. See, e.g., Robert A. Brookey, "A Community like *Philadelphia*," *Western Journal of Communication* 60 (1996): 40–56.

30. See, e.g., Shugart, "Reinventing."

31. Jonathan Bing, "The Metrosexual Mogul," *Variety*, September 8, 2003, 68.

32. E.g., Joshua Gamson, "The Intersection of Gay Street and Straight Street: Shopping, Social Class, and the New Gay Visibility," *Social Thought and Research* 26 (2005): 2–18; Heller, "Taking the Nation"; Sender, "Queens"; Helene A. Shugart, "Mediating Masculinity: The Metrosexual Moment," *Communication and Critical/Cultural Studies*, 5 (2008): 280–300.

33. See, esp., Sender, "Queens."

34. I would venture, too, that representations of lesbianism not articulated for the male gaze may be more transgressive for mainstream audiences than representations of gay male sexuality, which after all does not necessarily threaten male sexual prowess and access.

35. McGuigan, "Cultural Policy" and "The Cultural Public Sphere."

8
Citizenship, Freedom, and the Family
Public Access through Private Modalities

John M. Sloop

> Public and private life have always been mobile, situational, flickering and fragmented. We focus on automobility and information technology as two key elements of modernity that have ambivalent effects on cultures of democracy.
>
> —Mimi Sheller and John Urry, "Mobile Transformations of 'Public' and 'Private' Life"

During the spring of 2005, early childhood education specialist Mindy Holohan was traveling with her family of four on a road trip to visit her children's grandparents in Chicago. Midway through the trip, Holohan notes, her six-year-old daughter looked out her window and noticed a "rectangular box of light floating in mid-air, flashes of color darting across its surface—foreign yet familiar."[1] After observing that the television in the passing car "looked like magic," the child and her mother began playing a game of "How many TVs can we find in cars?" Later, as her daughter fell asleep, Holohan found herself with a growing sense of anxiety as she thought about the presence of portable televisions and DVD players in automobiles. It was not the threat to physical safety that primarily concerned Holohan—although she does mention the "sacred reverence" we each should have while driving—but rather the threat it represented to her family's (and other families') social dynamics.

After recalling the road trips she had taken as a child with her father, Holohan observed that only in the "sacred space" of the car's interior had she ever felt able to ask her father life's "big questions." In effect, Holohan mused, not only would such mobile media make ubiquitous what should be dosed out in small portions, but they would ultimately lead to the disappearance of a sublime arena for family interaction and "informal education." Holohan warns us that driving should never be equated with sitting on the living room couch as even a drive through the neighborhood provides "an opportunity to glimpse our environment outside of ourselves, to reflect on an experience that is uniquely human."[2] The space of mobility is here an arena worthy of argument.

Holohan's essay, to the degree that it is an example of a genre of reflections on the value and use of portable DVD players—especially as used in cars—is significant in a number of ways. First, on perhaps the most basic level, the article is a representative anecdote of the general cultural anxiety that consistently accompanies the growing use of any new medium (or new use of an existing medium). As Douglas Thomas and Marita Sturken put it, new communication technologies and new uses of existing technologies have been historically accompanied by both utopian claims concerning how they will improve our shared human condition and dystopian fears "that actual human connection has been irretrievably lost."[3]

More significantly, however, and I will pursue this concern throughout the chapter, Holohan's comments represent one side of a public debate over media use that ultimately concerns the contours of what Toby Miller has referred to as the "well-tempered self," that manageable, cultural subject formed and governed through institutions *and* discourses.[4] Given that the automobile and information technologies complicate the meanings of public and private (rather than having a solely destructive influence), as Mimi Sheller and John Urry point out in the opening epigraph, public debates over these technologies are, in effect, also arguments over what it means to be "in public" and how one is to behave publicly. As they are arguments, the meaning, indeed, changes over time.

While television since its inception has been understood as a technology through which individuals come to understand ideological norms and disciplinary images, automobiles—because of the ways they are regulated and disciplined by government rules, institutions, and public discourse—are also implicated in webs of ideological meaning. Hence, both television monitors and automobiles simultaneously act as individualizing prosthetics and purveyors of ideological norms and the regulations of govern-mentality. As a result, the public discussion over the costs/benefits of their joint usage should tell us something about contemporary values and norms of citizenship.

The link between technologies of mobility and communication quite rightly has taken center stage in many contemporary critical projects.[5] As Jeremy Packer puts it, the discourse surrounding mobility and the safety of mobile subjects ultimately concerns the safety, security, and good health of the citizen: "How we conduct ourselves as mobile subjects and how we construct mobilizations is related to how we enable ourselves as citizens, neighbors, and intellectuals."[6] For instance, in a reading of mass mediated representations of the introduction of the Segway, James Hay and Packer think through the ways "communication and transportation have been and are being conjugated and linked" and discussed in political terms of freedom and governance.[7] In general, technologies of physical movement and technologies of communication/information movement (e.g., CB radios, cell phones) are discussed both in terms of individual "freedom" and in terms of public safety/public responsibility. Packer and Hay moreover suggest that investigations of "the portability of media and communication technologies" and "the material attachment of these technologies to technologies of transport" are linked to discussions of what matters to a culture in terms of the well-behaved citizen.[8] Citizenship is not "dead" or in decline; the public is not dead; however, our understanding of each and their interconnections have been altered by public/private modalities. Perhaps we could speak, then, of "modalities of citizenship" rather than citizenship itself.

Given the multiple ties between the cultural understandings of our means of physical mobility (e.g., the way automobiles are understood ideologically and culturally) and metaphoric mobility (e.g., the ways media may be seen as "extensions of humanity" in space and time), the public discourse surrounding the use of television/DVD players within cars leads to discussions about the appropriate behavior of citizens in general. Moreover, given the large degree to which portable and mobile DVD players are utilized by children—highly regulated and protected citizens—it is also the case that the discourse surrounding the use of television/DVD players in cars tells us something about our contemporary expectations of, or battles over, proper child rearing. In effect, by investigating the discourse surrounding portable DVD players in cars, I provide a critical snapshot of our understanding of the appropriate ways in which citizens and budding citizens are expected to employ these particular mediated "prosthetic" devices as well as the ways these prosthetics are seen as shaping their "users." In the spirit of the introduction (by Daniel Brouwer and Robert Asen) to this volume, I want to stress that this snapshot is a framing of the values expected of citizens and their behavior. Moreover, the valence of these values is a mixed bag, encouraging the critic (here, me) to provide a reading that works according to my own concerns about how a collective people should behave.

In short, I am interested in public understandings and expectations of the employment of public modalities, or *mediated access to contemporary cultural ideology*, as a way to understand and take part in the argument over the values being articulated around the citizen/subject. Befitting this volume, I take "modalities" to refer to the individual digital media that we more and more commonly employ to provide access to those meanings and pleasures through which we make sense of our social world and our role as citizens. Like Sheller and Urry, I assume that changing technologies, including automobiles and digital media, neither destroy nor perfect the public sphere (and the citizen) so much as alter it, with the valence of this alteration being a subject of critical debate.

In the following, I first briefly situate my reading of the public discussion of mobile DVD players within historical and epistemological discussions of both television and automobiles within U.S. culture. Contemporary debates have a history that acts as a constraint on how contemporary public meanings can be understood. If we have access to public meanings through these private modalities and come to understand our roles as citizens in part through the use of these modalities, we do so partially by the way we are shaped by their function as prosthetics and partially by the ways these prosthetics are configured in public discourse. Because this configuration has a history, it is crucial that we touch upon that history as part of understanding the present.

Second, I investigate the public discussion through a reading of news reports derived through a database search concerning DVD players in cars.[9] I should stress here that my analysis and the included examples are taken from news reports rather than from advertising copy. While I assume a good degree of crossover between news and advertising that features mobile DVD players for a variety of reasons (e.g., marketing executives are quoted in the news reports, advertising often reflects consumer desires), the discourse I analyze here is drawn solely from news articles about personal, mobile DVD players, as I hope to capture a public sentiment about the technology that represents both adaptive and resistive viewpoints (advertising, of course, would always focus on the benefits of the product).[10] Moreover, I understand the public discussion of these DVD players within the critical framework designated by the term "disciplined mobility," an area of study that assumes that critics might fruitfully read this public discussion as a way of understanding the current struggle over public and private as well as general expectations for proper behavior. While we each have mediated access to contemporary culture, that access itself is not outside the bounds of ideology. The ways in which our movement—literal and metaphorical—is shaped and disciplined in multiple ways is one of the factors in the way we come to understand the world and our "selves."

The Automobile/Television Nexus

While there are countless histories of both television (as a medium, as a technology, and as an industry) and automobiles (as medium, industry, and design), I am most interested here in those which help explain the ways both media have been discussed publicly. Such background highlights the constraints now placed on the public discussion of either and on the nexus between the two. For this purpose, two of the most useful accounts of the history of television are Cecelia Tichi's *Electronic Hearth* and Lynn Spigel's *Welcome to the Dreamhouse.*[11] Two able and concise U.S. cultural histories of the automobile are Virginia Scharff's gendered history *Taking the Wheel* and Mark Foster's *A Nation on Wheels.*[12] While it is not my intent to recount full histories of the discourse concerning either technology, this summary explores the constraints that shape our current understandings.

Tichi suggests that the television has been consistently discussed in terms of how it was situated within heteronormative domestic settings. For example, early representations of the television in both advertising copy and news reports highlight the way broadcasts helped gather families together in the after-work/after-school evenings, offering a sanctuary where family members could reconnect.[13] The value of the family as an advertising theme proved so strong historically that ads concerning television hardware—especially portable sets—had to explicitly work against the possibility that television might evacuate its role as the "social hearth" of the family.[14] Indeed, Tichi argues that individual uses of the television were consistently explained as being for temporary use, a setup that would allow an eventual return to peaceful domesticity (e.g., couples had two different televisions but were physically together; the television set was with the entire family on a camping trip).[15]

In addition, marketers went to great lengths to suggest that broadcast content would serve, rather than disrupt, the "family atmosphere." Hence, when advertising copy featured a single person viewing television, she/he was illustrated as consuming images of domestic situations rather than images of, for example, war or violence: the single viewer "has to be shown as an individual ready to go back home, not as a murderous renegade individualist."[16]

Second, Spigel suggests that because social critics also expressed concern that television would turn "active citizens into passive consumers," advertisers worked to represent television as beneficial to civic life and to the physical health of the consumer (e.g., viewers were represented as being "on the go," mentally and physically active, even while utilizing the television).[17] Significantly, Spigel and others referred to this representation of television as "privatized mobility" in that it configured the medium-consumer relationship as one that allowed one's "window to the world" to provide company regardless of surrounding activities.[18]

Finally, a major concern expressed about television was its influence on children. While discussed by social critics as providing "brain candy" or as the "boob tube," advertisers worked to articulate the child consumer/viewer as "actively engaged with the on-screen image" or as "a toddler with a baccalaureate degree."[19]

Overall, such representations helped television's acceptance within American ideological formations, countering critical concerns that it would destroy dominant values. Various binarisms—domestic heteronormative family versus individualistic homoeroticism, physical activism versus physical passivity, mind candy for passive children versus educational medium for actively growing minds—act as constraints on the ways we continue to understand television and its relationship with or effect on different forms of behavior. To put it in Lynn Spigel's terms, although the public discussion of television historically worked to glorify a changing conception of a "new space age mobile family," it could only do so, only be acceptable, by being disciplined to other acceptable ideological frameworks which "harken back to residual ideas about gender roles and the division of spheres."[20] Current public arguments did not arise out of thin air; the constraints of past discussion weigh heavily on our current understandings.

Similarly, the history of public arguments over the automobile in U.S. culture are also constrained by historic ideological tensions. While dealing primarily with the early introduction of the automobile, Scharff notes that the automobile was "born in a masculine manger and when women sought to claim its power, they invaded a male domain."[21] As a result, similar binarisms are drawn forth: the distinction between public and private spaces, the gendered meanings attached with these spaces, the articulations between masculinity and functionality as well as femininity and the aesthetic. Hence, automobiles also have been discussed consistently in terms which upheld heteronormative, bigendered assumptions (e.g., what men and women differently "need" from a car in terms of power, space, and aesthetics).[22]

Covering a longer temporal range and a wider variety of values, Mark Foster highlights the many ways the automobile altered the U.S. landscape, as well as the way the U.S. ideological landscape shaped the meaning of the automobile. In Foster's eyes, not only did the automobile make the rather obvious changes of increasing the distances people could cover and freeing individuals from mass transit schedules, but it also created new geographic spaces (e.g., suburbs) and led to the standardization of many products (e.g., hotels, fast food) and the creation of new forms of consumerism (e.g., malls). What makes Foster's work so fascinating, however, is that while his overall project illustrates the multiple ways in which "the automobile has been an incredibly powerful, aggressive shaper of American culture,"[23] his argument is traced out within an ideological matrix in which similar concerns are repeatedly struggled over (e.g., gender binarisms, public/private spaces, public safety versus private freedoms). While the introduction of the automobile shifts social relations, it does so within a system of meanings that shape how the automobile and its purposes may be understood.

Like our understanding of the television, then, we rehearse on a cultural level our concerns with the overall influence these technologies have on those issues with which we are most concerned. As a result, while we may see both televisions and automobiles as prosthetics, in a McLuhanesque fashion, we cannot overlook the ways in which existing ideological arguments shape our understanding of the prosthetic *in use*. This is a complex and somewhat fluid discussion of meanings at the level of the body and at the level of ideology. The meaning of the individual citizen, then, and his/her connection to the social whole (i.e., the meaning of "public" and "private") are shaped by both the use of prosthetics and the public "meaning" of this usage. As Brouwer and Asen observe in the introduction to this volume, this turn to understanding the ways in which the process and medium of communication are valenced has far too often been slighted in communication studies research.

The introduction of a medium within a medium, the DVD/television inside the car, is an almost ideal location for the raising of ideological hackles. As each of us begins seeing increasing numbers of video monitors in passing automobiles, we engage in, or overhear, a number of conversations that concern such topics as the safety of viewing while driving and the potential interruptions to "family time" during trips. In asking such questions—as individuals, as experts on children, as family counselors, as government regulators—we are asking questions that impact how we behave as citizens, as well-mannered subjects, and how we engage with each other. Investigating such questions is especially important if, as Sheller and Urry observe, automobility and communication technologies have interconnected ambivalent effects on cultures of democracy. To investigate them together—and to shape this investigation through a critical reading—is to shape "the future of citizenship, democratic possibility."[24]

Disciplining "Private" Modalities: "Public" Concerns and Citizenship

In their discussion of technē in the introduction to this volume, Brouwer and Asen observe that public modalities invoke a tension between agency and structure. The public discussions regarding the employment of the hybrid DVD-automobile play themselves out along this tension, and it is along this tension that I will focus my attention. In what follows, I will take public discussions of onboard DVD players—personal entryways or modalities to larger cultural values—as evidence of a larger discussion of the concerns surrounding the mobile citizen and the specific ways in which we, as citizens rather than lawmakers, create our own governmental gaze on one another.[25] Ultimately, I will show in turn three major themes emerging in discussions of these DVD players, each of which plays out the individual's "right" to his or her own pleasures versus structural constraints on those impulses. First, the discourse surrounding mobile DVD players concerns the physical safety of the drivers, with direct concern being expressed for the safety of other drivers and pedestrians. Second, the discourse displays a modality of citizenship which is defined in part by a logic of friction-free choice of media content, technologies, and private modalities. Finally, the modality of citizenship articulated around these portable DVD players presents an argument about the "healthy" family that assumes a traditional, heteronormative configuration regardless of the positive or negative valence given the technology itself. In short, these themes provide us with access to the discourses by which the "well-tempered self" (as well as "well-tempered democracy") is being negotiated in a changing media environment.

Road Trip Dangers

Historically, new technologies are articulated as potentially dangerous in multiple ways—physically, intellectually, spiritually, or socially. The link between mobility and state regulation exists, Jeremy Packer argues, because "ultimately, it is the conduct of the individual, not devotion and loyalty, that strengthens the state, through increased production, longevity, and population growth."[26] Because citizens have access to different types of mobility, it is necessary for "govern-mentality" that the citizen be held in place in particular ways in order to remain productive and healthy.[27] Hence, "the goal of governing is not to simply guard against too much freedom, but to produce the type of freedom that accords with the expansive demands of culture and economy."[28] As a result, the very idea of learning to be a good driver cannot be fully separated from the notion of learning to be a good citizen, a good neighbor.[29] As I will illustrate here, we find that one theme worked out in this discourse is the balance between the structures/regulations of the state and the freedom of the individual. With the citizen subject configured as cyborg or posthuman, with the automobile as a prosthetic of spatial mobility and the DVD as "window on the world," the discourse under study here concerns structural/legal restraints on cyborg/posthuman agency.[30]

Many of these concerns are generalized by vague fears of how DVD players might distract drivers. From a *York Daily Record* article observing the ways in which having DirecTV in a car would endanger everyone on the road to a local Washington advice columnist insisting that DVD players are a distraction, a general consensus holds that the devices are a physical danger and should be regulated by law and by social censure.[31] These general concerns are accompanied by numerous citations of laws concerning DVD players and television screens and their placement beyond the eyesight of the driver. For example, the *Buffalo News* reports that it is illegal in New York to have a TV screen within the drivers' eyesight, as does the *Modesto Bee* concerning California law, while the *Daily Herald* and the *Telegraph-Herald* warn drivers about new laws enacted in Illinois.[32]

These reports are often accompanied by narratives illustrating the dangers that await those who utilize such technologies or those who encounter others who do. For instance, reporter John Bonfatti of the *Buffalo News* discusses a number of accidents that have occurred as the result of "media distractions": after reporting the death of a bicyclist at the hands of a text-messaging seventeen-year-old, Bonfatti discusses a local accident in which witnesses saw a driver weaving across the road as he looked at a map program on his front seat laptop.[33] In a separate case in New York, driver David McKay was convicted in a deadly crash in which he was driving an SUV and lost control, running into another car. While McKay was convicted in part because he was speeding and smoking marijuana, articles highlight that the SUV contained a DVD player which was showing the movie, "Meet the Fockers."[34] That is, rather than one aspect of the accident, the DVD player is the focus point as cause of the accident. Finally, reporter John Patterson highlights the irony of a case in which an Alaska man was charged with murder after his truck crossed the centerline and hit an oncoming car, killing all occupants, because the driver was watching the movie *Road Trip* rather than watching the road.[35] While this same essay notes, as do others, that "no scientific studies have been done on the dangers of watching TV and driving," it simultaneously highlights the activity as dangerous, as life threatening, above and beyond other distractions.

In this line of argument, then, the citizen subject is understood as impaired by the prosthetic. While the choices the mobile DVD player allows are articulated to the ideal of individual freedom, as I will show below, it is an agency that seemingly must be contained. Hence, while the automobile/DVD nexus is one step toward the McLuhanesque dream of extensions in space and time, this extension is placed in tension with the discipline of the citizen subject to remain productive and clearly identified within a set space.

Friction-Free Capitalism, or to Be American Is to Have Full Agency

In 1981, Jean Baudrillard observed that the combination of growth of digital technologies and the cultural logic of advertising (i.e., advertising not as an industry or practice but as a logic through which capitalist economies communicate) was leading to a cultural condition in which consumption in and of itself gets reconfigured as a political act. Hence, he prophesized a metaphoric merging of the phrases, "I vote, I participate, I am present, I am concerned" with "I buy, I consume, I take pleasure."[36] In effect, the proliferation of symbols and of simulation encourages a flattening of meaning to such a degree that the ability to have a variety of consumer choices becomes equalized as a political "freedom of choice." Citizenship, in short, becomes slowly equated with consumption—both symbolic and material—rather than with political action as more traditionally understood. As Toby Miller would have it, "the decisive postmodern guarantee falls in the area of providing access to the technologies of communication as crucial integers" in our contemporary understandings of citizenship and freedom.[37] Fittingly, then, one of the primary realms of discourse concerning portable DVD players is the way in which consumers praise their provision of a multitude of "choices" and "freedoms," or radical agency—both in terms of content choices and in terms of how one chooses to spend one's time. As I will illustrate, this logic equates choice and freedom of symbolic consumption with choice and freedom of "beliefs," and this equation is one that should give us pause.

In something of a popular culture reemergence of the "friction free capitalism" predicted by Bill Gates, much of the discussion about the benefits of portable DVD/media players focuses on freedom or agency—the freedom to consume images that one wants, when one wants, and where one wants.[38] For example, Peter Green, general manager of Intel's Extended Computing Division, notes in a report about newly marketed mobile media players that "just as VCRs gave consumers the *freedom* to view content when they want to, personal media players will give consumers the *freedom* to consume content where they want to."[39] These claims of freedom are articulated specifically to "America" in a news report that observes that the Sony corporation has installed portable DVD players on the next Space Shuttle *Discovery*, making it "the first in space, playing movies and music for the three astronauts," illustrating that DVD players can be used in *any* location in which consumers find themselves. Moreover, the articulation of seamless access with "citizenship" and "democracy" is solidified when the report observes that Sony is holding a contest in which those who purchase mobile DVD players will be allowed to "cast their vote on the contents of the first-ever DVD library in space."[40]

In addition to the articulation of mobile players with freedom in terms of mobility, they are also articulated with freedom in terms of content. For example, an essay in *Business Wire* observes that newer versions of personal media players will not only keep travelers entertained but will do so by holding an entire months' worth of "viewing and listening pleasure," assuring that travelers will never be bored.[41] Similarly, the *Houston Chronicle* observes that in the not so distant future, on "planes, trains and buses, we will see passengers carrying personal media players and watching several weeks' worth of favorite TV shows."[42] As if underlining the vision of a cyborg planet, Rudy Provoost, CEO of Philips Consumer Electronics, points out that the personal media players are the "next step in the realization of the connected planet, our vision of a world where consumers can access content anywhere, anytime."[43]

The articulation of geographic and content access to freedom is often directly made rather than implied. One headline observes that personal DVD players will give travelers "the freedom to take their favorite TV shows with them wherever they go."[44] Similarly, Seattle advertising consultant Phillip Torrone notes in the *Wall Street Journal* that what he loves about the portable DVDs is that they allow you to be free from "hostage time," giving you the freedom to "watch what you want, when you want and where you want."[45] I pause here to note that if we see mobile DVD players as the antidote to hostage time (i.e., time during which we generally can neither work nor play because we are in transit), the mobile DVD player becomes one means by which we allow even those spaces where we are alone and in transit to become useful or productive spaces, at least to the individual.

This wording concerning temporal and spatial access is repeated elsewhere in almost identical terms: in a discussion of a new TiVo based personal entertainment center, the author of a *PR Newswire* essay observes that the portable equipment—good for use in cars on long trips—will allow consumers to "watch what they want, when they want, and, now, where they want."[46] Ken Lowe, vice president of Strategic Marketing for Sigma Designs, sees the usage of personal media players as not simply a matter of atomized, dispersed consumer choices across myriad particular instances but as an index of a shift in the very structure of consumption itself: "With an endless choice of video, audio, photo, and other media, which consumers are collecting, products that conveniently access the entertainment library are quickly becoming a *necessity*."[47]

Again, the portable media centers, especially when tied to travel, provide a dream of a consumer world in which desires are "friction free"—access to product simultaneous with product desire. In the discursive world concerning the portable media center, much like in the promises of the Internet, one transcends the boundaries of time and space to new degrees, grabbing access to entertainment where one wishes and with no delay. Let me be clear: the logic of freedom, the logic of choice, is not simply about choice for the group of individuals in an automobile; it is about choice for each individual—truly private modalities. To wit: "Portable DVD players with tiny screens may not be good enough anymore. At the recent Consumer Electronics Show in Las Vegas, Panasonic showed off a dual-drive player with an 8-inch screen that will simultaneously let one back-seat passenger listen to a CD while another watches a movie."[48] Articulated with America and with freedom, consumption of images becomes a necessary right rather than a privilege; consumption of symbols, private access to public culture, and one's private modality are part of the meaning of the American citizen. Connected to the discourse on safety, then, this description of the free and expansive citizen is disciplined by the discourse of the safe and productive citizen. In brief, and in the language of values, the discourse concerning safety asks us to see our fellow citizens and ourselves as beholden to the safety of each other for the functioning of the community (its workers, its educators, etc.) as a whole.

Heteronormative Bliss

In addition to the tensions between freedom/access and constraint, the portable DVD player—especially as it is articulated with(in) the automobile—reaffirms the priority and value of the (heteronormative) family. Much as the histories of television and automobiles have always concerned the family and its influence on the health of the family, the discourse currently surrounding the ongoing evolution/intermingling of this medium within a medium raises similar themes. Regardless of the final outcome of debates over the proper use of these players, the concern raised focuses on the best route toward maintaining a physically and psychologically healthy family. These debates themselves play on the structure/agency tension. Either families make their own decisions within the context of the car as home, or we provide ideological, educational, or regulatory judgments of their usage of DVD players. It is again the dream of posthuman freedom, constrained by citizen safety.

Historically, Cecelia Tichi observes that the early use of the metaphor "electronic hearth" for the television signified its articulation within the domestic sphere. However, given that so many viewers began consuming television on an individual basis, television, especially to the degree that it was portable, was seen as a threat to the social order: "When positioned against the social hearth, individualist television can threaten the ideology of that hearth, contradicting it, betraying it and, at the same time, exposing private individual television as selfish, egoistic, . . . and, most disconcerting of all, subversive."[49] Likewise, while arguing that the mix with family and gender roles is far more complicated—both reifying and challenging gender/domestic roles—Lynn Spigel notes that the portable television and its representations offered a challenge to how the family would be constituted, as well as the proper ways to raise children and structure a family.[50] The discursive situation is further complicated by the fact that the automobile, given its ability to move people from the domestic sphere and into the public sphere (and, indeed, to create new spheres), coupled with its links with masculinity, always threatened to trouble gender, sexuality, and the heteronormative family.[51] As a result, discourse about the automobile consistently disciplined it into the realm of traditional gender and domestic roles.

The most interesting ideological aspects of the automobile and DVD player in the realm of gender, then, derive in part from the fact that both technologies/prosthetics have been read historically as potentially troubling to, or supportive of, domesticity. While automobiles can literally rearrange where bodies can be, the television has been consistently articulated as a danger to the domestic sphere to the degree that it diverts children's attention and divides family members along different programming interests. Given that the portable DVD player/television is generally positioned to be viewed from the backseat, the majority of domestic issues raised about the portable DVD player center on the occasion of the "family trip." As I will illustrate, discussions about the use of DVD players on family trips focus largely on a cultural argument over the "best interests of the family" in terms of safety and family "togetherness." To be clear, in every case, the family articulated within this discussion is a heteronormative family; the car is potentially a space for traveling domestic bliss. The DVD player's role in creating or damaging this bliss is argued along the lines of either excessive disruption of the family or agitating lack (i.e., if there is no activity in a car, without the DVD players, families engage in fighting).[52]

On the one hand, then, as with the narrative that begins this chapter, parents and interest groups focus on the portable media player as disruptive to the family sphere in that excessive television keeps individual members of the family from interacting. For example, and echoing Mindy Holohan, parent Tammy Zmyewski notes in the *Chicago Sun-Times* that when her three sons, aged seven through twelve, asked for a DVD player in their car, she and her husband decided against installing one because "children don't interact with each other or anybody else when they're watching a movie. We wouldn't have people singing. We wouldn't have the jokes. I like the togetherness."[53] Similarly, psychologist Harriet Ainbinder, while endorsing the players for some lengthier trips, worries that the DVD players separate "parents from children. . . . It's just one more place where there is not a relationship."[54] An essay in the *Wisconsin State Journal* refers to the portable DVD players as "mobile pacifiers" and observes that many parents curse the very idea of the players as "another example of mass media infiltrating life's every moment."[55] Similarly, Bram Groeneveld decided against purchasing a DVD system for his car, "fearing it would undermine conversation and sightseeing. 'It's a one-way medium with a child staring at a screen. There's no interaction or looking down the road.'"[56] Finally, Nancy Dowling also opted out of the use of a DVD player because she feared it would put an end to the "cocooney" place to talk about parent-child issues that the car had been in the past.[57]

Examples of such discourse are so vast that one begins to get the sense that the car has become a more valued "domestic" family sphere than the traditional home. Hence, a *Lincoln Journal Star* essay about the DVD players observes that "parenting purists may frown upon all this mind-numbing gadgetry" as it "stops all our family communication."[58] More pointedly, the *Spokesman Review* provides a forum to think about the value of the DVD players in cars, providing quotations from a number of parents concerning why they have chosen not to put the players in their automobiles. A sampling reveals that "kids don't look outside the car. *It's just like they're at home.* It isn't an adventure" and, more sardonically, "no longer are children made to suffer through countless miles of endless natural beauty."[59]

Child care experts are often drawn in as experts on the use of DVD players in cars. Tonya Altmann, a board member of the American Academy of Pediatrics, provides a prescription in which DVD players might be used for thirty minutes on a two-hour car trip but not used by children under two.[60] Others noted that the players harmed the chances for "serendipitous family bonding" and for reading.[61] Finally, Harriet Shaklee, a University of Idaho family development specialist, is invoked to observe that the DVD players cost families an opportunity for conversation.[62] Even if we ignore the implication that such parents have seemingly turned the home over to television sets (i.e., "It's just like home"), we see here an emphasis on family and a representation of DVD players as dangerous to family health.

There are a number of critical nodal points around the configuration of family implied in these articulations that demand attention. First, we can note the ways in which healthy "family behavior" is defined primarily by conversation and television/DVD viewing is posited as a solo experience, something to be experienced in isolation in that parents and children do not seem to be able to watch and discuss the shows positioned in these examples. The television/DVD player is positioned metaphorically as a consuming/controlling medium. Second, when parents note that "it's just like they're at home," the home is positioned as a location of familial dissolution. That is, each time one makes reference to the automobile as the last space for family interaction, we notice that the "home" is being articulated as absent that status.

On the other hand, but also supportive of the value of the heteronormative family, portable DVD players are simultaneously understood as a means by which families might maintain domestic tranquility during long trips, a tranquility that allows a safer trip and a more satisfying domesticity after the trip is complete. In this articulation, as a culture, we could use more DVD players rather than fewer. For example, in a *New York Times* essay entitled "Boredom Busters for the Youngest Travelers," Patrick McGeehan discusses his decision to purchase a portable DVD player for travel with his children.[63] After mulling over a number of humorous alternatives to the DVD player (e.g., providing his children with sedatives, tying them into body bags), McGeehan suggests that the safest legal means for keeping his children quiet, comfortable, and happy for long periods of time is a portable DVD player. The player, he notes, allows the children to arrive "rested and tension-free." Moreover, McGeehan observes that, after his first use of the DVD player, the benefits to domestic tranquility were so obvious that he would never hesitate to use one again. Similarly, in an essay in the *Austin American Statesman*, Vasin Douglas notes that the mobile DVD system's effect on children will lead to family "driving bliss."[64]

Similarly, Patrick Beach provides a rather compelling but humorous list of the reasons he has chosen to purchase a DVD for his car.[65] Beach, too, positions the DVD player as a metaphorical sedative for the children, one that ultimately benefits the entire family. To those who claim that DVDs in a car are a bad idea, Beach counters that "stopping at every minor emergency clinic on the route for sutures is worse." Indeed, drawing on gendered norms, Beach observes that the "natural state of boys is violence—dirty, vicious, senseless violence," but the DVD player acts as an "onboard digital anesthetic," keeping his sons calm and safe.[66] This same theme emerges repeatedly in the discourse about the portable DVD players. For example, in the *Modesto Bee*, Patrick Giblin quotes AAA spokesperson Sean Comey observing that, in addition to "safety equipment" such as a first aid kit, parents should consider bringing along a DVD player in car trips because "any parent knows the true value of 90 minutes of silence."[67] Moreover, Doug Erickson of the *Wisconsin State Journal* refers to the players as "mobile pacifiers" and a gift "from the parenting gods" that keeps children from fighting and hence maintains family happiness.[68] Similarly, James Cummings of the *Dayton Daily News* observes that the DVD players are "safety features" for a family in the sense that not only is there no bickering but, due to the use of headphones, passengers can quietly enjoy the players without disturbing the drivers.[69] Finally, Erin Andersen of the *Lincoln Journal Star* observes that portable DVD players put an end to backseat bickering and fighting, with hundreds of miles of peace, while parent Nicole Christie observes that she and her husband will never return to the pre-DVD days as, with the DVD, they "usually don't hear a peep out of [their son] unless he laughs."[70]

A quick perusal of a number of other essays reaffirms this point. Hence, *Pittsburgh Post-Gazette* writer Mackenzie Carpenter observes that on a recent trip, his children watched a movie, laughed, "and never complained about the flat landscape," allowing a happier family trip than would normally be the case.[71] Cynthia L. Miller of the *Grand Rapids Press* refers to the DVD player as a "modern little marvel" and provides a story of a recent trip in which her children sat patiently and quietly in the backseat of their car.[72] Michael Kitschka, a car salesperson, notes in the same essay that the DVD players help kids "settle down" and hence operate as a way to help the entire family maintain "peace of mind."[73] Parent Holly Sims tells the *Spokesman Review* that she could not imagine life again without the portable DVD players because "it saves our sanity," while parent Kathy Altieri observes that, after remembering horrible fighting and bickering on car trips, she finds that DVD players are ultimately helpful because "anything to keep the peace and quiet during a long car trip is welcome."[74] In nearly every case, we see memories of car trips when children's screaming and fighting ruined harmonious family trips, followed by the DVD player being prescribed as a route by which peace and harmony might be maintained.

Here, then, whether discussed as a danger or an aid to the family, the assumption of the family—and the idea of a peaceful and talkative family—remains a commonsense priority. In both negative and positive evaluations, the primary concern is the maintenance of a fruitful and peaceful family within the context of new media technology. While there are disagreements about how a family should conduct itself while traveling, there is no disagreement that the family—in every case a heteronormative family—should ultimately be engaged in peaceful conversation. The tension is between the freedom of the family and the safety/protection of the citizen.

Conclusion

While there are a number of specific conclusions that one might draw from this case study, I would like to begin with the most general: a renewed call for critical work that refocuses on public disciplining of mobility. James Hay has recently noted that "the mobility and portability of communication technology require, perhaps more than ever, an analytic that recognizes the rituals of communication as maps that move and are danced."[75] In effect, we need to think not only of the ways in which mobile media are prosthetics but also of the ways in which our discussions of these technologies are part of the cultural communication ritual by which we understand ourselves and our relations to one another. These "private modalities" and the ways we discuss them are routes by which we both understand citizenship and participate in publics. That is, these cases provide a clean lens on both "media determined" changes and ideological/discursive ones.

Second, discussions of the meanings of new media technologies are disciplined in both senses of the word: the discussions not only limit certain understandings of these technologies and of our desires as citizens but are also productive maps of our desires and roles as citizens (in this formulation, after all, they provide access to contemporary cultural ideology). As Sheller and Urry observe, "rather than a straightforward colonization of the public sphere by private interests, there is, we argue, a more complex de-territorialization of publics and privates, each constantly shifting and being performed in rapid flashes within less anchored spaces."[76] One effective way for us to think through the meaning of contemporary citizenship, then, is to think about the ways we discuss the safety and productivity of communication and transportation technologies, the way this new space allows new performances. If we return here to Toby Miller's conception of the "well-tempered self,"[77] we can find the discussions around mobile DVD players conjuring a citizen encouraged to act upon his/her citizenship through the pursuit of unlimited consumption and to do so within the context of family. While there is always space for change within these categories, they do set a theme through which change must begin.

It may be useful here to also tie this point to Robert Asen's "discourse theory of citizenship."[78] Herewith, Asen, building largely from a Deweyan version of pragmatism that would fit comfortably with Foucauldian discourse theory, articulates citizenship as a fluid and quotidian enactment that emerges in the tension between "individual action" and the existing medium of ideology. One of the points Asen stresses, and one with which I fully concur, is that such a theory of citizenship problematizes current claims that social involvement has declined. Rather, in that citizenship is not an essence but a discourse, we are all "always already" involved, although our modes of involvement change. Taking such a perspective encourages us, as critics, to think about the changing meaning of citizenship rather than to presume its decline.

Third, while I have no interest in questioning the value of any form of supportive family, the fact that only one form of family was represented in these narratives—narratives that, indeed, center on the health of American families—is telling of the ways in which commonsense understandings of families work as supports for the same notions of family largely supported by governmental policy. Implicitly siding with legal definitions of families which would exclude, say, gay couples with children, the discussion of the DVD players endorses heteronormativity. When, in his discussion of the contemporary citizen, Miller reminds us that "cultural criticism is a mode of self-formation inscribing incompleteness—but potential for something more—in an inexorable relationship that is the touchstone of the claim made by the humanities to manufacture civic subjects,"[79] we are reminded in this case that this "something more" may well be an expansive notion of family. If the governmentality found at the nexus of communication technologies and transportation is one locus where productive and safe citizenry is defined, it is a location that emphasizes the stability of heteronormative families.

Finally, and as I stressed earlier, it seems imperative that cultural critics continue to probe the deterioration of the democratic space in which "freedom" has come to mean freedom of product/entertainment choice rather than freedom of political behavior. In his recent discussion of disciplined mobility, Jeremy Packer observes that "media can be and are used to aid in the creation of very undemocratic systems of meaning and communities."[80] While I am not suggesting that "media" are creating "undemocratic systems," and while I do not wish to take up Cass Sunstein's or Robert Putnam's concerns that contemporary technologies lead to a deterioration of the public sphere, I am concerned about the ways in which the discussions surrounding these technologies reinforce the notion of consumer choices over political choices.[81] Regardless of contestations we may have concerning ontology, I would like to join with Cass Sunstein in opposing "a conception that sees consumption choices by individuals as the very embodiment of freedom."[82] When we—as cultural critics—allow ongoing public disputes to take place in which freedom is tightly articulated to freedom of consumption, we are complicit in affirming definitions that work against change outside of the idea of increased consumption and, as we have seen, increased calls for regulation of that consumption.

Notes

1. Mindy Holohan, "Portable DVDs Intrude on Drive Time," *Grand Rapids Review*, June 12, 2005, C1.
2. Holohan, "Portable DVDs."

3. Douglas Thomas and Marita Sturken, "Introduction: Technological Visions and the Rhetoric of the New," in *Technological Visions: The Hopes and Fears that Shape New Technologies*, ed. Marita Sturken, Douglas Thomas, and Sandra J. Ball-Rokeach (Philadelphia: Temple University Press, 2004), 3. See Langdon Winner's chapter, "Sow's Ears from Silk Purses: The Strange Alchemy of Technological Visions," in the same collection, for utopian views of new technologies.

4. Toby Miller, *The Well-Tempered Self: Citizenship, Culture, and the Postmodern Subject* (Baltimore: Johns Hopkins University Press, 1993), ix.

5. In a number of important works, Jeremy Packer and James Hay (separately and jointly) investigate some of these links between automobility, communication media, and freedom/citizenship. Drawing from a similar Foucauldian tradition, they, like Toby Miller in his investigation of the "well-tempered self," are interested in both the rules and regulations created by government institutions and the technologies of "self-governance" through which individuals recognize their concerns and behavior as shared with that of the public. See Miller, *Well-Tempered*, xxi. Another important and influential take on "mobility studies"—indeed, an attempt to create said field of study—is John Urry, *Mobilities* (Malden, MA: Polity Press, 2007).

6. Jeremy Packer, "Disciplining Mobility: Governing and Safety," in *Foucault, Cultural Studies, and Governmentality*, ed. Jack Bratich, Jeremy Packer, and Cameron McCarthy (Albany: State University of New York Press, 2003), 157.

7. James Hay and Jeremy Packer, "Crossing the Media(-n): Auto-mobility, the Transported Self and Technologies of Freedom," in *MediaSpace: Scale and Culture in a Media Age*, ed. Nick Couldry and Anna McCarthy (New York: Routledge, 2004), 211.

8. Hay and Packer, "Crossing," 212. Similarly, Toby Miller points to road/traffic signs as one way that the citizen is protected (*Well-Tempered*, 212).

9. I utilized LexisNexis and coupled "DVD" with "Car," "Automobile," and "Travel," providing me with over fifty articles.

10. To clarify, while I realize that a number of resistant or alternative values and understandings of citizenship are always present, I am interested in the dominant or mainstream representations, as defined by the database choices I have made.

11. Cecelia Tichi, *Electronic Hearth: Creating an American Television Culture* (New York: Oxford University Press, 1992); Lynn Spigel, *Welcome to the Dreamhouse: Popular Media and Postwar Suburbs* (Durham, NC: Duke University Press, 2001).

12. Virginia Scharff, *Taking the Wheel: Women and the Coming of the Motor Car* (Alburquerque: University of New Mexico Press, 1991); Mark Foster, *A Nation on Wheels: The Automobile Culture in America since 1945* (Belmont, CA: Wadworth/Thompson Learning, 2003).

13. Tichi, *Electronic Hearth*, 48; Spigel, *Welcome*, 117.

14. Tichi, *Electronic Hearth*, 63.

15. Moreover, as Spigel stresses, advertising had to subtly indicate that television

would not be used for autoerotic behavior, again so that it would not interfere with domestic tranquility. Tichi, *Electronic Hearth*, 63; Spigel, *Welcome*, 54.

16. Tichi, *Electronic Hearth*, 83.

17. Spigel, *Welcome*, 4, 97–98.

18. Ibid., 121.

19. Spigel, *Welcome*, 104, 192.

20. Spigel, *Welcome*, 134–35.

21. Scharff, *Taking*, 13.

22. Ibid., 122–38.

23. Foster, *A Nation*, viii.

24. Mimi Sheller and John Urry, "Mobile Transformations of 'Public' and 'Private' Life," *Theory, Culture & Society* 20 (2003): 122.

25. Utilizing Proquest and Lexis/Nexis, I put together a number of combinations of terms such as "automobile," "car," "portable media," "DVD players," etc., and was able to find over one hundred articles concerning the use of portable DVD players in automobiles in the United States.

26. Packer, "Disciplining," 136.

27. For a robust discussion of govern-mentality that situates the arguments within communication studies, see Ronald Walter Greene, "Another Materialist Rhetoric," *Critical Studies in Media Communication* 15 (1998): 21–40.

28. Packer, "Disciplining," 140.

29. Ibid., 153. See also Albert W. Whitney, *Man and the Motorcar* (New York: J. L. Little and Company, 1936).

30. Packer, "Disciplining," 157.

31. "Popular High-tech Mods," *York Daily Record*, May 21, 2006, 3/07; Jeff Switzer, "The Car's No Place to Watch Television," *Daily Herald*, March 20, 2006, B1. See also Ben Van der Meer, "DVD Players Entertaining to Distraction on the Road," *Modesto Bee*, February 27, 2006, A1.

32. John F. Bonfatti, "Risk of Driving While Distracted," *Buffalo News*, February 27, 2006, A1; Van der Meer, "DVD," A1; see also Bob Keefe, "Wired on Wheels," *Palm Beach Post*, January 29, 2006, 4F; John Patterson, "State Says Turn Off That Television in the Front Seat," *Daily Herald*, November 27, 2005, B1; "New Illinois Laws Ready to Take Effect," *Telegraph-Herald*, January 1, 2006, A11.

33. Bonfatti, "Risk," A1.

34. Bob Gardinier, "Driver Convicted in Deadly Crash," *Times Union*, December 17, 2005, B3; see also Bob Gardinier, "Teen Charged in Fatal Crash Testifies," *Times Union*, December 13, 2005, B7.

35. Patterson, "State," B1.

36. Jean Baudrillard, *Simulacra and Simulations* (Ann Arbor: University of Michigan Press, 1994), 91.

37. Miller, *Well-Tempered*, 134.

38. Bill Gates, *The Road Ahead* (New York: Penguin, 1996), 180.

39. "Intel Corporation," *M2 Presswire*, January 10, 2003, 1 (emphasis added).

40. "Sony Takes One Small Step for Man, One Giant Leap for DVD," *Business Wire*, February 15, 2001, 1.

41. "PQI Corporation's New mPack Tops Portable Multimedia Player Field with More Formats, Higher Resolution, Live TV Recording," *Business Wire*, January 5, 2005, 1. See also "Philips and Microsoft to Bridge Consumer Electronics and PC Worlds for Digital Entertainment," *Business Wire*, May 11, 2005, 1.

42. "A Traveler's Next Best Friend," *Houston Chronicle*, October 10, 2004, B5.

43. "Philips and Microsoft," 1.

44. "Tune In and Enjoy the Ride," *Newswire*, June 8, 2005.

45. Phillip Torrone quoted in Elizabeth Bernstein, "Travel—Gadgets," *Wall Street Journal*, December 3, 2004, W24.

46. "TiVo Unveils Next Generation Service Strategy at CES," *PRNewswire*, January 6, 2005, 1. See also "First Portable DVD Player with Wireless Headphone and TV Tuner for Easy Travel or Game Watching at the Stadium," *PR Newswire*, January 6, 2005, 1.

47. "Portable Media Devices Hit the Streets Using Sigma Media Processors," *Business Wire*, November 1, 2004, 1 (emphasis added).

48. Bob Keefe, "Wired on Wheels," *Palm Beach Post*, January 29, 2006, 4F.

49. Tichi, *Electronic Hearth*, 63. Moreover, to the degree that television shows were consumed by children in the home, Tichi notes, television was seen as a "third vector, commanding the children's attention directly, usurping the prerogatives of the Guardians, who must now struggle to retain or recapture their authority" (201).

50. Spigel, *Welcome*, 149.

51. These are rather large claims, of course, but they are the subject of, or a large part of the subject of, several books, including Scharff's *Taking the Wheel;* and Sean O'Connell's *The Car and British Society: Class, Gender, and Motoring, 1896–1939* (New York: Manchester University Press, 1998). Moreover, in his work on U.S. Southern male homosexuality, John Howard trenchantly argues that the existence of the automobile allowed for entirely new social spaces for homosexual culture, reshaping it radically. See John Howard, *Men Like That: A Southern Queer History* (Chicago: University of Chicago Press, 1999).

52. In a recent essay, Jeremy Packer observes that this "lack vs. excess" argument emerges with all new technologies, especially as they are linked to transportation. For example, either we need more cell phones in cars because they increase safety or the excessive use of cell phones distracts drivers. Either we need radios in all cars as a way of warning driver's about impending bad weather or the music on radios distracts drivers. See Packer, "Disciplining," 84.

53. Tammy Zmyewski quoted in Edward L. Kennedy, "More Car Buyers Getting the Picture with DVDs," *Chicago Sun-Times*, March 28, 2004, B6.

54. Harriet Ainbinder quoted in Kennedy, "More Car Buyers," B6.

55. Doug Erickson, "Miracle Device," *Wisconsin State Journal*, July 4, 2004, A1. For another use of the pacifier metaphor, see Patterson, "State," A1.

56. Bram Groeneveld quoted in Erickson, "Miracle," A1.

57. Nancy Dowling quoted in Katherine Snow Smith, "Voices from the Backseat Let Us Hear Heart, Mind," *St. Petersburg Times*, February 27, 2005, B8.

58. Erin Andersen, "Vacation . . . ," *Lincoln Journal Star*, July 16, 2004, A2.

59. Paul Turner, "At the Crossroads," *Spokesman Review*, June 5, 2005, D1.

60. Smith, "Voices," B8.

61. Turner, "Crossroads," D1.

62. Ibid.

63. Patrick McGeehan, "Boredom Busters for the Youngest Travelers," *New York Times*, November 20, 2003, G3. See also Meryl Schoenbaum, "Travel DVDs for Kids on the Go," *Home Media Retailing*, May 1–7, 2005, 16.

64. Vasin Omer Douglas, "Road Trip Reels," *Austin American Statesman*, April 15, 2006, D1.

65. Patrick Beach, "No Movies in the Car?" *Austin American Statesman*, June 1, 2004, D1. See also Kennedy, "More Car Buyers," B6; and "Notebook Travel Harness Allows In-Auto DVD Theater," *Twice*, April 5, 2004, 40.

66. Beach, "No Movies," D1.

67. Sean Comey quoted in Patrick Giblin, "Get Going with Gadgets," *Modesto Bee*, June 17, 2004, D1.

68. Erickson, "Miracle," A1. See also Michael O'Rourke, "DVD Players Bring New Era of Auto Road Trips," *San Antonio Express-News*, October 22, 2005, E1.

69. James Cummings, "Player's a Perfect Travel Buddy," *Dayton Daily News*, July 15, 2001, L1.

70. Andersen, "Vacation," A2.

71. Mackenzie Carpenter, "Western Wonders," *Pittsburgh Post-Gazette*, August 22, 2004, F1.

72. Cynthia L. Miller, "Vehicle Video Systems Sales Rise as Families Travel More," *Grand Rapids Press*, October 3, 2004, N8.

73. Michael Kitschka, quoted in ibid., N8.

74. Turner, "Crossroads," D1.

75. James Hay, "Between Cultural Materialism and Spiritual Materialism: James Carey's Writing about Communication," in *Thinking with James Carey: Essays on Communications, Transportation, History*, ed. Jeremy Packer and Craig Robertson (New York: Peter Lang, 2006), 49.

76. Sheller and Urry, "Mobile Transformations," 108.

77. Miller, *Well-Tempered*, ix.

78. Robert Asen, "A Discourse Theory of Citizenship," *Quarterly Journal of Speech* 90 (2004): 189–211.

79. Miller, *Well-Tempered*, 49.

80. Jeremy Packer, "Rethinking Dependency: New Relations of Transportation and

Communication," in *Thinking with James Carey: Essays on Communications, Transportation, History*, ed. Jeremy Packer and Craig Robertson (New York: Peter Lang, 2006), 97.

81. See Cass Sunstein, *Republic.com* (Princeton: Princeton University Press, 2001); Robert Putnam, *Bowling Alone* (New York: Simon & Schuster, 2000).

82. Sunstein, *Republic.com*, 15.

9
Risibility Politics
Camp Humor in HIV/AIDS Zines

Daniel C. Brouwer

Writing in *Artforum* in 1987, Edmund White addressed the status of humor as an aesthetic mode in the context of the AIDS epidemic. "If art is to confront AIDS more honestly than the media have done, it must begin in tact, avoid humor, and end in anger," he asserted. "Humor suggests that AIDS is just another calamity to befall Mother Camp, whereas in truth AIDS is not one more item in a sequence, but a rupture in meaning itself."[1] Using White's sober proscription as a foil, activist David Feinberg countered with an embrace of the possibilities of humor for those who, like him, are AIDS-diagnosed. "Humor is a survival tactic, a defense mechanism, a way of lessening the horror"; it is a means for asserting control over disease and a distancing mechanism.[2] Artists and activists alike have frequently embodied Feinberg's ludic stance toward humor, inflecting their works with irony, camp, and gallows humor. In one emblematic event in 1997, audience members at a comedy club in New York City selected via applause acclamation "The Funniest HIV-Positive Person in New York" at a competition and fund-raiser sponsored by *POZ Magazine*.[3] Humor's general persistence in the AIDS epidemic suggests the important task of exploring the reasons why and the specific ways in which humor has functioned as a mode through which people infected with or affected by HIV make sense of the virus and the syndrome.

In this chapter, I explore deployments of humor about HIV/AIDS by gay men with HIV/AIDS. In multiple media—novels, theater, movies, stand-up comedy routines, even *AIDS! The Musical!*—gay men with HIV/AIDS use humor to perform multiple functions. From among these media, I focus on humor in two zines (truncated from "magazines") in the United States—*Infected Faggot Perspectives* (*IFP*) and *Diseased Pariah News* (*DPN*). Print-based, "underground" publications spanning ten years of the epidemic (1990–1999), these zines serve as sites of gay men's cultural production. Elsewhere, Thomas Long has adumbrated the transgressive strategies of these zines and fruitfully described the relations between the zines' production values and their political commitments.[4] Elsewhere, I have explicated the specific ways in which these zines constitute counterpublics, focusing on the corporeal modes of the erotic and the grotesque. Neither of those investigations, however, has fully explored humor, specifically, camp humor, as a modality of (counter)publicity.[5] Such a study of risibility politics in the face of HIV/AIDS is warranted by both the need to understand actual communication practices in conditions of significant crisis and the persistent scholarly call to recognize the value of plural modes of constituting public culture.

In this chapter, I first explore camp humor's ambivalent career, focusing on its potential to mediate important relations between symbolic and material politics. Next, I offer a sketch of the role of humor in constituting the zines as a particular kind of place. Attending to *glamour* as an exemplary theme of camp humor, I then offer a reading of both "AIDS Barbie," a figure whose fall from glamour is dramatized in a disturbing mock advertisement, and personal narratives from zine writers who describe their own struggles to maintain glamour in the face of AIDS. Along the way, I advance three main positions: First, neither inherently subversive nor inherently ineffectual, humor's critical potential is best studied in historical specificity, paying particular attention to the conditions of its emergence, circulation, and reception. Second, camp humor about AIDS produced by infected gay men in the pages of *IFP* and *DPN* should be read as acts of counterpublicity that articulate and circulate oppositional meanings of infection. Third, camp humor in the zines addresses material politics on two significant and overlapping levels—the materiality of the body and its relation to discourse, and the economic conditions that structure everyday life.

Camp Humor's Ambivalent Career

During a dream sequence in *Angels in America*, protagonist Prior Walter sits before a mirror and grows increasingly frustrated with his inability to make up his AIDS-ravaged face into the semblance of his former drag queen beauty. With a mixture of rage and drollery, he concludes, "Oh my queen; you know you've hit rock-bottom when even drag is a drag."[6] This painful scene advances the specter of the eclipse of symbolic politics by the dimming force of material, bodily conditions. As such, this scene simultaneously illuminates the challenge of forwarding camp humor as a valuable modality of counterpublicity, one that can productively mediate relations between symbolic and material politics.

In this section, I argue that camp enables its practitioners to pursue both symbolic and material politics. This argument proceeds in recognition that regardless of the form that it takes—irony, satire, wit, etc.—humor operates within and thus indexes an existing set of social relations.[7] Indeed, discernment of what counts as humor, who is permitted to perform and appreciate it, and in what contexts or settings it is permitted reveals relations of power. Ambivalent, humor can reify or challenge dominant ideologies and discourses.[8] This recognition prevents global and reductive assessments of humor as, on the one hand, tragically ineffectual or, on the other hand, relentlessly subversive.[9] Further, my argument depends in part on an examination of the historically specific conditions of camp humor's emergence, circulation, and reception. Such an examination will contextualize the critical potential of camp by exposing the concern that camp has not always successfully mediated symbolic and material politics and by forwarding criteria for assessing camp's successful mediation.

Although camp was named and practiced earlier, Susan Sontag's 1964 essay "Notes on 'Camp'" provided contemporary intellectual warrant for its study and interrogation.[10] Since then, scholarship on camp has sometimes directed recognition toward its historically specific emergence as a form of "solely queer discourse" and toward its historically shifting functions and significance.[11] Moe Meyer carefully charts the ways in which publicity of the Oscar Wilde trials in the early twentieth century produced a new homosexual figure, arguing that in the aftermath of the trials, "camp emerges as an identifiable performative phenomenon and the means for constituting a homosexual identity."[12] That is, homosexual men learned to read and express themselves—and a general population learned to read homosexuals—through camp signifiers of excessive gesturation.[13] Further iteration of camp's homosexual tendencies resides in historian George Chauncey's study of gay male culture in New York City at the turn of the twentieth century. Chauncey shows how camp functioned as a critical, cultural strategy to challenge social categories (like biological kinship) and as an idiom of sexuality for gay men.[14] Embedded within sociopolitical and cultural milieux that ignored, denounced, or marginalized homosexuality and its expressions, gay men employed camp humor as a means of personal and collective survival, as a way of expressing publicly one's queerness and as a performative critical stance against domination.

Central to recognition of camp's historical specificity is its shifting critical potential based on the conditions of its emergence, circulation, and reception and its status in a matrix of symbolic and material politics. The distinction between material politics and symbolic politics rests largely on a distinction between economic redistribution and cultural interventions.[15] In recent LGBTQ (lesbian, gay, bisexual, transgender, queer) politics, the work of the Gay and Lesbian Alliance Against Defamation (GLAAD) to challenge harmful media portrayals might exemplify symbolic politics, whereas some of the work by the AIDS Coalition to Unleash Power (ACT UP) to alter the conduct of HIV/AIDS research, to increase the affordability and availability of HIV/AIDS treatments, and to secure affordable housing for people with HIV/AIDS might represent a materialist political project. Under this distinction, camp becomes intelligible as a means for conducting symbolic politics with its critical potential determined, in part, by its relation to materialist politics and by the conditions of its production, circulation, and reception.

According to Andrew Ross, the shifting functions and, in his view, diminished critical capacity of camp humor in the 1960s correlate with shifting modes of cultural production.[16] Particularly damaging to camp's critical status is the claim that as a result of shifting cultural conditions gay male camp conducts depoliticized nostalgia that directs its audiences toward positive remembrances of a more glorious past rather than toward courses of present action to secure a materially and symbolically better future.[17] Along this line, Ross claims that "the traditional gay camp sensibility was an *imaginary* expression of a relation to real conditions, both past and present—an ideology, if you like—while it functions today, in the 'liberated' gay and straight world, as a kind of imaginary challenge to the new *symbolic* conditions of gay identity."[18] As a mode of symbolic politics, camp has untethered itself from material politics. In this view, camp is retrograde and regressive; it has lost much of its critical potential. As a result, camp can be easily dismissed as silly posturing or wit that engages in "misdirected aggression."[19] This challenge to the critical potential of camp presumes, of course, that camp gestures are intelligible to their audiences. When audiences are not culturally competent to recognize and understand camp, its critical potential is further delimited.[20]

Given the early and enduring intersections between gay men and HIV/AIDS and given the enduring intersections between gay men and camp humor, it should not be surprising that gay men have deployed camp humor in their personal, social, and political experiences of HIV/AIDS. Indeed, for gay men confronting HIV/AIDS, camp humor was a cultural idiom ready for deployment.[21] However, given shifting cultural conditions, the ability of camp to serve a critical function in the service of AIDS activist politics has come under challenge. David Román offers the most nuanced critique. Comparing three stage dramatizations with AIDS plotlines, he determines that,

> unlike, say, *I Could Go On Lip Synching* or *The Lisbon Traviata*, where camp emerges as a possible intervention into the crisis of (gay male) representation in the age of AIDS only to be subsumed by the larger ideological effects of either compulsory heterosexuality or the politics of nostalgia, *AIDS! The Musical!* manages to maintain both camp's outrageousness and its efficacy as a survivalist discourse. *AIDS! The Musical!* demonstrates how the theatre can accommodate both entertainment and activism, or more precisely, how camp can serve AIDS activist politics through the medium of theatre.[22]

Importantly, Román both distinguishes among disparate functions that camp performs and locates camp's more critical functions in survivalist rather than nostalgic modes. Additionally, he warns that camp's potential complicity with heteronormativity and its partial inscrutability to certain audiences complicate its critical career. With these distillations of camp's critical potential in mind, I explore the career of camp humor in *Infected Faggot Perspectives* and *Diseased Pariah News*.

Zines, Camp Humor, and Counterpublicity

Dramatizing humor as a dominant mode of expression in the zines, a cartoon strip in issue 5 of *DPN* features its mascot Oncomouse in a hallway with many doors, wondering to himself which of the organizations housed in this space will give him the kind of support for which he is looking. At the first three doors that he approaches, he encounters very unsatisfying creatures who consecutively demand to "share the exquisite agony of your noble affliction," blame Oncomouse's bad attitude for his affliction, and offer to hug him while he dies. Reaching the final door, which announces "*DPN*," Oncomouse encounters a handsome man in a turtleneck and an unfortunate haircut who tells him, "Hi, welcome to DPN! Come on in, have a doughnut, and get over it."[23] This depiction of *DPN* as a place separate from others, one in which camp modes of intimacy replace exploitative and censorious relations with people with HIV/AIDS, suggests that the zines function as a counterpublic for gay men with HIV/AIDS.[24]

Viewed from the perspective of a counterpublic, humor can serve a variety of purposes: it aids in the construction of an oppositional or alternative reality, it impacts attitudes and influences behavior, unites groups through the formation of a collective identity, and fosters a climate in which the power and control of dominant institutions and their representatives are destabilized and denaturalized.[25] In moments of inward address, humor can function as an "insulated means of argument to challenge the dominant view of the social order."[26] And when participation in dominant publics necessitates the practice of earnest reason, the use of culturally specific modes of humor affirms marginal publics' expressive idioms and exposes "one of the most powerful ruses of the dominant[:] to pretend that critique can only exist in the language of 'reason,' 'pure knowledge' and 'seriousness.'"[27] One should not underestimate the significance of these functions of humor for collectives that perceive themselves as counterpublics in opposition to dominant publics.

Each zine employs a range of visual and linguistic representations. Topics, tones, and attitudes vary within and between the zines. But humor, often macabre, biting, and absurd, abounds in both. Consider, for example, Wayne Karr's promisingly empowering "The AIDS Survival Guide: A Long-Termer Shares His Secrets," in which he dispenses the following advice: "BE WHITE! . . . BE MALE! . . . HAVE A GOOD INSURANCE POLICY! . . . BE RICH or GET RICH QUICK."[28] These suggestions are (to varying degrees) out of the range of individuals' agency: their ludicrousness dramatizes material advantages conferred through structures of race, sex, and class privilege in the United States. Regardless of its form, humor plays an important role in making sense of AIDS. Echoing Emma Goldman, Aunt Kaposi, one of *DPN*'s most eloquent writers, affirms the power of humor in the fight against AIDS: "A revolution without laughter is like a wedding without love."[29]

Thus, for example, alongside necessarily sober, earnest, and outraged framings of "the AIDS crisis" as a crisis of inhumane disparities in access to medical care, a crisis of global pharmaceutical profiteering, or a crisis of compassion, zine writers invite us to lament the AIDS crisis as a crisis of glamour. From among the numerous occurrences of camp humor in *IFP* and *DPN*, then, I focus on the recurrent camp theme of *glamour*. Such a focus provides fertile terrain for examining the performativity and gestural production of camp and offers a surprising and complex distillation of camp humor's labor as a mediator between symbolic and material politics. In the next section, I first conduct a reading of the disarming figure of "AIDS Barbie" and her fall from glamour. I then offer a reading of zine writers Trixie Trash's and Pansy Ass Faggot's overt meditations on their own glamour crises; in conjunction with that reading, I interrogate the politics and poetics of *noms de plume* as a particular manner of conducting camp humor.

Glamour

The connection between Barbie and glamour would seem to be obvious: indeed, while Barbie has stood for many things,[30] one of the things that she has especially stood for is glamour. A prevailing way in which Barbie circulates in the national popular imagination is as an icon of white, heterosexual, middle-class, feminine beauty:[31] she is an impossibly leggy, svelte, and busty woman whose feet are perpetually frozen into a glamorous high-heel position. Her long flowing hair, the endless number of outfits, her cars, houses, friends, and boyfriends let us know that Barbie has it made. But in an eye-catching *Diseased Pariah News* advertisement, Barbie has clearly run into trouble. Confronting an issue that existed far away from the idyll of her Malibu dream world, Barbie now finds herself a smiling, yet marked and defiled, "victim" of AIDS.[32]

The *DPN* advertisement promotes a new and profoundly grotesque product on the market: it is *AIDS Barbie!* in three different forms. Consumers can choose from AIDS Barbie with Kaposi's sarcoma and shingles, AIDS Barbie with malignant lymphoma and gynecological complications, or AIDS Barbie with wasting syndrome and CMV (cytomegalovirus) retinitis. The text of the advertisement reads: "Nice girls don't use condoms. Nice girls can't say 'No!' Now, for all of those nice girls, there's . . . AIDS Barbie! And she thought that math class was tough! Don't forget to accessorize AIDS Barbie with her own elegant Estée Lauder 'European Mystique' oxygen gurney, Krups HI-FLO automated IV rack, and glamorous Bob Mackie designed bedpan with rhinestone accents!"[33] Three naked, smiling Barbie dolls, one waving to the reader, sit close together on what appears to be a bench or a hospital bed. All three are smiling, but one of the Barbies is blind. Her eyes have been whited-out, and X's have been placed over them, signifying the death of her vision from CMV retinitis. Still, she smiles despite the gross disfigurement of her right leg and arm, apparently placed in a flame by the makers of the advertisement in order to make her flesh shrivel into a signifier of wasting syndrome. Perhaps she smiles because she does not have it as bad as AIDS Barbie with Kaposi's sarcoma and shingles. *This* Barbie is missing her right hand and is hooked up to the Krups HI-FLO automated IV rack. This Barbie's legs, like the legs of her wasting syndrome sister, have been intentionally disfigured with what appear to be burn marks. The third Barbie seems the friendliest, for she is able to wave at the reader, perhaps because she suffers the least visibly. Manifesting a dozen lumps around her throat and armpits (regions of the lymph nodes) and closely cropped hair, AIDS Barbie with malignant lymphoma and gynecological complications seems to be recovering from chemotherapy.

These AIDS Barbies are grotesque. They may be difficult to look at or to comprehend; they may produce a visceral, wincing, pained reaction. Indeed, the citation of grotesque AIDS signifiers upon the slick, smooth, plastic skin of fantastic, "*emphatic femininity*" produces a disturbing incongruity, punctuated by that imperturbable, inappropriate (slightly insane?) smile.[34] AIDS Barbies follow Bakhtin's "essential principle of grotesque realism," that of degradation of hegemonic spiritual or social ideals through the medium of the body.[35] With their lesions, blindness, wasting, and more, these figures denounce normative prescriptions for femininity—"niceness," or passivity, in contrast to assertiveness, for example—that place women at risk of HIV infection. Yet grotesque realism also demands change, a new ordering of values and power relations.[36] Here, AIDS Barbies call for a world that psychologically, socially, and institutionally supports women's bodily autonomy.

Despite her abjection, AIDS Barbie compels laughter. I suggest that Bakhtin's "festive laughter" helps to explain this ambivalence. Festive laughter is "gay, triumphant, and at the same time mocking, deriding. It asserts and denies, it buries and revives."[37] In sympathy with the grotesque, such laughter celebrates the base puns and vulgar displays of bodies because of their demystifying and destabilizing effects. Zine readers are invited to celebrate the ambivalence—the parody and the criticism, the humor and the earnestness.[38]

Her glamour compromised by grotesque symptoms of AIDS, Barbie mediates at least two different meanings of glamour, for glamour has both failed her and may save her. Implied in the ad is that Barbie dangerously believed that the glamorous conditions of her life would protect her from infection, that her status as a "nice girl" would keep AIDS at bay. The ad thus functions as a warning against such thinking, even as it fails to interrogate the social conditions that produce women's variegated forms and degrees of agency.[39] Notably, the false prophylaxis of glamour undermined in this ad has a real-life analogue in which glamour was promoted as a guarantor of HIV immunity. Much controversy arose when a January 1988 *Cosmopolitan* article, "Reassuring News about AIDS: A Doctor Tells You Why You May Not Be at Risk," by Robert E. Gould, dispelled the possibility of heterosexual transmission of HIV from men to women. The Women's Committee of ACT UP demonstrated against *Cosmopolitan*, a glamour magazine targeting a well-to-do or aspiring audience of women, for providing a forum for "lethal advice . . . based entirely on ignorance and prejudice."[40] Demonstrators decried *Cosmo's* complicity in rendering women vulnerable to infection.

The second meaning of glamour that Barbie mediates is the more obviously campy but not inconsequential one. While glamour will not protect one from AIDS, once one *has* AIDS, he or she can do it up glamorously. In the AIDS Barbie ad, it is possible that the AIDS *victim* can become an AIDS *diva* simply by accessorizing smartly with brand-name hospital accoutrements (Bob Mackie designs dresses for Cher, for goodness' sake). The emphasis on glamour in dealing with AIDS is an assault on sociocultural perceptions of what it means to be AIDS-diagnosed. The bases of the Denver Principles that were formulated at the first meeting of the National Association of People with AIDS (1983) were that people with AIDS were not "AIDS victims" and that only sometimes could they be defined as "AIDS patients" (that is, in hospital or medical care settings); mostly, these activists defined themselves as "living with AIDS." For zine writers, gay men in the second decade of the AIDS epidemic, living with AIDS often means engaging in a glamorous, campy performativity that simultaneously derides and revives; it means claiming glamour as a vital attitude toward AIDS; and it inspires the presentation of counter-hegemonic images of the AIDS body, a grotesque body that fosters the disconcerting festive laugh of the carnival.

Can we talk? You should know: to do AIDS right, honey, sometimes you need a little glamour. Crypta la Coccus the advice columnist, Trixie Trash, and Pansy Ass Faggot all speak to the need of the person with AIDS to recover, hoard, or simply find anew some of the glamour that makes living with AIDS tolerable.[41] Glamour means several things simultaneously to zine writers: a magic spell or enchantment, as in the archaic sense; physical composition, put together just so, as in a glamorous appearance; and a "vital attitude" toward AIDS.[42] Trixie Trash writes:

> Are you slipping. .girl? Is it getting harder to work that "AIDS Glamour" in this day of AIDS Awareness? Has the change in the Old AIDS Defi-

> nition created too much competition for you. .girl?[43] Has some queen stole your Glamour Spot? Well I am here to tell you how to get it back!
>
> Let's face it girl, the days of Unlimited Glamour are over. The good Old Days when a flash of a lesion would bring you looks of admiration or a particularly Hideos [*sic*] herpes sore "worn proudly" would bring you instant fame are gone. So remember girls. .Glamour is the only commodity left to us Infected Girls, since sympathy went out in the '80s.
>
> So A GIRL[']S GOT TO GRAB WHAT A GIRL CAN GET![44]

Trixie's nostalgia for better days periodizes affect in the epidemic. In the earliest years of the epidemic, activists, medical providers, and others countered phobic responses to AIDS and people with AIDS by establishing lines of identification, including sympathy, toward people with AIDS. Parallel to sympathy in the mainstream, Trixie suggests, was a kind of morbid admiration that one could earn from one's fellow and sororal sufferers. As people with HIV/AIDS benefited from increasing social legitimacy and medical and political empowerment, morbid admiration and sympathy were no longer adequate for earning distinction; thus, "glamour" names a newly possible affective positionality, albeit one under duress. Trixie Trash is likely writing after the Centers for Disease Control and Prevention expanded its definition of AIDS effective January 1993 to include a measure of CD4+ T-lymphocytes ("T cells") and more AIDS-defining conditions. These changes resulted in an immediate increase in the number of people diagnosed with AIDS and thus, to Trixie Trash's chagrin, the number of people in competition over the limited resource of "glamour." Since it is no small feat to reframe AIDS from stigmatizing to glamorizing, it must have been frustrating for Trixie Trash to witness such symbolic labor undermined by glamour's diffusion.

In this excerpt, Trixie invokes two types of materiality—bodily survival and economic sympathy. Despite Trixie's explicit link between glamour and nostalgia, glamour functions for her as a survivalist discourse. While one of the problems that Trixie addresses is demotion in social status, she begins her monologue with an expression of concern about the problem of "slipping"—dissipation, losing control, losing composure. Glamour thus appears as a way of keeping it together—gaining control, composing oneself, continuing to live. Second, while Trixie laments the scarcity of sympathy as an interpersonal or social dynamic, her description of sympathy as a commodity triggers recognition that sympathy is also a structural dynamic that delivers federal, state, and local funds for prevention and treatment of HIV infection and AIDS diagnosis; anonymity or confidentiality of HIV-antibody positive test results; and more. Like glamour, structural sympathy emerges as a necessity for doing AIDS right. In this instance, Trixie articulates (albeit weakly) a relation between symbolic politics and material politics.

Zine writers obviously describe glamour in humorous ways, but glamour is neither ridiculous nor inconsequential. Indeed, as a survivalist discourse glamour just might prolong your life; it will certainly enhance your quality of life, however long or short. Pansy Ass Faggot suggests:

> To all you queens who thought I'd be gone by now . . . I'm not! So there!! Didn't you know. . Evil Girls don't die young, we hang around while all the goodies go quick. . . . Now what['']s wrong with you queens dropping like flies? Don't you know all you have to do is refuse to die—decide not to go! . . . So the next time that big and bad AIDS monster visits you thinking you are going to be easy prey just let it know girl, "it ain't happening" sister. Put all that cranky, mean, nasty energy we queens are full of into use. . . . So even though your [*sic*] shaking in your hospital gown (or if you have any glamour, strike a pose in your silk shift. . . . , show a little leg and BAT your eyes. While you've thrown it off guard Open that Big Scary mouth of yours and yell FUCK YOU! I ain't going. .yet . . . This queen isn't thru! What[']s it going to do. KILL YOU. . Duh. Wait and see, you'll surely get well.[45]

This character casts a glamour—a spell, a distraction. She enacts a queer habitus, composing herself before a personified, embodied enemy. With a wry awareness that death approaches, she offers the ironic assertion that merely saying no to AIDS will stop it in its tracks. She seems delusional, and perhaps she is, but that is not the point. She asserts: I am going to be glamorous until the end; through the pain and the nausea and the slow creeping sounds of the approach of death, I will maintain dignity through composition; I will not dissipate. More broadly, in her confrontation with AIDS, Pansy Ass Faggot demonstrates that "in some cases, the fearful is made harmless through being made comic."[46]

Clearly, the zines aspire to be a site for cultivating AIDS-diagnosed gay men's oppositional articulations of infection by training them in how to discover, find, reclaim, or create their own glamour. "Stigma with style," Aunt Kaposi encourages.[47] Notably, zine writers frequently articulate glamour through the use of *noms de plume*. In queer culture, we might call this "writing in drag." The metaphor of modality reminds us that style or manner matters; in that spirit, I interrogate the politics and poetics of writing in drag as a particular manner of conducting camp humor.

The use of noms de plume or pseudonyms has a rich history, serving disparate functions for disparate constituencies. For the male agitators of the American Revolution, for example, pseudonyms such as Cato, Brutus, and Philo Publicus permitted agitators to evade retribution and persecution for their claims, to assume a position of high moral ground in debate, and to frame their defense of revolution in terms of venerated antiquity.[48] Other familiar functions of the pseudonym include perpetration of fraud, mediation of antagonistic relations with audiences, and, for women writers, avoidance of ridicule and facilitation of publication.[49] Rejecting key presumptions about the motives and effects of pseudonyms, however, Margaret Ezell argues that in the genre of seventeenth-century English coterie literature, a genre constituted by self-selected intimates and peripheral to commercial purposes, writers deployed pseudonyms in order to facilitate dynamic, playful interactions with readers, to affirm characteristics of a social group and signal membership in it, and to suggest the permeability between fiction and "the real."[50]

Zine writers' noms de plume function in ways similar to their functions in coterie literature. Zines like *IFP* and *DPN* are seldom commercial publications, and they typically enjoy a highly self-selected readership. As such, *IFP* and *DPN* cultivate intimacy with their readers. Like pseudonyms in coterie literature, pseudonyms in *IFP* and *DPN* function "not as a cloak or a mask, but as a password to signal membership in an exclusive and much desired group."[51] The drag queen/drag writer performs in camp idioms that are presumably familiar to zine readers (who are presumed to be familiar with queer culture). Although her position in queer culture is complicated,[52] her performances can express solidarity with members of her community.

Writing in drag retains key elements of camp's origins as a form of self-reflexive gestural production. In Meyer's account of the emergence of male homosexuality in the aftermath of the Oscar Wilde trial, homosexuality came to be diagnosed as a "pathology of fashion and gesture" in that homosexuals became legible through their excessive gesturation and cross-dressing. Meyer names as "camp" gay men's self-reflexive deployments of gesture and fashion to craft a "vehicle of social agency."[53] Like male cross-dressing, writing in drag articulates femininity onto a male body, raising important questions about the critical potential of drag performance. Judith Butler understands drag as a form of citational performativity of gender, by which she means that drag performs the "*sign* of gender" and that drag exposes "the 'normal' constitution of gender presentation." Butler has clarified her famously contended position on drag, describing drag as "ambivalent" and asserting that it bears no necessary relationship to subversion. As a criterion for assessing drag's critical potential, Butler maintains that drag must interrogate the "imitative structure by which hegemonic gender is itself produced," perhaps through "parodic inhabitance" of the laws of normative gender performances.[54] Recognizing the gravity of charges that drag is necessarily (or at least tends toward) misogyny, I follow Butler in her recognition of drag's ambivalence.[55]

I want to argue that writing in drag performs a queer trope on the prophylaxis of self-abstraction that noms de plume offer up. Michael Warner notes how in the bourgeois public sphere the appropriation of a persona or of a "mass subject" allowed male writers and speakers to construct a "prosthetic" person, which deflected critique away from the individual and also allowed the individual to be judged on the basis of what he said and not who he was.[56] In the zines, we find what appears to be the appropriation of "prophylactic subjectivities." Thus, for example, Cory Roberts Auli, Wayne Karr, and Michael Botkin write sometimes not under these, their birth names, but under the camp personae of Crypta la Coccus, Pansy Ass Faggot, La Sidosa, or Aunt Kaposi. These appropriations of dramatic personae are dissociating in the sense that they create a prosthetic persona for the writer: there is a "real person with AIDS" behind the persona, but the writer chooses to "hide" behind the persona. But the prosthetic personae also dramatize the gay male AIDS body—its functions, its capacities, its limitations, its multiple and various (and sometimes nefarious) possibilities. The noms de plume create camp personae that offer self-abstraction, yet that distance is almost always refused: it is used to comment back on the body, a body that is not fully fictional and not fully real.

The third space between the real and fictional body facilitates a kind of critical, "parodic inhabitance." Richard Schechner's extension of the psychoanalytic concepts of "not me"/"not not me" to the dynamics of performance workshops and rehearsals is instructive here: any character that a performer embodies is both not the performer (not me) and not completely distinct from the performer (not not me). This condition Schechner describes as a "liminal realm of double negativity."[57] I want to extend this notion to refer to drag performance, including writing in drag. When carnivalized by grotesque, visible symptomologies, a body diagnosed with AIDS functions as a figure of abjection, the excluded difference that haunts intelligible bodies, reminding them of their imperfection.[58] Enough traces of the abject, real bodies of zine writers (not not me) remain for the drag bodies (not me) to function as figures of abjection themselves. Drag personae suffer from diarrhea, neuropathy, a boil on the nose, even death (Crypta writes her advice column from the grave). Although Pansy Ass Faggot, Aunt Kaposi, and others strive for glamour, they can hardly accomplish it; glamour is almost always deferred. This is how writing in drag engages in parodic—I would say *absurd*—"inhabitance" of normative, glamorous femininity.

Conclusions

It could be easy to dismiss celebrations of glamour and deployments of noms de plume as enervated or fatally misdirected efforts to confront HIV/AIDS. Particularly when political activities are viewed as discrete acts rather than as constellated and interanimating acts and when formal political forums are posited as the primary loci of efficacy, humorous acts akin to drawing mustaches on the images of leaders seem feeble, indeed. Further, when a contrast between symbolic and material politics is heightened or when the relationship between symbolic and material politics is unclear, the potentially critical work of cultural interventions might be underappreciated. While I want to assert that it would be ridiculous to claim that specific acts of writing in drag promote justice by causing economic redistribution, I also want to underscore the important ways in which camp humor mediates symbolic and material politics in *Infected Faggot Perspectives* and *Diseased Pariah News*.

Carole Blair has outlined three ways in which rhetorical scholars have treated materiality: "the material conditions of discourse, . . . the lived-in body as a condition and consequence of discourse, and . . . rhetoric itself as material."[59] If we recognize these varieties of materiality, then we can see how the symbolic politics of glamour and noms de plume address the material in two distinct senses. On the materiality of the lived-in body, zine readers observe that as AIDS carnivalizes bodies and renders them grotesque, glamour, as an extant idiom among gay men, gets deployed. Glamour permits the infected to reframe what their infected bodies mean, and the unexpected signification of AIDS on glamorous bodies facilitates exposure and critique of damaging social codes. Zine writers also address the materiality of the body in their advocacy of glamour as a mode of self-presentation that can, if not save, improve the quality of one's life. One need not subscribe fully to psychoneuroimmunology or holistic medicine in order to treat as tenable a correlation between psychological and physical health. Further, reminders by zine writers that their temperamental health produces an irregular production schedule demonstrate profoundly how bodily conditions effect the ability to circulate discourse.

The second sense of materiality that zine writers address is the economic structuring of the conditions for discourse. On this front, both of the zines dramatize the advantages of insurance, advantages that significantly shape access to expert medical discourses about HIV/AIDS. Additionally, writers from both zines indicate economic disadvantage at some point or the other: *IFP* editors occasionally refer to themselves as welfare queens, and by the final issue of *DPN* Beowulf Thorne reports that he has been on the dole. *IFP* is especially attuned to class, race, ethnicity, and nationality and the ways in which economic disparities structure the experience of HIV/AIDS. Much more frequent in *IFP* are expressions of political outrage and calls to mobilize for direct action in pursuit of social justice: "March - Touch - Complain - Explode - Remember - Agitate"; "CREATE REVOLUTION WHERE EVER YOU GO BY ANY MEANS NECESSARY"; "END RACISM!! IN OUR LIFETIME."[60]

Ultimately, however, cultural interventions in the camp modalities of glamour and writing in drag produce a limited program for one of the most significant versions of material—that of economic redistribution. This limitation is significant but not fatal. In her book-length monograph on Barbie and symbolic rearticulations of Barbie, Erica Rand insists that "justice requires redistribution of resources and power, which neither studying nor subverting Barbie can effect." Indeed, Rand writes, "If we measure cultural interventions and strategies of resistance by whether they catalyze big social changes by themselves and fast, Barbie subversions, like most, will not" suffice. Rand's points hold for cultural interventions more generally. This leads to questions: If glamorous, campy provocations cannot produce a program for material distribution, then what good are they? More, why study them? Rand answers this with the compelling assertion that "cultural products need political attention. Political battles are fought over and through the manipulation of cultural symbols. People use them to signal political identities, to effect political coalitions, to disrupt and challenge beliefs and connections that have come to seem natural."[61] In my view, one of the important lessons of *Infected Faggot Perspectives* and *Diseased Pariah News* is that counterpublic discourse in the alternative media forum of zines can circulate oppositional understandings of infection, promote the occupation of resistant subject positions, and cultivate resistant frames, all work that can be preparatory for and concurrent with the improvement of economic conditions. That for gay men this work often occurs through the culturally relevant idiom of camp humor suggests the need for critical attention to risibility politics.

In parting, I assert that a comparative approach that interrogates the emergence, circulation, and reception of HIV/AIDS humor beyond the world of the zines appears as a valuable but unfinished project.[62] Such a project would examine the intelligibilities and functions of humor and humor's disparately localized expressions of symbolic and material politics. As a gesture toward that project, I outline an articulation of glamour in a different national and global context. Since 2002, the annual "Miss HIV Stigma-Free" beauty pageants in Botswana have mobilized and reoccupied the format of the pageant to stage cultural and material interventions. Contestants, women who are either infected with or significantly affected by HIV, enact common pageant forms with national and global inflections. In 2005, for example, women in the competition staged the nation through the wearing of traditional clothing in addition to the wearing of evening gowns familiar to pageants of the West. More, in a nation wherein 37–38 percent of the adult population is HIV positive, contestants in the pageant are judged "in large part on their knowledge of HIV/AIDS, its treatment and related issues."[63] This criterion recognizes the exigence of the nation and fosters the urgent need for competent advocacy. In a different vein, the media narrative of 2003 winner Kgalalelo Ntsepe's ability to participate in the pageant dramatizes both a national and a global inflection to the pageant format. Significantly ill and AIDS-diagnosed in 2001, Ntsepe's health improved immensely after beginning a regimen of HIV antiretroviral drugs provided for free by the government of Botswana.[64] Its provision of free antiretroviral drugs sets Botswana apart from most other countries' drug policies and counters pharmaceutical companies' global efforts to protect patents and prevent more affordable production and distribution of anti-HIV drugs. In the narrative of Kgalalelo Ntsepe one can discern the operation of material politics at global and national levels in a specific body dramatized in the format of a glamorous cultural production.

Acknowledgments

I offer my gratitude to several colleagues who read or heard full versions or portions of this chapter and offered critical commentary, most notably Robert Asen, John M. Sloop, Phaedra Pezzullo, and Fabian Holt. In revising this chapter, I additionally benefited from the comments and criticism of graduate students and faculty at an October 2008 colloquium sponsored by the Department of Communication Studies at the University of Texas at Austin.

Notes

1. Edmund White quoted in David B. Feinberg, "AIDS in Humor," in *Queer and Loathing: Rants and Raves of a Raging AIDS Clone* (New York: Viking, 1994), 84.

2. Feinberg, "AIDS in Humor," 85.

3. Laura Engle, "Is HIV a Laughing Matter? A Report from the First Comedy Contest for HIV Positive People in New York," *Body Positive*, June 1997, http://www.thebody.com/bp/june97/aids_laugh.html (accessed September 26, 2004).

4. Thomas L. Long, "Plague of Pariahs: AIDS 'Zines and the Rhetoric of Transgression," *Journal of Communication Inquiry* 24 (2000): 401–11.

5. Daniel C. Brouwer, "Counterpublicity and Corporeality in HIV/AIDS Zines," *Critical Studies in Media Communication* 22 (2005): 351–71. In that essay, I situated *IFP* and *DPN* within the universe of alternative media, provided details about their production and circulation, characterized their distinct political projects, and assessed their relations with other publics.

6. Tony Kushner, *Angels in America: A Gay Fantasia on National Themes. Part One: Millennium Approaches* (New York: Theatre Communications Group, 1993), 31.

7. Mary Douglas, "Jokes," in *Implicit Meanings: Essays in Anthropology* (London: Routledge, Kegan & Paul, 1975), 98.

8. See Chris Powell and George E. C. Paton, "Introduction," in *Humour in Society: Resistance and Control*, ed. Chris Powell and George E. C. Paton (New York: St. Martin's Press, 1988), xiii–xxii. See also Stephen A. Smith, "Humor as Rhetoric and Cultural Argument," *Journal of American Culture* 16 (1993): 51–63.

9. Commentary on humor and AIDS recognizes humor's ambivalent career. Dundes catalogues the emergence of cruel, phobic AIDS jokes and diagnoses them as "a kind of collective mental hygienic defense mechanism." See Alan Dundes, "At Ease, Disease—AIDS Jokes as Sick Humor," *American Behavioral Scientist* 30 (1987): 73. Others have explored humor as a potentially efficacious mode in HIV prevention programs, as a phenomenon among HIV/AIDS health care workers, and as a mode of response among the diagnosed and in the queer community generally. These works are, consecutively, Kathleen J. Welch, "Correlates of Alcohol and/or Drug Use among HIV-Infected Individuals," *AIDS Patient Care & STDs* 14 (2000): 317–23; Stella Dorz, Caterina Novara, Claudio Sica, and Ezio Sanavio, "Predicting Burnout among HIV/AIDS and Oncology Health Care Workers," *Psychology & Health* 18 (2000): 677–84; and Ruth Grossman Dean, "Stories of AIDS: The Use of Narrative as an Approach to Understanding in an AIDS Support Group," *Clinical Social Work Journal* 2 (1995): 287–304; Feinberg, "AIDS in Humor"; and Engle, "Is HIV a Laughing Matter?"

10. Susan Sontag, "Notes on 'Camp,'" *Partisan Review* 31 (1964): 515–30.

11. Moe Meyer, "The Signifying Invert: Camp and the Performance of Nineteenth-Century Sexology," *Text and Performance Quarterly* 15 (1995): 278. While camp may have emerged as a "solely queer" discourse, it should no longer be treated, descriptively or normatively, as such. Certainly, camp is available to and practiced by other constituencies. Patrick P. Garlinger and H. Rosi Song argue that consideration of camp in Spain challenges both Sontag's depoliticized or apolitical rendering of camp and Meyer's narrow rendering of camp as solely queer. See Patrick Paul Garlinger and H. Rosi Song, "Camp: What's Spain Got to Do with It?" *Journal of Spanish Cultural Studies* 5 (2004): 4.

12. Meyer, "The Signifying Invert," 277.

13. Ibid., 265–66.

14. George Chauncey, *Gay New York* (New York: Basic Books, 1994), 290.

15. See Alberto Melucci, "The Symbolic Challenge of Contemporary Social Movements," *Social Research* 52 (1985): 789–816; see also Dana L. Cloud, "Doing Away with Suharto—and the Twin Myths of Globalization and New Social Movements," in *Counterpublics and the State,* ed. Robert Asen and Daniel C. Brouwer (Albany: State University of New York Press, 2001), 235–63.

16. Andrew Ross, "Uses of Camp," in *No Respect: Intellectuals and Popular Culture* (New York: Routledge, 1989), 135–70.

17. David Román, "'It's My Party and I'll Die If I Want To!': Gay Men, AIDS, and the Circulation of Camp in U.S. Theatre," *Theatre Journal* 44 (1992): 311–16.

18. Ross, "Uses of Camp," 137.

19. Mary M. Garrett, "Wit, Power, and Oppositional Groups: A Case Study of 'Pure Talk,'" *Quarterly Journal of Speech* 79 (1993): 312.

20. It should be noted that, at tactical moments, being unintelligible to a wider public might constitute the primary reason for deployment of camp gestures. "Style performs membership," Michael Warner claims, and one might perform one's queer membership through camp gestures in order to short-circuit authorized codes of meaning making. Nevertheless, it is important to recognize that camp's social and political efficacy is linked to its intelligibility. Additionally chastening is the disparate availability of camp as a critical tool. Corroborating and extending Andrew Ross's recognition that camp functions differently for constituencies distinguished by sex, sexuality, class, and more, E. Patrick Johnson examines gestural performances of SNAP!—the artful combination of snapping fingers and full forearm motion with roots in African American culture—and argues that SNAP! performances by white people expose the critical limits of camp humor. When SNAP! is imagined as part of a camp repertoire, whites' appropriative performances of it risk offensive parody and stereotyping. See Michael Warner, "Styles of Intellectual Publics," in *Publics and Counterpublics* (New York: Zone Books, 2002), 142; and E. Patrick Johnson, "SNAP! Culture: A Different Kind of 'Reading,'" *Text and Performance Quarterly* 15 (1995): 122–42.

21. Here, I supplement my earlier reference to the AIDS Coalition to Unleash

Power (ACT UP) and its interventions in material politics with recognition that ACT UP sometimes employed camp humor in its conduct of material politics. ACT UP's early enactments of camp politics have been fruitfully chronicled in John Goss's 1989 activist video, *Stiff Sheets*, and in Douglas Crimp and Adam Rolston, *AIDS DemoGraphics* (Seattle: Bay Press, 1990).

22. Román, "'It's My Party,'" 319.

23. "I Wonder If Any of These Organizations Will Offer Me the Support I'm Looking For," *Diseased Pariah News* 5 (1992): 14.

24. For an extensive demonstration of the ways in which *Infected Faggot Perspectives* and *Diseased Pariah News* constitute counterpublics, see Brouwer, "Counterpublicity and Corporeality."

25. Powell and Paton, "Introduction," xv; Chauncey, *Gay New York*, 290.

26. Smith, "Humor as Rhetoric," 51.

27. Peter Stallybrass and Allon White, *The Politics and Poetics of Transgression* (London: Methuen, 1986), 43.

28. W. Wayne Karr, "The AIDS Survival Guide: A Long-Termer Shares His Secrets," *Infected Faggot Perspectives* 3 (1991): 11.

29. Aunt Kaposi, "Advice for the Loveworn: Ask Aunt Kaposi," *Diseased Pariah News* 5 (1992): 14.

30. For discussion of Barbie's multiple cultural articulations, see Erica Rand, *Barbie's Queer Accessories* (Durham, NC: Duke University Press, 1995); Mary F. Rogers, *Barbie Culture* (Thousand Oaks, CA: Sage Publications, 1999); and Susan Stern, *Barbie Nation*, VHS (New York: New Day Films, 1998).

31. Rogers, *Barbie Culture*, 11.

32. "AIDS Barbie!" *Diseased Pariah News* 8 (1993): 1.

33. Ibid.

34. Rogers, *Barbie Culture*, 14.

35. Mikhail M. Bakhtin, *Rabelais and His World*, trans. Hélène Iswolsky (Bloomington: Indiana University Press, 1984), 19.

36. Bakhtin, *Rabelais*, 48.

37. Ibid., 11.

38. Zine readers were invited to continue their festive laughter in issues 9 and 10 of *Diseased Pariah News*, both of which featured back-page advertisements for additional AIDS Barbie products: AIDS Barbie's Dream Hospice and KS [Kaposi's sarcoma] Ken.

39. Indeed, one might say that this flattening of women's variegated agencies indexes Barbie's investments in whiteness; in the ad, even as Barbie's commitments to norms of femininity contribute to her infection, she is still imagined in a social matrix that would authorize her to refuse sexual activity or to negotiate condom use.

40. Crimp and Rolston, *AIDS DemoGraphics*, 38–39.

41. Crypta la Coccus, "Crypta from the Crypt," *Infected Faggot Perspectives* 10 (1992): 2; Trixie Trash, "Trixie's Holiday Tips for Girls in Need of Glamour!" *Infected*

Faggot Perspectives 12 (1993): 8, 13–15; Pansy Ass Faggot, "Just Say No," *Infected Faggot Perspectives* 12 (1993): 4–5.

42. I thank Linda Park-Fuller for drawing my attention to the significance of glamour as a spell in my reading of this passage.

43. In the United States, the Centers for Disease Control and Prevention has amended the definition of AIDS several times during the epidemic—in 1985, 1987, 1992, 1994, and 2008. Trixie's implied concern about deindividuation of the experience of AIDS through its increasingly "mass" characteristics resonates with Foucault's distinction between "morbid" (individuated, expressive) and "macabre" (mass, impersonal) diseases. See Michel Foucault, *The Birth of the Clinic: An Archaeology of Medical Perception*, trans. A. M. Sheridan Smith (New York: Vintage Books, 1994), 171.

44. Trixie Trash, "Trixie's Holiday Tips," 8. To avoid interruptive editorial marks, I have retained the original punctuation for this quotation.

45. Pansy Ass Faggot, "Just Say No," 4–5. To avoid interruptive editorial marks, I have retained the original punctuation for this quotation.

46. Sander Gilman, *Disease and Representation: Images of Illness from Madness to AIDS* (Ithaca, NY: Cornell University Press, 1988), 3.

47. Aunt Kaposi, "Advice for the Loveworn," 14.

48. Eran Shalev, "Ancient Masks, American Fathers: Classical Pseudonyms during the American Revolution and Early Republic," *Journal of the Early Republic* 23 (2003): 153–54.

49. Margaret J. M. Ezell, "Reading Pseudonyms in Seventeenth-Century English Coterie Literature," *Essays in Literature* 21 (1994): 14–25. See also Maureen E. Mulvihill, "'Butterfly' of the Restoration Court: A Preview of Lady Mary Villiers, the New 'Ephelia' Candidate," *ANQ* 9 (1996): 36.

50. Ezell, "Reading Pseudonyms," 19–23.

51. Ibid., 21.

52. Writing about gender performance in gay male collectives, Johnson claims that "effeminacy . . . is not valued outside of camp and humor in most of these communities." See Johnson, "SNAP! Culture," 128. I do not have space in this chapter to interrogate this important claim.

53. Meyer, "The Signifying Invert," 270, 277.

54. Judith Butler, *Bodies That Matter* (New York: Routledge, 1993), 235–37, 125, 122.

55. The specter of misogyny raises the question, Why would *Diseased Pariah News* editors choose Barbie as a vehicle for their commentary about glamour and sexual politics? Barbie's possible status as a drag queen provides a response. Rogers notes, "As an icon of drag, Barbie illustrates what many feminists and cultural critics have been saying for some years[,] . . . that femininity is a manufactured reality." See Rogers, *Barbie Culture*, 42. In my view, *DPN*'s AIDS Barbie ads are sympathetic to Barbie as a person with AIDS; the mockery of Barbie functions critically as a mockery of the gender norms to which she is subjected.

56. Michael Warner, "The Mass Public and the Mass Subject," in *Habermas and the Public Sphere*, ed. Craig Calhoun (Cambridge: Massachusetts Institute of Technology Press, 1992), 377–401.

57. Richard Schechner, "Restoration of Behavior," in *Between Theater and Anthropology* (Philadelphia: University of Pennsylvania Press, 1985), 35–116, quote on 97. I wish to thank Linda Park-Fuller for drawing the connection between writing in drag and "not me"/"not not me."

58. Butler, *Bodies That Matter*, xi.

59. Carole Blair, "Reflections on Criticism and Bodies: Parables from Public Places," *Western Journal of Communication* 65 (2001): 288.

60. These appear consecutively in Richard Gray, *Infected Faggot Perspectives* 3 (1991): 6; *Infected Faggot Perspectives* 9 (1992): 23; and *Infected Faggot Perspectives* 9 (1992): 25.

61. Rand, *Barbie's Queer Accessories*, 5, 161, 5.

62. More broadly—that is, without specific reference to HIV/AIDS—I encourage a comparative approach to the study of camp humor among various collectives. Note, for example, the differing conditions of emergence, circulation, and reception of camp as a mode of critique against Francoist culture in Spain (Garlinger and Song), camp embodied in Cubana dyke performances (Muñoz), and camp in lesbian cultural productions in the United States (Cvetkovich). See Garlinger and Song, "Camp," 3–10; José Esteban Muñoz, "Sister Acts: Ela Troyano and Carmelita Tropicana," in *Disidentifications: Queers of Color and the Performance of Politics* (Minneapolis: University of Minnesota Press, 1999), 119–41; and Ann Cvetkovich, "In the Archive of Lesbian Feelings," in *An Archive of Feelings: Trauma, Sexuality, and Lesbian Public Cultures* (Durham, NC: Duke University Press, 2003), 239–71.

63. Challiss McDonough, "Botswana Crowns 'Miss HIV Stigma-Free,'" VOANews.com, September 9, 2003, http://www.voanews.com/english/africa/ (accessed March 2, 2005).

64. Ibid.

10
The Vernacular Mode
Locating the Non-institutional in the Practice of Citizenship

Robert Glenn Howard

Near the dawning of the age of participatory media, an ironic discursive moment demonstrates how participatory media can facilitate a vernacular mode that encourages transformative discourse. During John Kerry's 2004 bid for U.S. president, the Democratic Party created a Web site titled the Official Kerry-Edwards Blog. Cultivating an informal tone on the site, party officials chronicled minor campaign happenings in periodic dated entries. One official noted the quality of the baked goods at the "Baking for Barnstormers" event and even posted a snapshot of a tasty-looking cake.[1] Elsewhere on the site, this informal ethos was evoked with personal posts like this one: "Congrats Shanna! Right now John Kerry is in the front seat talking with Shanna Williams from Chicago, Illinois—she's a local Kerry supporter . . . and she's getting married this fall."[2] Only identified as "davidwade," this entry was written by David Wade, Kerry's national press secretary for the campaign and the communications director for Kerry's U.S. Senate office.

Underneath these "official" blog entries, the site offered its audience the opportunity to post their own informal comments and responses. In response to "Congrats Shanna!" the site's blog-savvy audience ignored David Wade and used the comments section of his entry to continue a heated debate from previous posts. Just a month before, Howard Dean had lost the Democratic Party's nomination to Kerry. After his loss, Dean supporters began posting comments on Kerry's site. Because Dean had made an early entry into the realm of online campaigning, some Dean supporters called Kerry a "copycat" for creating the Official Kerry-Edwards Blog. Arguing that the Dean supporters were just jealous of the newly remodeled Kerry site, one participant mused on the nature of Internet media: "Dean didn't invent the internet, after all. The net is for everyone—it's just another form of media. . . . The medium is just an interpreter for this—the messages people care about, their feelings about what's going on, and what they want to change."[3] Celebrating the vernacular expression that this Web site's comments sections fostered, the audience member ignored David Wade, the powerful institutional agent behind the blog—as did almost everyone who commented in response to the "Congrats Shanna!" entry. Out of fifty-two responses, only three addressed the actual topic of Wade's post: Shanna and her impending marriage. This ironic discursive moment functions as an early example of how the most ubiquitous form of participatory media in the first decade after the year 2000 (the "blog") can encourage discourse in a vernacular mode.

Heralded as marking a new era of "participatory culture," the number of Web pages considered "blogs" exploded in the early twenty-first century.[4] In July of 2002, 3 percent of Internet users reported having their own blog. By November of 2005, that number had jumped to 10 percent. At that time, 27 percent read other people's blogs and 19 percent of teenage Internet users maintained their own blogs.[5] Meanwhile, it has been estimated that seventy thousand new blogs and about seven hundred thousand new posts to existing blogs are appearing everyday.[6]

This explosion has fueled (and been fueled by) a growing diversity of participatory forms of online media. Famously termed "Web 2.0" by computer media CEO Tim O'Reilly, these media have emerged from ongoing innovations in network communication technologies.[7] With the development of more robust network protocols and languages, it became easier for Web users to create and alter Web site content. From wikis to social networking, photo sharing, folksonomy, and blogs themselves, these sorts of Web use occur across network locations where individual actors and institutional structures intermingle in whole new kinds of communication processes. In these processes, old distinctions between private and public, personal and commercial, and vernacular and institutional are blurred. Imagining these processes in terms of the preexisting theories of the vernacular does not fully account for the discursive blurring participatory media foster.

By returning to its classical meanings, however, the vernacular can be reimagined as a dialectical modality of discourse. This structural conception of the vernacular can help account for the common resource of non-institutional expression that individuals are engaging online while acknowledging that even institutional agents can speak in a vernacular mode. Because of its dialectical structure, the vernacular necessitates that those who deploy it express alterity to the dominant institutions. Though the vernacular does not necessarily oppose institutions, it holds open the door for such opposition because it insists on maintaining access to an alternate authority, and this door opens even when an institutional agent performs the vernacular.

In this chapter, I argue that conceptualizing the vernacular as a dialectical modality of discourse can help researchers of communication and rhetoric account for the blurring of the distinction between vernacular and institutional agencies and agents occurring in online participatory media. In the first section, I explore the two primary theories of the vernacular in communication research. While one relies on a distinction between vernacular and institutional agents, the other relies on a distinction between vernacular and institutional agencies. Participatory media, however, blur the distinction in both agents and agencies. A third conception of the vernacular is needed to account for this blurring. In the next section, I deploy the ancient meanings of the term to imagine the vernacular as a dialectical mode of discourse hybridizing not just texts but also discursive agents and the agencies they deploy. Next, I demonstrate how this conception can account for the complex confluence of agents and agencies occurring on and around the example of the Official Kerry-Edwards Blog. The institutional agents on the site successfully initiated a vernacular dialectic that expressed support for Kerry. However, when Democratic Party officials were perceived by their audience to be reducing the alternate views expressed on the site by moderating its collaborative mechanisms, their ability to deploy a vernacular modality was called into question. Across an emergent web of network locations, the blogging community asserted a redefined alterity beyond the reach of the Official Kerry-Edwards Blog.

In online participatory media, opportunities for new kinds of public expression have emerged. While much of this discourse is mundane, that does not necessarily mean that it is incapable of functioning as a means for social change. As Robert Asen has noted, "Discourse practices present potentially accessible and powerful everyday enactments of citizenship. Even regular voters can vote only periodically. . . . By contrast, discourse practices suggest a frequency and sustainability to civic engagement."[8] The conception of a vernacular mode of public discourse helps account for the discourse practices that are arising in participatory media. These new communication technologies are increasing the means available to speak and the audiences who can be addressed. As a result, they are increasing the opportunities for engagement in the processes of discursive citizenship.

The Vernacular as Non-institutional

After Margaret Lantis introduced the term to cultural theorists in 1960, "vernacular" has come to refer to non-institutional cultural forms and practices. This usage has become common in several fields, including anthropology, architecture, religion, and literary studies.[9] Since the late 1990s, researchers in communication studies have taken a growing interest in the concept. Reacting against the traditional emphasis on the great speakers tradition, Kent Ono and John Sloop imagined a subaltern "vernacular discourse." Four years later, Gerard Hauser imagined a common resource of "vernacular rhetoric." As Dana Cloud has demonstrated, Hauser's and Ono's and Sloop's conceptions of vernacularity diverge significantly.[10] Hauser refers to a diffuse set of communication practices generally available, while Ono and Sloop imagine the vernacular in reference to historically disempowered groups. While these two views are not entirely reconcilable, they both imagine the vernacular as defined by its non-institutional nature.[11] In the case of Hauser, that non-institutional nature adheres in an agency commonly available to discursive participants. In the case of Ono and Sloop, that nature adheres in the agents who are able to deploy a pastiche of cultural forms to their specific vernacular ends.

To imagine this distinction, agents and agencies must not be conflated. "Agent" refers to the entity that carries out an action. In the case of discourse, the agent is the subject deploying language to create a documentable communication behavior. "Agency," on the other hand, refers to the capacity to assert influence or power. Any documented communication may include many or only one agent. In the same way, discourse can emerge as the manifestation of one or several different capacities for expressive power or "agencies."

Focusing on vernacular agents in 1995, Ono and Sloop called for critics to explore "vernacular discourse" that "resonates within and from historically oppressed communities."[12] In the introduction to their book *Shifting Borders*, Ono and Sloop specifically define vernacular discourses as those that "emerge from discussions between members of self-identified smaller communities within the larger civic community."[13] From this perspective, vernacular discourse is that discourse which is produced by individuals who are imagined as alternate to the larger "civic community" by identifying with a historically subordinated group. With this emphasis on the historically disenfranchised, Ono and Sloop's "vernacular discourse" became associated with subaltern agents.[14]

Ono and Sloop are correct to emphasize that "vernacular discourse does not, by definition, enable constituents of vernacular cultures to articulate liberatory political identities and subject positions." Using rap and jazz as examples, they note that the discourse produced by vernacular agents often assimilates and redeploys institutionally produced discourse. Emphasizing that vernacular discourse can be a "pastiche" in this sense, they explicitly disavow the valorization of the vernacular as something extra-institutional and thus non-repressed, virtuous, and pure.[15] Their most enduring point may be that the vernacular is open to critique at least because it sometimes acts to support hegemonic power structures.

Even when it does act in favor of the hegemonic, however, the vernacular's definitive trait lies in the agents who produce the discourse. The vernacular may redeploy institutional discourse, and it may even function in support of hegemony, but it must always be "discourse that emanates from specific localized communities."[16] For Ono and Sloop, the vernacular lies in the identity of the discursive agents who produce the discourse instead of in the structuration caused by the agencies that agents (subaltern, local, or institutional) employ. In this sense, their definition of the vernacular relies on the imagined identity of the speaker. This suggests that institutionally empowered agents like those producing the Kerry blog are not able to produce vernacular discourse. As I noted at the outset, however, the institutional producers of that blog did (for a time) successfully speak in a vernacular mode.

In his 1999 *Vernacular Voices*, Gerard Hauser articulated a different conception of the vernacular. Hauser argued that "publics are emergences manifested through vernacular rhetoric." Hauser's "vernacular" is the dialogic force of the community. This force emerges in what he calls the "mundane transactions of words and gestures that allow us to negotiate our way through our quotidian encounters." Used as a source of invention, the vernacular is here an agency that adheres in the commonplace. Differentiating vernacular agency from that of formal public speaking associated with institutional discourse, Hauser argues that publics, "are not formal exchanges of the podium; they are vernacular expressions of who we are, what we need and hope for, what we are willing to accept, and our commitment to reciprocity."[17] From this perspective, the vernacular is associated with the *doxa, sensus communis,* or "common sense" that is accessed through informal discourse.[18]

Imagining the vernacular in reference to one or both of these conceptions, researchers in communication and rhetorical studies have generated excellent scholarship focusing on African American vernacular discourse.[19] Other scholars looked at how Latina/o vernaculars voice counter-hegemonic political interests.[20] The success of these explorations spurred a reassessment of the place of the vernacular in public address generally.[21] From there, researchers focusing on communication and rhetoric have explored the vernacular in terms of education, film, performance studies, religion, subcultures, and Internet-based discourse.[22]

Applying these two conceptions of the vernacular to communication occurring online today, Hauser's and Ono and Sloop's vernaculars address different qualities of these new media. Deploying Ono and Sloop's concept of vernacular discourse, participatory media can be seen to offer subaltern agents who have access to the necessary technologies the chance to express themselves in different ways and to new audiences. In cases where agents may be clearly identifiable members of a historically subordinated community, Ono and Sloop's conception of the vernacular may be activated. As the Official Kerry-Edwards Blog demonstrates, however, sometimes openly institutional agents deploy a vernacular modality of discourse. In participatory media, individuals often express themselves as alternate to institutions but without reference to any local community or historically subordinated group. In these cases, their discourse cannot be defined as "vernacular" based on the imagined identity of agents enacting the discourse.

Deploying Hauser's concept, participatory media can be seen increasing the occasions when the informal communal agency of vernacular rhetoric can be enacted in discourse. This vernacular voice is particularly evident in the collaborative features on blog Web sites. The technologies deployed in these "guest books" and "comments sections" allow audience members to post their responses underneath the blog owner's main entries. Because it is public, typically informal, and the product of multiple agents acting together, this discourse enacts Hauser's vernacular rhetoric. However, Hauser's concept suggests that multiple non-institutional agents act together to generate a vernacular agency for the generative discourse of publics. While the discourse produced in participatory media is typically the result of multiple agents, this multiplicity is not the result of non-institutional agencies alone. In the case of the Official Kerry-Edwards Blog, the institution of the Democratic Party provides the agency by which these multiple agents engage vernacular rhetoric. With many institutions offering similar collaborative features on their Web sites, participatory media often blur the distinction between institutional and non-institutional agencies.

In terms of agency, the vernacular blurs into the institutional because the technologies that make multiplicity possible are themselves institutional products. Here, the proprietary hardware and software used as the means for creating the network locations for vernacular discourse inscribe institutional power into vernacular expression. In terms of agents, the institutional can blur into the vernacular. With the wide adoption of the term of "blog," it has come to refer to a particular genre that carries with it specific audience expectations. Seeking to reach the audiences that create and consume discourse in this genre, institutional agents have begun to term their Web sites "blogs." Because the genre is expected to include comments sections or guest books, these institutional sites often include collaborative features. With the inclusion of those features, institutional agents deploy a vernacular modality to their own ends.

The social factors that have operated to form communication technologies result in institutional intentions becoming embedded in online vernacular discourse.[23] As theorists of technology have long recognized, technologies carry ideological components because they are the result of the social factors that operated to form them. As those technologies shape future action they, in turn, reproduce elements of those social factors and their ideologies.[24] In this sense, the computer products necessary to create and access participatory media extend the influence of the institutional intentions that operated to create those technologies. This occurs first through the physical machines that make computer-mediated communication possible.[25] More profoundly, however, it also occurs as individuals access the software applications through which their personal Web sites are created and hosted. In the case of blogs, this influence has been well documented.

In 1999, several companies released software designed to automate Web site creation in an effort to harness the growing popularity of "weblogs." The most successful of these ventures was the "Blogger" software of Blogger.com.[26] In exchange for placing third-party advertising on the personal Web sites it hosted, Blogger.com offered a service that made it very easy for even computer novices to put personal content online.[27] The software was primarily designed to put diary-like entries on a Web site. It paid little attention to making network links to other Web sites. At the time, this angered many amateur and hobbyist Web users because they felt that the value of the "weblog" (the term for blogs current at that time) was in its ability to create links between multiple network locations. However, the power of this clever corporate strategy as well as an effective software design allowed Blogger.com to define the basic features of the new genre of blogs.

With Blogger.com, the sheer numbers of individuals able to create blogs rendered the previous conception of weblogs obsolete. As well-known blogger and scholar of communication Rebecca Blood has described it, "With the overwhelming adoption of Blogger, and without an interface that emphasized links as the central element of the form, the blog-style Weblog was born."[28] Reverse-dated personal entries dominated this style, and the term "weblog" gave way to "blog."[29] With its emphasis on individually posted entries, the Blogger.com software can be seen to have carried that institution's intentions into the vernacular discourse that it made possible.

In terms of agents, participatory media blur the distinction between the vernacular and the institutional when institutions deploy forms associated with the vernacular to their own discursive ends. As blogs came to emphasize individual entries written by a single agent over collections of links to other sites, blogs became a medium well suited for monologic discourse. This made it a better medium for the formal statements of institutions. Typically, the entries posted by a blog owner define the character and content of the blog. The audience going to the network location is, to a great extent, drawn by the choices the blog owner has made. On completely personal blogs, this central agent can be considered vernacular. As blogging became more popular, however, institutions began to term some of their institutional media "blogs."

In cases like that of the well-known GM *Fastlane Blog* of General Motors or the blogs of *New York Times* columnists, the blogger speaks as a representative of her or his institution.[30] Here, the entries are often polished pieces of editorial, journalistic, scientific, or other discourse. Because these cases lack the informality or communal nature of vernacular rhetoric, many blog sites may not activate Hauser's conception of communal agency. At the same time, these blogs are not created by vernacular agents and are thus not properly considered vernacular discourse as it is defined by Ono and Sloop.

Such sites can, however, enact discourse in a vernacular mode when they seek to deploy the dialogic agencies of collaborative participatory media to their own institutional ends. As the blog stabilized into a genre in the first decade after the year 2000, blogging included tools that made it easy to create collaborative media features like comments sections. As a result, both the creators and readers of blogs expected these collaborative features to be included on a Web site or page termed a "blog." Including such comments sections and using the informal language common in these collaborative discursive media, institutional agents deployed a vernacular agency to their own ends.

The agency that collaborative features facilitate on institutional Web sites is not, however, strictly vernacular. The agents of the institution technically control any comment posted on their institutional site. Even if we imagine the collaborative sections of blogs as texts wholly separate from the more formal entries, the blog owner or owners typically retain the technical ability to limit, edit, or even remove any or all of the comments posted by the audience. As a result, even the comments sections on institutional sites taken by themselves blur the institutional agency of monologic discourse with the vernacular agency of informal dialogic discourse: that of the audience-poster and that of the blog owner who chooses to retain, edit, or remove audience-posted comments.

Even in the case of the most vernacular blog possible, the institutional nature of participatory media themselves shapes the possibilities of the discourse enacted in those media. So doing, they allow (as did the Blogger.com software described above) institutional intentions to shape the discourse. In a blog that is controlled by an unquestionably vernacular agent who includes collaborative features for a vernacular audience to enact dialogic discourse, the participatory media still blur the distinction between institutional and vernacular agencies as the proprietary products that make the blog possible exert their institutional influence on the kinds of communication that can be enacted in those media.

As participatory media blur the distinction between vernacular and institutional in both agents and the agencies they deploy, defining the vernacular on the basis of either a vernacular agent or a vernacular agency becomes problematic. A third conception of the vernacular, however, can help account for this blurring by emphasizing the structural definition of the vernacular as a mode of discourse instead of emphasizing either the identity of the speakers or the nature of the agency deployed by those speakers.

In this conception, the vernacular becomes distinct in communication processes whenever non-institutional authority is invoked. In this sense, it is a structural result of specific kinds of rhetorical tactics. When an agent claims the non-institutional as a source of authority, she or he speaks in a vernacular mode. As a necessary result of this structural definition, however, the vernacular becomes a mode of discourse available even to institutional agents. This fact allows a dialectical conception of the vernacular to account for the deployment of a vernacular mode even on an institutional Web site such as the Kerry blog. In the next section, the classical meanings of the term are explored to help imagine this modal vernacular. From this exploration, it becomes clear that the ancient meanings of the vernacular can account for the blurring of the distinction at a structural level because any expression in a vernacular mode must simultaneously invoke both vernacular and institutional as a dialectical pair.

The Vernacular as Dialectic

As a mode of discourse, the expression of alterity to the institutional is a resource open to any who have access to the means of communication. Even claims to vernacular authority that are enacted by institutional agents can attempt to generate acceptance of a non-institutional authority. In these cases, the vernacular can advocate for (or even speak as) an institution insofar as it can maintain a perception that its agency is alternate to that of the institution it supports. In this conception, an institutional agent is not necessarily excluded from the vernacular because vernacularity emerges dialectically whenever expressive discourse situates itself as alternate to the institutional.

However, this conception necessarily imagines the vernacular not just as hybrid discourse but as hybrid at a structural level because agents must invoke the institutional as a prior term from which to distinguish their alternate authority. In this dialectic, the vernacular acknowledges the priority of the institutional in order to garner its alternate authority. As a result, the vernacular is necessarily also an extension of the institutional that has made it possible. This dialectical sense of the vernacular is rooted in its meaning from classical antiquity.

The Latin word "vernacular" is derived from the Classical Greek word *oikogenes* that literally means "home-genetic." In extant Greek writings, an *oikotrips* is a "home-born" slave. A distinguishing quality of the oikotrips was her or his ability to speak Greek. This meaning is made clear in Plato's *Meno* when Socrates asks Meno to provide a "retainer" for an experiment in learning. Meno brings a boy forward, and Socrates asks, "He is a Greek and speaks our language?" Meno responds, "Indeed yes—born and bred in the house [literally, 'yes, he is home-genetic']."[31] By the Roman period, Latin had come to dominate the colonial holdings of the Republic and later the Empire. At this time, "Vulgar Latin" was a blanket term covering the many spoken dialects of Latinate languages that were spread across Western Europe. These more diverse kinds of Latin were distinguished from the institutional languages of Classical Latin and the still common Classical Greek. These were the written languages of Roman institutions, and it is from this usage that we get the modern meanings of "vernacular."

Verna, in Roman Latin, is a noun specifically referring to slaves that were born and raised in a Roman home. Sometimes literally a hybrid between a Roman master and an enslaved servant, the verna was always a cultural hybrid. The verna was a native to Roman culture but was also the offspring of a sublimated non-Roman ethnic or culture group. In Roman society, most slaves were seized during wars, during the suppression of colonial insurrections, or even through outright piracy. The majority of these slaves did not read or write Classical Latin or Greek. Since any person born to a slave woman (without regard to the social position of the father) was automatically a slave, female slaves were encouraged to have children to increase the master's slave stock.[32] These vernas could become even more valuable than their mothers when they were trained as native users of the institutional languages and could then engage in more technical kinds of work. Subordinated in relation to the institutions, their access to institutional languages made them more powerful than the average slave. Unlike their masters, however, they were typically also native speakers of their own cultural languages. In this sense, they were hybrid.

The Latin term *hibrida* was closely related to *verna*. Not necessarily referring to a slave, hibrida referred to individual livestock that were a cross between a domesticated animal and a "wild" animal. In its most ancient meaning, hibrida seems to refer to the offspring of a domesticated sow and a wild boar. The boar was emblematic of a masculine ideal in both Greece and Rome. Considered a dangerous and worthy adversary, it was one of the most prized and respected animals of the hunt.[33] When applied to a person, however, it suggested an individual with parents from two different ethnicities. In particular, the term was applied to individuals who acted in Roman institutions but were not of Roman birth.[34] While the authentically Roman was seen as civilizing its counterpart, the non-institutional had access to an alternate authority.

The verna would have been perceived as only partially tame because its non-Roman elements were seen as wild. At the same time, that wildness was wild precisely because it granted access to something outside of the institutions of Rome. In one of its earliest uses to describe expressive human behavior, Cicero suggested that the "vernacular" was a means to persuasive power. In one of his works on rhetoric, *Brutus*, he wrote of vernacular as an "indescribable flavor" that rendered a particular speaker persuasive.[35] Cicero understood the vernacular, linked to participation in a particular community, as set in opposition to what he and other Roman politicians saw as the institutional elements of persuasive communication available through the formal study of Roman history, literature, and philosophy.

Unlike the arts of oratory, the vernacular existed and was learned outside of formal Roman education. The non-institutional aspect of the hybrid verna was seen as powerful by institutional Rome precisely because it was both able to act in institutional modes of communication, Latin, and had access to something beyond those institutional powers. The vernacular is powerful because it can introduce something other than the institutional into an institutional realm. This ability is the result of its hybrid nature because it is its hybridity that gave the verna access to the combined authority of its nativity and the institutional. This hybridity is embedded in the structure of the vernacular mode of expression because the vernacular needs the institutional from which to differentiate itself. Even as it expresses its alterity, it acknowledges the priority (the dominance) of its masters: the institutional forms that allow its voice to be heard as alternate.

Because the vernacular comes into meaning as a result of being rendered distinct from that to which it is a subordinate, it can never be a complete alternate to the institutional. As a result, it is never completely separate from institutions. Instead, the institutional authorizes the vernacular in the sense that all vernacularity relies on the institutional to create the grounds on which the vernacular can enact its distinction. In this way, the vernacular emerges only when it imagines its dialectical twin as prior: the institutional. At this structural level, the vernacular is necessarily hybrid in that it must contain the institutional from which to express alterity.

While this conception of a dialectical vernacular does not necessarily supersede or exclude previous theories, it deploys the classical origins of the term to imagine a more inclusive structural vernacularity. It emphasizes the ways vernacular expression emerges structurally bound up with its subordinating institutional powers. This emphasis is particularly useful when attempting to account for the blurring of agencies and agents common in participatory media because it does not try to render the institutional and non-institutional distinct. Instead, it recognizes that part of what empowers the vernacular is the inclusion of its subordinating alternate. The verna was empowered only in so far as she or he deployed the forms that carried institutional power. Writing a bill of sale or counting a master's profits, the verna forwarded the same cultural forms that gave the institutional its dominance.

For those who have access to participatory media today, the situation is far less dire than it was for the verna. The verna could typically do very little to express alterity. Today, however, individuals with enough social and financial privilege to access new communication technologies can choose to situate their discursive expression in the vernacular mode. They can evoke an authority alternate to institutionally empowered communication.[36] In participatory media, institutional power persists in such communications to the degree that institutions have participated in creating the network locations from where the alternate speaks. When institutional participation is only in the form of the proprietary hardware and software used to enact the communication, its influence is relatively weak. In a case where an institution has created a Web site and then allowed some of its audience members to post comments, its influence is much stronger.

When an institutional Web site engages a vernacular modality by including collaborative features, it invokes the authority of the communal voice. Even just the use of the term "blog" by an institutional Web site incites audience expectations that the site will include mechanisms through which alternate voices can be expressed. In the following section, these expectations account for why the participants in the blogging community that supported John Kerry's 2004 presidential campaign felt betrayed when the overtly institutional Web site removed its links to a controversial online supporter. Because Kerry's site was titled a blog and incorporated the expected collaborative features, it demonstrates that even an institutional agent can deploy the vernacular modality. At the same time, however, because its vernacularity was ultimately discredited in the eyes of many, this case also demonstrates that if that agent does not fulfill the expectations of vernacularity, its claims to alterity can lose their credibility.

Vernacular Expectations

In 2003, with his eye on the nomination to run for U.S. president by the Democratic Party, Howard Dean attended a public gathering that was organized through the Web site Meetup.com. Recognizing the potential of the Internet for building support, Dean's campaign quickly started its own meet-up group. In March of 2003, the Dean for President group became the largest on the Web site with 15,000 members. By mid-November, it had over 140,000 members. That year, Dean broke the standing record for the most money raised in a single quarter for a Democratic presidential campaign: over 15 million dollars.[37] Despite these efforts, John Kerry won the Democratic nomination and chose John Edwards as his running mate.

Meanwhile, the Republicans had already developed a robust deployment of Internet technologies in their campaign. The Republican Party created a site titled Bush-Cheney '04 Official Campaign Blog, linked to the official campaign Web site. Terming it a "blog" suggested that collaborative features might be present. In this sense, the site invoked the vernacular. However, this invocation was in name only. While the audience could email the Bush campaign, subscribe to email lists, and contribute money, that audience could not post comments.[38]

Though they had created a blog that offered official information, Bush-Cheney's main Internet strategy was to use email lists and local contacts to get voters involved. While this strategy proved to be a significant factor in the campaign, it did not offer any significant collaborative media features.[39] Without such features, the site remained highly monologic and institutional. There was no invocation of the dialectical vernacular beyond the term "blog" itself, and it seems that few expectations of vernacularity were aroused in the site's audience.

Facing the formidable machinery already put in place by Bush, Kerry poured funding into Internet media designed to primarily follow Dean's example and garner support through interactive media on the Internet.[40] Central to that effort was the Official Kerry-Edwards Blog. In August of 2003, the Official Kerry-Edwards Blog was linked from John Kerry's official site.[41] The top of the front page was dominated by a graphic that included two pictures of John Kerry (one thoughtful and one waving and smiling) and a picture of the White House with elements of an American flag swirling tastefully around it. In later versions of the site, the official Kerry campaign logo was used as a banner image across the top of the page with a title-line for the blog. In May of 2004, that title-line read, "The Official John Kerry Blog." In August of 2004, that text was changed to "the official Kerry-Edwards blog."[42]

In both titles, the Web site overtly identified itself as "official." Official actors wrote the main blog entries. The majority of these entries were by Dick Bell. Bell was employed by the John Kerry campaign under the official title "Blogmaster." First hired by the Democratic National Party in 1993, he oversaw the development of the official party Web sites. During the last three months of the Kerry campaign, Bell reported having fifteen assistants working full time to maintain the Official Kerry-Edwards Blog.[43] These aspects clearly made the discourse on the site a product of the Democratic Party as an institution. However, the site also included significant collaborative features. So doing, it operated in a vernacular mode even though it was produced by institutional agents.

Unlike the singularly institutional Bush-Cheney '04 Official Campaign Blog, the Official Kerry-Edwards Blog offered community members the ability to post their comments underneath each of the official blog entries. By including this feature, the site gave a vernacular voice to everyday Kerry supporters. While the Web site appealed to institutional authority by its official association with the Democratic Party, it also invoked alternate authority by its association with the medium of blogs and, in particular, the inclusion of responses and comments posted by its audience members in the collaborative sections of the site.

By including this collaborative feature, the Official Kerry-Edwards Blog initiated the dialectical definition characteristic of communication in a vernacular mode. With that process in motion, specific expectations emerged in its audience. When a significant controversy arose, the site failed to deliver on those expectations. Recognizing this failure, the vernacular agents who were thwarted on the institutional site itself loudly reasserted their side of the dialectic elsewhere.

The controversy began in July of 2004 when the Official Kerry-Edwards Blog announced it was removing all links to a very popular blog named Daily Kos. On Daily Kos, a Kerry supporter named Markos Zuniga made incendiary comments about American contractors who were videotaped as they were burnt, dragged from their car, and their bodies hung on a bridge during the military conflict in Iraq. The Kerry campaign dubbed Zuniga's comments "unpresidential language" and removed all links from its site to Daily Kos. Outrage erupted in the pro-Kerry blogging community.[44]

When the Official Kerry-Edwards Blog administrators decided to de-link themselves from Daily Kos's "unpresidential language," it became clear that the blog valued its institutional authority over the vernacular modality enacted by its collaborative features. The community of bloggers supporting Kerry, however, had come to expect the inclusion of alternate voices. As a result, the Kerry campaign's choice to remove its off-site links seemed like a betrayal. In an ensuing storm of commentary, Kerry's blogging supporters vented their outrage across a web of pro-Kerry blogging sites.

One popular liberal blogger summed up the response, saying, "[It] shows they're not ready to really have a blog and interact with the rest of the blog world. They should just pull down all their links."[45] On another blog, lesser-known bloggers weighed in with more blunt language: "Kerry is a wuss and a hawk."[46] Another commenter on a still different blog called Kerry "clueless and worrisome." A second participant expanded on that with this comment: "Pathetic indeed. No wonder we [Democratic supporters] get our asses handed to us by the right year in and year out."[47]

As the outcry continued to grow on the sites in the larger pro-Kerry blogging community, no evidence of the controversy appeared on the Official Kerry-Edwards Blog itself—even in the collaborative sections. By then, it seemed to have become clear that the Kerry campaign was quietly moderating the audience comments posted to their site. Specifically claiming that his posts to the Official Kerry-Edwards Blog were removed, one blogger posted on his own Web site, saying, "Apparently Kerry's people don't want to allow people to read anything that they don't have control over." He continued: "As you know I have strongly supported every aspect of the Democratic Party's effort to elect John Kerry and John Edwards. But this universal idea and thought that if someone goes on a message board or blog and posts something that those running the site don't agree with, that it's okay to remove the post or ban the person, is ridiculous. . . . With regard to the censorship practices going on, I would only respond that this is not what America is supposed to be about."[48]

Among many bloggers, it seemed that the Kerry campaign had rejected the vernacular in favor of institutional control; and, in response, community members voiced their rejection of the site's claim to alternate authority. With this institutional outing, the Official Kerry-Edwards Blog was judged more "official" than "blog," and the vernacular authority that the institutional site had dialectically invoked now turned against it. Censored from the site itself, expressions of alterity diffused outward across a web of network locations beyond the reach of the Democratic Party.

The case of the Official Kerry-Edwards Blog demonstrates how a dialectical conception of the vernacular can help account for the blurring of vernacular and institutional agents and agencies occurring in participatory media. Its self-identification as a blog and its inclusion of collaborative features show how the vernacular mode of public discourse is a resource available even to an overtly official site. However, the invocation of a dialectical vernacular enabled that agency to move through participatory media and out of the control of the institution that had invoked it. As the alterity of the Official Kerry-Edwards Blog seemed to fade into just another outlet for institutional monologues, the blogging community dialectically reasserted a stronger alterity at a variety of different network locations. Alterity erupted into a vernacular web of network-based discourse.

The Transformative Potential of Discourse in the Vernacular Mode

In this chapter, I have argued for conceptualizing the vernacular as a mode of discourse. This structurally dialectical vernacular emerges whenever non-institutional authority is invoked. More than a pastiche text, it is structurally hybrid because the vernacular must contain the institutional as the prior authority from which to assert its alterity. Not grounded in any specific capacity or identity, this modality can be engaged by even institutional agents. While this may be disconcerting, the advantage of a dialectical conception of the vernacular is that it accounts for rhetorical tactics that invoke a non-institutional authority without either essentializing the agents engaging it or homogenizing their agencies.

Avoiding the need to establish the vernacularity of discursive agents or agencies, the dialectical vernacular can account for the blurring of the distinction between vernacular and institutional typical of participatory media. Though this conception of the vernacular acknowledges its availability to institutional agents, that should not be seen as weakening some previous, more pure vernacular. Instead, recognizing that the vernacular is dialectical is a recognition that it is also always already hybrid.

Participatory media hold open the possibility for transformation through discourse by offering inexpensive and seemingly endless avenues for everyday people to participate in public discourse. As long as alternate ideas can be expressed, those alternatives have some hope of finding their way into institutions. Even in the cases like that of the Official Kerry-Edwards Blog, where the institutional reduces the authority of vernacular expression, participatory media offer a myriad of other locations for alterity to emerge. Through these vernacular webs of communication, the expression of alterity can retain its transformative potential even when it is under threat from institutional power.

Re-imagining the vernacular as a dialectical mode is an important step toward accounting for the rapidly transforming nature of communication in the twenty-first century. As network-mediated discourse becomes more and more embedded in the daily lives of North Americans, those technologies are exported and transformed throughout the globe. Participatory media with its collaborative potential will increasingly present researchers of communication and rhetoric with significant challenges. As more individuals access television shows side by side with homemade digital video on YouTube or read the *New York Times* after following a link made by a teenage blogger, maintaining distinctions between commercial and personal, institutional and vernacular, and complicit and oppositional in any given discursive fragment will become more and more difficult.

With these changes, it is more important than ever before for researchers and critics to avoid romanticizing the vernacular as held wholly separate from any taint of institutional power. Instead, a dialectical vernacular acknowledges that the institutional forms the grounds from whence the vernacular can speak and, so doing, hybridizes both the agents and agencies of vernacular expression.

In an age of participatory media, this hybridity is a source of hope. Institutional power calls for a vernacular response (either in affirmation or denial) as every vernacular response assumes an institution. The two emerge together as they are invoked. So long as institutions produce discourse, vernacular voices will have the grounds to rise up and voice their alternate authority. Today, participatory media are giving those voices new means to speak, new audiences to address, and new opportunities to engage in the myriad of small acts of citizenship that are necessary for social transformation—if they so choose.

Notes

1. Kerry-Edwards, "Barnstorm Report: Day Three," Official Kerry-Edwards Blog, http://www.blog.johnkerry.com/blog/archives/000315.html (accessed October 10, 2004).

2. Kerry-Edwards, "Week of 08/03/03 Archive," Official Kerry-Edwards Blog, http:www.blog.johnkerry.com/blog/archives/week_2003_08_03.html (accessed October 27, 2004).

3. Ibid.

4. Henry Jenkins, Katie Clinton, Ravi Purushotma, Alice J. Robinson, and Margaret Weigel, "Confronting the Challenges of Participatory Culture: Media Education for the 21st Century," 2006 MacArthur Foundation Digital Media and Learning, http://www.digitallearning.macfound.org/site/c.enJLKQNlFiG/b.2108773/apps/nl/content2.asp?content_id=%7BCD911571-0240-4714-A93B-1-DoC07C7B6C1%7D&notoc=1 (accessed January 19, 2007).

5. Amanda Lenhart, John Horrigan, and Deborah Fallows, "Content Creation Online," Pew Internet & American Life Project, February 29, 2004, http://www.pewinternet.org/pdfs/PIP_Content_Creation_Report.pdf (accessed January 6, 2006); Pew Internet & American Life Project, "January 2005, Daily Tracking Survey," February 11, 2005, http://www.pewinternet.org/datasets/Jan%202005%20tracking%20topline.zip (accessed January 6, 2006); Pew Internet & American Life Project, "The Internet and American Life Daily Tracking Survey, March 2000," March 18, 2001,

http://www.pewinternet.org/datasets/banners.March2000.zip (accessed January 6, 2006); Pew Internet & American Life Project and Mary Madden, "Teen Content Creators and Consumers, November 2, 2005," www.pewinternet.org/pdfs/PIP_Teens_Content_Creation.pdf (accessed January 6, 2006).

6. Technorati Data, "About Technorati," Technorati, January 6, 2006, http://www.technorati.com/about/ (accessed January 6, 2006).

7. Tim O'Reilly, "What Is Web 2.0: Design Patterns and Business Models for the Next Generation of Software," OReillyNet, September 30, 2005, http://www.oreillynet.com/lpt/a/6228 (accessed November 10, 2006).

8. Robert Asen, "A Discourse Theory of Citizenship," *Quarterly Journal of Speech* 90 (2004): 207.

9. For vernacular in anthropology, see Margaret Lantis, "Vernacular Culture," *American Anthropologist* 60 (1962): 202–16. For vernacular in architecture, see Henry Glassie, *Vernacular Architecture* (Bloomington: Indiana University Press, 2000); Amos Rapoport, *House Form and Culture* (Englewood Cliffs, NJ: Prentice-Hall, 1969). For vernacular in religion, see Leonard Norman Primiano, "Vernacular Religion and the Search for Method in Religious Folklife," *Western Folklore* 54 (1995): 37–56. For vernacular in literary studies, see Henry Louis Gates, *The Signifying Monkey: A Theory of African-American Literary Criticism* (Oxford: Oxford University Press, 1988).

10. Dana Cloud, "Which Voices? Whose Democracy?" review of *Vernacular Voices: The Rhetoric of Publics and Public Spheres*, by Gerard Hauser, *Argumentation and Advocacy* 37 (2001): 201–13.

11. Robert Glenn Howard, "The Vernacular Web of Participatory Media," *Critical Studies in Media Communication* 25 (2008): 490–512.

12. Kent A. Ono and John M. Sloop, "The Critique of Vernacular Discourse," *Communication Monographs* 62 (1995): 20.

13. Kent A. Ono and John M. Sloop, *Shifting Borders: Rhetoric, Immigration, and California's Proposition 187* (Philadelphia: Temple University Press, 2002), 13.

14. Ono and Sloop rightly question Trinh T. Min-ha's use of the term "subaltern." Here, however, I associate Ono and Sloop's vernacular with the more robust and original sense of the "subaltern" forwarded by Antonio Gramsci in *Selections from the Prison Notebooks*, ed. and trans. Q. Hoare and G. Nowell Smith (New York: International Publishers, 1971).

15. Ono and Sloop, "The Critique of Vernacular Discourse," 25.

16. Ibid., 39.

17. Gerard A. Hauser, *Vernacular Voices: The Rhetoric of Publics and Public Spheres* (Columbia: University of South Carolina Press, 1999), 14, 11.

18. John D. Schaeffer, *Sensus Communis: Vico, Rhetoric, and the Limits of Relativism* (Durham, NC: Duke University Press, 1990).

19. Todd Boyd, *Am I Black Enough for You? Popular Culture from the Hood and Beyond* (Bloomington: Indiana University Press, 1997); Susan Kates, "The Embodied Rhetoric of Hallie Quinn Brown," *College English* 59 (1997): 59–71.

20. Bernadette Marie Calafell and Fernando P. Delgado, "Reading Latina/o Images: Interrogating Americanos," *Critical Studies in Media Communication* 21 (2004): 1–21; Lisa Flores, "Creating Discursive Space through a Rhetoric of Difference: Chicana Feminists Craft a Homeland," *Quarterly Journal of Speech* 82 (1996): 142–56; Lisa Flores and Marouf Hasian, "Returning to Aztlán and La Raza: Political Communication and the Vernacular Construction of Chicano/a Nationalism," in *Politics, Communication, and Culture*, ed. Alberto Gonzalez and Dolores V. Tanno (Thousand Oaks, CA: Sage Publications, 1997), 186–200.

21. Steven R. Goldzwig, "Demagoguery, Democratic Dissent, and 'Re-Visioning Democracy,'" *Rhetoric and Public Affairs* 9 (2006): 471–78; Steven R. Goldzwig and Patricia A. Sullivan, "Narrative and Counternarrative in Print-Mediated Coverage of Milwaukee Alderman Michael McGee," *Quarterly Journal of Speech* 86 (2000): 215–31; Samuel McCorkmick, "Earning One's Inheritance: Rhetorical Criticism, Everyday Talk, and the Analysis of Public Discourse," *Quarterly Journal of Speech* 89 (2003): 109–31; Jennifer R. Mercieca and James Arnt Aune, "A Vernacular Republican Rhetoric: William Manning's Key of Liberty," *Quarterly Journal of Speech* 91 (2005): 119–43

22. For a discussion of the vernacular in education, see A. Suresh Canagarajah, "Safe Houses in the Contact Zone: Coping Strategies of African American Students in the Academy," *College Composition and Communication* 48 (1997): 173–96. For the vernacular in film, see Erin M. Reer, "Strategies of Negotiation in Mainstream Media: Vernacular Discourse and Masculinity in *The Full Monty*," *Popular Communication* 3 (2005): 217–37. For the vernacular in performance studies, see Dwight Conquergood, "Performance Studies Interventions and Radical Research," *Drama Review* 46 (2002): 145–56; D. Soyini Madison, "Performance, Personal Narratives, and the Politics of Possibility," in *The Future of Performance Studies: Visions and Revisions*, ed. Sheron J. Dailey (Annandale, VA: National Communication Association, 1998), 276–86. For the vernacular in religion, see Robert Glenn Howard, "Apocalypse in Your In-Box: End Times Communication on the Internet," *Western Folklore* 56 (1997): 295–315; Robert Glenn Howard, "On-Line Ethnography of Dispensationalist Discourse: Revealed versus Negotiated Truth," in *Religion on the Internet*, ed. Douglas Cowan and Jeffery K. Hadden (New York: Elsevier Press, 2000), 225–46; Robert Glenn Howard, "Sustainability and Narrative Plasticity in Online Apocalyptic Discourse after September 11, 2001," *Journal of Media and Religion* 5 (2006): 25–47. For the vernacular in subcultures, see Derek R. Sweet, "More Than Goth: The Rhetorical Reclamation of the Subcultural Self," *Popular Communication* 3 (2005): 239–64. For the vernacular in Internet-based discourse, see Daniel C. Brouwer and Aaron Hess, "Making Sense of 'God Hates Fags' and 'Thank God for 9/11': A Thematic Analysis of Milbloggers' Responses to Reverend Fred Phelps and the Westboro Baptist Church," *Western Journal of Communication* 71 (2007): 69–90; Robert Glenn Howard, "A Theory of Vernacular Rhetoric: The Case of the 'Sinner's Prayer' Online," *Folklore* 116 (2005): 175–91; Robert Glenn Howard, "Toward a Theory of the World Wide Web Vernacular: The

Case for Pet Cloning," *Journal of Folklore Research* 42 (2005): 323–60; Robert Glenn Howard, "Electronic Hybridity: The Persistent Processes of the Vernacular Web," *Journal of American Folklore* 121 (2008): 192–418.

23. Howard, "Toward a Theory."

24. Donald McKenzie and Judy Wajcman, "Introduction," in *The Social Shaping of Technology*, ed. Donald McKenzie and Judy Wajcman (Philadelphia: Open University Press, 1999), 3–27; Langdon Winner, *The Whale and the Reactor: A Search for Limits in an Age of High Technology* (Chicago: University of Chicago Press, 1986).

25. Peter D. Schaefer and Meenakshi Gigi Durham, "On the Social Implications of Invisibility: The iMac G5 and the Effacement of the Technological Object," *Critical Studies in Media Communication* 24 (2007): 39–56.

26. Rebecca Blood, "How Blogging Software Reshapes the Online Community," *Communications of the Association for Computer Machinery* 47 (2004): 53–55.

27. Howard, "Toward a Theory," 323.

28. Blood, "How Blogging Software," 53.

29. Robert Asteroff, "Searching for the Library: University Home Page Design and Missing Links," *Information Technology and Libraries* 20 (2001): 93–99; Andrew Dillon and Barbara A. Gushrowski, "Genres and the Web: Is the Personal Home Page the First Uniquely Digital Genre?" *Journal of the American Society for Information Science and Technology* 51 (200): 202–205; Carolyn Miller and Dawn Shepherd, "Blogging as Social Action: A Genre Analysis of the Weblog," in *Into the Blogosphere: Rhetoric, Community, and Culture of Weblogs*, ed. Laura J. Gurak, Smiljana Antonijevic, Laurie Johnson, Clancey Ratliff, and Jessica Reyman, http://blog.lib.umn.edu/blogosphere/blogging_as_social_action_a_genre_analysis_of_the_weblog.html (accessed January 11, 2006).

30. Howard, "The Vernacular Web."

31. Plato, "Meno," in *Collected Dialogues of Plato,* ed. Edith Hamilton and trans. W. K. C. Guthrie (Princeton: Princeton University Press, 1989), 365.

32. Keith Bradley, "On the Roman Slave Supply and Slave Breeding," in *Classical Slavery*, ed. Moses Finley (London: Cass Publishers, 1987), 42–64.

33. Xenophon, *Xenophon: Scripta Minora,* vol. 7, trans. E. C. Marchant and G. W. Bowersock (Cambridge, MA: Harvard University Press, 1968), 429.

34. Pliny the Elder, *The Natural History,* trans. John Bostock and H. T. Riley (London: Taylor and Francis Publishing, 1855), 2346.

35. Cicero, *Brutus and Orator,* trans. G. L. Hendrickson (Cambridge, MA: Harvard University Press, 1971), 147.

36. Mia Consalvo, "Cyber-Slaying Media Fans: Code, Digital Poaching, and Corporate Control of the Internet," *Journal of Communication Inquiry* 27 (2003): 67–86; Mia Consalvo, *Cheating: Gaining Advantage in Video Games* (Cambridge: Massachusetts Institute of Technology Press, 2007).

37. Joe Trippi, *The Revolution Will Not Be Televised: Democracy, the Internet, and the Overthrow of Everything* (New York: Harper Collins, 2004); Gary Wolf, "How the

Internet Invented Howard Dean," *Wired News* 12 (January 2004), http://www.wired.com/wired/archive/12.01/dean_pr.html (accessed February 1, 2004).

38. Bush-Cheney Presidential Campaign, "Blog," Bush-Cheney '04 Official Campaign Blog, http://www.georgewbush.com/blog/ (accessed on October 21, 2004).

39. Lee Rainie, Micheal Cornfield, and John Horrigan, "The Internet and Campaign 2004," Pew Internet and American Life Project, 2005, http://www.pewinternet.org/pdfs/PIP_2004_Campaign.pdf (accessed April 6, 2007).

40. Philip Howard, *New Media Campaigns and the Managed Citizen* (Cambridge: Cambridge University Press, 2006), 17.

41. Kerry-Edwards, "Blog Archives," Official Kerry-Edwards Blog, 2004, http://www.blog.johnkerry.com/archives.html (accessed October 17, 2004).

42. Kerry-Edwards, "We Will Beat Bush," Official Kerry-Edwards Blog, 2004, http://www.blog.johnkerry.com/blog/archives/000333.html (acessed October 20, 2004).

43. Kerry-Edwards, "John Kerry-Campaign Organization General Election Edition: A Sketch of the Kerry Organization in Fall 2004," Democracy in Action: P2004 Site Index, 2004, http://www.gwu.edu/~action/2004/kerry/kerrorggen.html (accessed October 20, 2006).

44. Adam Penenberg, "Kerry and the Lost Kos," *Wired News*, July 7, 2004, http://www.wired.com/news/culture/0,1284,64113,00.html (accessed October 30, 2005).

45. Atrios, "Some Changes," Eschaton, April 4, 2004, http://atrios.blogspot.com/2004_04_04_atrios_archive.html#108110402749163310 (accessed October 30, 2006).

46. Bob, "Kerry Is a Wuss and a Hawk," Bob's Links and Rants, April 5, 2004, http://www.personal.umich.edu/~bgoodsel/post911/2004/04/kerry-is-wuss-and-hawk-in-light-of.htm (accessed October 30, 2006).

47. Metafilter, "Comments on 32202," Community Blog, April 3, 2004, http://www.metafilter.com/mefi/32202 (accessed October 30, 2006).

48. Huck, "John Kerry's Blog Is Undemocratic & No Different Than Others," What the Huck? September 13, 2004, http://www.s5000.com/what_the_huck/565/john_kerry_blog.php (accessed October 19, 2005).

Contributors

Robert Asen is Professor of Communication Arts at the University of Wisconsin–Madison. His research focuses on the relationship among social and economic inequalities and public deliberation. He is the author of *Visions of Poverty: Welfare Policy and Political Imagination* and *Invoking the Invisible Hand: Social Security and the Privatization Debates*.

Daniel C. Brouwer is Associate Professor of Human Communication at Arizona State University. His research explores theories and practices of publics, rhetorics, and cultural performances. He is a co-editor of *Counterpublics and the State* and the author of recent essays in *Rhetoric and Public Affairs* and *Critical Studies in Media Communication*.

Stephen P. Depoe is Professor of Communication at the University of Cincinnati. His research examines environmental and risk communication. He currently edits the journal *Environmental Communication* and has co-edited the books *Nuclear Legacies: Communication, Controversy, and the U.S. Nuclear Weapons Complex* and *Communication and Public Participation in Environmental Decision Making*.

Joshua Gunn is Assistant Professor of Communication Studies at the University of Texas at Austin. He is the author of the book *Modern Occult Rhetoric: Mass Media and the Drama of Secrecy in the Twentieth Century* and numerous articles on psychoanalysis, rhetorical theory, and theological forms in public culture.

Radha S. Hegde is Associate Professor of Media, Culture, and Communication at New York University. Her scholarship on globalization, diasporic identities, representations of violence, and postcolonial feminism has appeared in *Communication Theory*, *Women's Studies in Communication*, *Feminist Media Studies*, *Violence against Women*, and *Critical Studies in Media Communication*.

Robert Glenn Howard is Associate Professor of Communication Arts and Associate Director of the Folklore program at the University of Wisconsin–Madison. His research explores the possibilities and limits of everyday expression on the Internet. He has published in such journals as *Critical Studies in Media Communication* and *New Media & Society*.

Sara McKinnon is Instructor of Communication and Journalism at the University of New Mexico. Her research focuses on questions of subjectivity, agency, and belonging within refugee and asylum-seeking communities, utilizing textual analysis, participant observation, interviews, and performance methods. Her essays have appeared in *Liminalities*, *Text and Performance Quarterly*, and *Howard Journal of Communications*.

Phaedra C. Pezzullo is Associate Professor of Communication and Culture at Indiana University. Her research interests include environmental communication and social movement studies. She is the author of *Toxic Tourism: Rhetorics of Pollution, Travel, and Environmental Justice* and co-editor of *Environmental Justice and Environmentalism: The Social Justice Challenge to the Environmental Movement*.

Helene A. Shugart is Associate Professor of Communication at the University of Utah. Her research investigates the intersections of rhetoric, media, gender, sexuality, and critical theory. She is the co-author of *Making Camp: Rhetorics of Transgression in U.S. Popular Culture* and has published in such journals as *Communication and Critical/Cultural Studies* and *Feminist Media Studies*.

John M. Sloop is Professor of Communication and Associate Dean of the College of Arts and Science at Vanderbilt University. His research addresses the intersections of rhetoric, culture, and media. He is the author of *The Cul-*

tural Prison: Discourse, Prisoners, and Punishment and co-author of *Shifting Borders: Rhetoric, Immigration, and California's Proposition 187*.

DALE SMITH is a doctoral candidate in Rhetoric and Writing at the University of Texas at Austin. His research examines poetry's engagement with the public sphere to constitute social change. His poems and essays have appeared in *Black Stone, The Flood & the Garden, New American Writing*, and the *Chicago Review*.

ERIC KING WATTS is Associate Professor of Communication at the University of North Carolina, Chapel Hill. His research explores how public voice is invented, performed, consumed, and suppressed. He has published in such journals as the *Quarterly Journal of Speech, Critical Studies in Media Communication*, and *Rhetoric and Public Affairs*.

Index